STYLE FOR LIVING

Style for Living

How to Make Where You Live You

by ALEXANDRA STODDARD

Illustrated by Bill Goldsmith

DOUBLEDAY & COMPANY, INC., GARDEN CITY, NEW YORK
1974

Library of Congress Cataloging in Publication Data

Stoddard, Alexandra.
　Style for living.

　1. Interior decoration.　I.　Title.
NK2115.S698　　747'.213
ISBN 0-385-08252-5
Library of Congress Catalog Card Number 73–82250

Excerpt from *A God Within* by René Dubos. Copyright © 1972 by René Dubos. Reprinted by permission of Charles Scribner's Sons.

Excerpt from *The Beautiful and Damned* by F. Scott Fitzgerald. Copyright © 1922 by Charles Scribner's Sons. Reprinted by permission of Charles Scribner's Sons.

Excerpt from *Gift From the Sea* by Anne Morrow Lindbergh. Copyright © 1955 by Anne Morrow Lindbergh. Reprinted by permission of Pantheon Books, a division of Random House, Inc.

Excerpt from *The Second American Revolution* by John D. Rockefeller III. Reprinted by permission of Harper & Row, Publishers, Inc.

Excerpt from *Letters to a Young Poet* by Rainer Maria Rilke, translated by M. D. Herter Norton, revised edition. Copyright © 1954 by W. W. Norton Company, Inc. Reprinted by permission of the publisher.

Excerpts from *New Dictionary of Thought* (La Rochefoucauld and Parkhurst). Published by Standard Book Company.

The quotation from the poem "Joy of Living" reprinted by courtesy of Jenny B. Derwich and Quality Industries, Inc.

Excerpts from *Design As Art* by Bruno Munari. Reprinted by permission of Gius Laterza & Figli-Bari.

Excerpted from *The Modulor* by Le Corbusier. Reprinted by permission of Harvard University Press.

Excerpt from *The New Spirit* by Havelock Ellis from *Familiar Quotations* by John Bartlett, published by Little, Brown and Company, 1968.

To Mrs. Archibald Manning Brown

CONTENTS

FOREWORD

You are the reason I wrote this book. I want to take you on an adventure in design, and you are the one who will determine where we go and what interior design will result.

I have been an interior designer for eleven years, at McMillen, Inc., in New York City, and from my work I've learned how important it is for each person to live in an environment that reflects his particular, individual feelings about life and also his personality. Your environment needs go far beyond merely having a decorated space. We all need to establish our own philosophy and style of living and have them reflected in our home environments. You can design and create a unique environment of beauty and joy, an environment that reflects you, that nourishes you in all kinds of circumstances, moods and changing situations, if you will become intimately involved with all the dimensions of your surroundings.

Who is more qualified to create your personal environment than you? You know your real priorities, your functional and emotional needs. You understand your aesthetic sensibilities. You know how you want your place to comfort those you love and those you want to welcome.

In fact, you are the *only* one who can determine the total design concept that will work best for your life style and personality. Space design is inner directed, deeply rooted and involves building a living surrounding which is both dynamic and organic. Your private place should reflect a continuity and interrelationship between you, your place, your things and the time in which you live.

This book has been in the works for a long time and comes out of my experience working with the designers at McMillen and with clients, who have created wonderfully personal, meaningful, private worlds, houses and apartments that weren't designed to be photographed for *House and Garden* or to impress you. Private havens that grew out of the life and breath, the personal styles of the people who live in them. This book is my effort to pass on to you some of the things I've learned about interior design.

You and I are going to enter into a dialogue. In this book I'll try to give you the tools you will need to help you design your very personal environment, a space that will reflect the many facets of your life. Your involvement with the creation of your house or apartment should be one of the joy-filled experiences of your life. It should not be, as it is for so many, a hair-raising, frustrating ordeal, one to be gotten over quickly. I hope through this book to give you the confidence to carry out your own dreams and plans for your space.

The book is divided into three main parts. In Part One, we'll get to know you better, to know what you want from your interior design, how you might think about your space. What your priorities are in terms of your living place, and how your life style will dictate elements in it. Then, in Part Two, we'll talk about the design "building blocks," from which you can select the design for your own particular space—about what you might do about windows, lighting, color, etc. In Part Three, we'll put all the rooms together. My aim in the book is to help you get started at making where you live you.

It is something to be able to paint a particular
picture or to carve a statue, and so to make a
few objects beautiful, but it is far more glorious
to carve and paint the very atmosphere and
medium through which we look . . . To affect
the quality of the day—that is the highest of arts.

HENRY DAVID THOREAU

STYLE FOR LIVING

Part One

Place

. . . life of the individual man needs to relate his innate genius to the spirit of the place in which he lives.

RENÉ DUBOS
A God Within

. . . use, to express yourself, the things in your environment, the images from your dreams, and the objects of your memory. . . . for to the creator there is no poverty and no poor indifferent place.

RAINER MARIA RILKE
Letters to a Young Poet
Translated by M. D. Herter Norton

YOUR PLACE IS YOUR ESSENCE

Our surroundings are of prime importance to our sense of well being and contentment. They can make all the difference in the quality of our lives. I've seen whole personalities uplifted by improved physical surroundings. And we have all seen the ill effects caused by dark, cramped, depressing living places where man is unable to feel dignified.

Oscar Newman's book *Defensible Space*, subtitled "Crime Prevention Through Urban Designs," was reviewed in the New York *Times* by Ada Louise Huxtable as a "supremely significant study" illustrating how environment and design affect behavior. "While design cannot create behavior it can to a significant extent modify and control it."

You can create a better environment through design which will enrich your life. It is actually in your hands to create a dynamic, uplifting place where happiness is a natural state of mind. Our relationship to our place establishes patterns, shapes the style and determines the framework of our lives. Our clothes, our speech, our thoughts, our handwriting are all extensions of self. So, too, we cannot escape our commitment to our place because it is where we house our lives. A fitting place is one which nourishes your mind, body and soul. It is high time we incorporated our standards and values into a specific physical place, identifying with it on the most basic terms. It not only gives us security and identification, but it provides us with a place where we can be private or not, depending on our wishes.

Where we live is our niche, it's where we fit, and our places should fill the wide range of our needs. It is our core, our focal point. When one place is truly yours, you can fit into the complex of social and cultural conditions affecting you each day. You can move from it to take your place in and deal effectively with the outside world.

LIVING IN YOUR OWN PLACE

Being responsible for and living in your own creation is a most satisfying experience. The only way to find fulfillment in your physical surroundings is to understand them as a dynamic design, realize their potential as an environment which enriches *you*. There must be solid design principles allowing for flexibility and growth. A keen understanding of your own human needs and how they relate to and overlap with the needs of others is absolutely essential in order to design a place that will work for you.

I'd like to help you get started in executing an original design for your own place. In planning your design, keep three things in mind: function, integrity to your self and unity. It all should relate to the times. To elevate your place above the average you have to make an emotional commitment to it. I can assist you with the technical know-how, but only you can determine what your place should be.

The truth is you have to put your life and blood into your designing in order to envision the full potential. Sara Lee might do your baking but only you can create your own master place plan, so you feel joy in your surroundings.

The word "environment" is overused and not yet understood in terms of design. Your physical shelter should become an inner-directed environment, by design, so it incorporates all your circumstances and hopes into your immediate surroundings. Build into your living place, by your design, attitudes and characteristics of your unique personality. Our physical extension can bring satisfying, harmonious results when we thoughtfully analyze the problems and limitations and overcome them with inventive solutions. An ironing board on a hinge inside your closet for last minute touch-ups can lighten your days. It's handy if men's shirts are visible on open shelves built inside a closet. We should build into our designs hundreds of humble conveniences.

The challenge is to make your environment a growing, living set of attitudes which continue to move with you as you step from one season to the next. It is important to allow for growth, to analyze the future and make sure your decisions project forward into the unknown.

MODERN MAN, MODERN SOCIETY

How is it possible to think freely about design without all the voices of the past, of family upbringing, haunting every move? Who says you have to continue along the same path, live with the same oriental runners in your halls, the comb, brush and mirror set on your dressing table and who says you have to carry on the same conventional decorations when they have no meaning for you?

Time and space create change. You, your circumstances and all the places you know are undergoing changes. Our contemporary life styles and tastes are vastly different from our predecessors; we see a whole new world in this society. Everything is extremely complex in every area of our living. We are all greatly influenced by the turbulent circumstances of our times, and our designs should reflect these changes and forecast future needs.

Every particle in your surroundings is important to the rest. The changed circumstances and attitudes from yesterday to today boggle the mind. Instead of using the obvious Chippendale vs. plastic as an example of changed attitudes, let's look at jewelry. My favorite bracelet is two bent silver circles linked together. The clasp is a screw. My favorite necklace is thin gold circles all hammered by hand, each circle interlocking with the next circle and soldered smooth. Both pieces are modest and unassuming. Both pieces are basically continuous round forms. Think of a circle when you think of your physical surroundings: continuity, integrity, a feeling of converging. The interconnecting decisions and elements in your background make the circle an appropriate image for your design structure. A circle is a comfortable, relaxed form—your place should be too.

What are the presiding influences of our time on domestic design? A shortage of money, time and space have forced new approaches to the way we live. A total living concept, one where we are attempting to integrate all aspects of our surroundings into our lives, is the most appealing and satisfying way for us to live now.

MEMORABLE EVENTS

No longer are we removed from the daily details of domestic life; we're all involved in every way. Our basic everyday chores are more out in the open, and can and should be enjoyed. The most obvious example is enjoying the preparation of food. Now it's possible to cook in front of your guests (even letting them share in the preparations) and delight in cooking a beautiful, colorful meal. Preparing a beautiful meal, setting a dazzling table, lighting candles, playing music you love, having fresh flowers all add to the joy of a meal. If you have light from a fireplace it adds to the atmosphere. Have a scented candle burning. Have green plants hanging in your bathroom. Use lemon or your favorite almond soap. Use flowered sheets. All these simple pleasures add luxury. Romance. They set a mood. They elevate an everyday function into an event. Your design plan should consider how you spend each hour of your time. Romance and elegance can be present in your design continually when they are the essential extension of your personality.

FIND YOUR OWN ISLAND OF CALM—
AND IT WILL WORK FOR OTHERS

A basic need is to find a place where we can leave ourselves alone. If we can't putter about and feel joy in our own home, where can we go? Your home environment should be able to rejuvenate, restore you. When a room is assembled out of love and caring, it can be enjoyed by all people. No one claims he can create an atmosphere that will be livable for every friend, relative and business associate. The only thing you can possibly do to please most people most of the time is to please yourself. Let me give you an example. A friend of mine has an overpoweringly critical and difficult mother-in-law. Penny was desperate for her mother-in-law's approval and always did just what she thought her mother-in-law would expect of her. They had basic conflicts to begin with because the mother-in-law didn't see how Penny and Robert could possibly live in the city, didn't understand Penny's working, didn't approve of their "liberal" friends. What earthly difference would it make what furniture Penny chose, when everything else seemed wrong?

Penny decided to admit her limitations and instead of trying to please Robert's mother, she and Robert decided to simplify their lives by removing everything they didn't really love. Out went the cobwebs from his past, the pretenses of an era Penny and Robert weren't part of. Onward they marched into the twenty-first century. To end the story quickly, Penny and Robert made some important discoveries about their own lives and, happily, learned that Robert's mother could admire them and support them completely. She said, "I think it's so exciting when the young today find their own style and seem to be so much more content than we were in our roles. I wish I could live my youth over; I'd make a lot of changes."

When you're a guest in someone else's house, the style of his house doesn't matter, the important thing is that you feel welcome. When people love where they live their pride and enthusiasm is infectious and there is automatically a good, comfortable feeling. It's when people try to make a "good" impression and don't really decide for themselves what they want that rooms with personality problems are created. A perfectly put together room might be cold; a simple modest room could be as explosive as dynamite. Think about this. Ersatz rooms have no soul and therefore lack life and when the important elements are missing the impression is uninviting.

Suppose you have a young child and have to find a school for him; your job is to pick a stimulating, secure environment most suited for your child's personality and needs. A guided tour of the physical plant can't guarantee Johnny's future career success but you can get a feeling and pretty accurate reading of whether the atmosphere is a compatible one for your child. Schools are meant to be an extension of the home atmosphere. Certainly the home atmosphere is meant to be a true and honest continuation of the family living there.

YOUR CHOICE OF PLACE IS HIGHLY SUBJECTIVE AND AN EMOTIONAL DECISION

Where and how you live at home consumes your life's time and therefore has the most penetrating influence on your entire being. The atmosphere where we sleep influences the quality of our rest, the mood where we eat determines our dining pleasure, and the places where we spend our leisure and gather socially determines the possibilities for pleasure. Most of us live in very ordinary places and it is up to us to imbue them with a spirit which has the power to transform drab, dull interior spaces into private havens.

Identification with your physical place is the beginning. Find a place that seems right for you; no one cares what you select for yourself so long as it delights and feeds you. Have the courage to select an unusual place and mold it to your own habits. People enjoy living on boats, in barns, on farms, in windmills, in lofts, old houses, new houses, town houses, high rises, floor-through apartments and condominiums. Don't stop your search until you find a place with which you can identify.

Before you select a specific house or apartment you have to decide *where* you want to live. All of us move around a good deal now, but in a specific place one can find roots. Within a community or city you might make three or more moves before you "settle down" in your forever place. I don't believe in lively people worrying about "forever" places; it's difficult to make lifetime projections. Ten years are a long-enough period to plan for and even ten years may be too long a time period for most of us. The worst thing to endure is waiting to move; when you're in that state, progress is impossible. Even two years in one place can be spent in a settled, orderly and functional way with as many of the aesthetic improvements being portable as possible. Whatever your situation is, don't make the mistake of drifting until you move. If you do you'll find the move overwhelming. The biggest trauma in relocation is fear of change. We fear we won't be able to make new friends, get along as well with our shopping and, most important, we fear we won't be able to deal with our space.

Question your location needs. Are you happy with your neighborhood? Is it convenient to the children's schools? Your office? Are you generally pleased with your house or building? Do you feel reasonably safe after dark (which, by the way, is the ultimate freedom). Do you feel uplifted when you return home? Is the community stimulating to you? Are the people you and your children see interesting and fun to be with? Are there parks and play areas? What about churches and libraries? Is there a restaurant or neighboring tavern where you enjoy going when you are alone? Is there sunlight? Are there trees and flowers nearby?

These personal needs for you and your family will help give order to your location priorities. All of these decisions have to do with place.

IS GEOGRAPHIC LOCATION RELEVANT?

I always enjoy a contiguous, compatible landscape, architecturally speaking. Southern California is a superb example of Hollywood make-believe. Driving around Bel Air, you go from Italy to Spain to France, and cover centuries, in a matter of seconds. One stage setting after another flashes before you until you end the movie by leaving. The Taj Mahal is appropriately located in Agra, India, and would have no place in New England.

Relatively few of us get involved in the actual building of our places; we are stuck with the selection at hand. If we live in an ugly house it's not our fault, we didn't design and build it. What we *are* responsible for and should concern ourselves with is what goes on inside.

Only concern yourself with suitability to yourself, not to the period or style of your house or apartment. Why limit yourself to a 1792 environment just because you live in an old frame house? Don't ever let your place dictate limitations and restrictions on your ideas and style. A perfect example of this is the old idea that there is a city way and a country way to live and act. Look how that has got all mixed up!

Try to select a house or apartment which lends itself to your ideas, certainly, but this is not always possible. Availability and cost make your job tougher than ever. If you end up buying or renting an ugly house, have a ball with the inside and don't worry about how it fits with the outside. If you try to go on with the look of the house you'll have a horror on your hands.

ESTABLISHING ESSENTIAL INGREDIENTS

Where to live. It doesn't matter what elements you put into your decision, it is an emotional decision. After weighing cost, location, convenience, safety, zoning, schools, church, commuting, space, light and charm, you have to feel the space is terrific. You have to believe in its potential. The only thing that will transform an ordinary situation into magic is your belief in its suitability. All the drawbacks, limitations, financial strains and design restrictions become a challenge when you know it's your place.

Accept those things you can't change and don't settle for anything you can't improve through change.

It is hardest to begin because no house or apartment is ever ideal and it takes courage to commit oneself to a compromising situation. If only there were one more bathroom. If only there were a dining room. If only there were two more feet on the width of the living room. If only it weren't so far uptown.

Attitude is everything. At some point you have to look on the plus side and go. Your commitment can turn a routine builder's house into a beauty or apartment 3L into a home.

WE'RE ABLE TO CONTROL OUR INTERIOR ENVIRONMENT

Not only are we able to have light and heat twenty-four hours a day, we're also able to determine personally and artificially everything about our surroundings and what goes on inside them. You can alter the physical space within your place—move walls, change windows.

YOU SHOULD NEVER BE "FINISHED"

When one has a new house or apartment one races around frantically trying to get settled. Mothers tell children to relax, that as soon as they're finished fixing up one place, they're likely to move to another and be back in the same boat. You keep working and when it seems just right, you may have to move on to a new challenge. There isn't any need to have every project completed. Interior decoration is like traveling; half the joy is the excitement and anticipation. The planning. This can last for months, even years.

Future projects bring hope. If you don't take much pleasure in domestic puttering and you want to feel settled quickly you are limiting yourself to instant atmosphere which will get you by but not go any further. Don't have getting it all done as a goal. Progress yes, but not finishing.

Do those things that drive you crazy and leave undone other things until they too drive you crazy. Who says you should be settled three months after you move? Learn to live with work in progress. Seeing the continuing growth and gradual change is so much a part of your eventual enjoyment because you put so much of yourself into each room.

Do one room at a time and don't move on to the next until you're satisfied. Years ago there was money enough to do several rooms at once. Not any more.

It's more than money too. It takes time to think out a room. When you get all your ideas in order and come up with your design, floor plan, color scheme, furniture decisions, lighting, materials and flooring, you'll find there's no way you'll be able to afford to do everything at once. What's the difference between waiting for a coffee table you absolutely love and a painting to hang over your sofa? We've got to unlearn these out-of-date notions about having everything just so and in place. Whom are we trying to impress? Whom are we kidding?

When we patiently see one room executed to our delight it gives us hope to move on to another mountain.

COMFORT IS EVERYTHING

I've been slapped down over and over again when I plead that our living places should be comfortable. People say, "We don't want to be so comfortable, Sandie." There must be a misunderstanding of the word or no one could possibly make such a statement. Webster's New International Dictionary defines comfort as: "affording comfort, consolatory or encouraging. Fairly adequate, sufficient, but not in excess. A state of consolation, *cheerful*. In a state of content, at ease. Free from pain or distress." Is there anyone of us alive who doesn't want to be *comfortable?*

If you love stiff uncomfortable chairs, they'll make you comfortable. If you're 6 feet 4 inches tall and you love old houses with beams that you bash into, you'll be comfortable in such a house. If you have a sensitive back, you'll want to feel comfortable in your sofa and chairs. If you have a friend whom you care deeply for and she comes often for tea, it will make you feel comfortable to have your tea service close at hand. If a friend brings a house present for your new room and it just misses, it will make you comfortable to keep it front and center on your coffee table because you love him and it reminds you of that love. Using your grandmother's old mahogany banister as a coffee table base might be your ultimate comfort.

With some inward thought we can all determine what it is that is most comfortable for us to have around us.

UPKEEP IS UNDERSTOOD

The other disadvantage to being "finished" is the upkeep. Once everything is established then it has to be maintained.

I have a separate chapter on maintenance so I will only say here that nothing can destroy a room quicker than letting it go. When the freshness is gone it is as off putting as a bunch of dead flowers. There isn't anything rigid or formal about a well-maintained place. It is a smile.

Half your budget will go into the less romantic, less visually pleasing, more rudimentary, functional aspects of building a nest. Vacuum cleaners, ice crushers, Water Piks, floor waxers, pots, pans, garbage cans. Brooms, mops, sponges. Scissors.

When someone comes to me with a specific budget, I remind him of all the shelf paper he'll need, and all the equipment needed to maintain and store his possessions. Don't underestimate the value of having aesthetically pleasing household equipment. You may laugh at me but wait!

Certainly this is a shift. Think of the ugly industrial designs of the past when the help handled everything versus today when we all do everything ourselves. Designers are caring as much about an ironing board as they are about a piece of jewelry. Housewares are museum pieces in design excellence. Electric heaters that are handsome and compact are made now. Why have an ugly heater? Coffee makers are available in many colors; so are tea kettles.

You can't say you don't care what your kitchen drawers look like or your linen closet or your ice crusher or your wooden spoons or your towel rack. These are the things you confront each day and they should be pleasing, well shaped, aesthetic and totally functional. When something is beautiful, tactile and does its job well, it is an aid to us and makes our time spent an enjoyable experience instead of a drudgery, a chore.

Discover for yourself the pleasures of having the inside of your closets, shelves and drawers inviting and gracious. Buy the best-looking broom you can find. Hold out until you find the right color garbage can. Who sees it? *You* do, day in and day out.

Indulge in industrial glass jars for your refrigerator. The shapes are so beautiful. Your food looks attractive when you see it through clear glass shapes. Great for chilling your white table wine too.

The ultimate enjoyment is to have all your domestic details a delight. The designs are available at last. Remember that the person who sees these things and works with them is the most important one of all. An artist buys the best materials he can afford. So should you.

TOUCHES, TOUCHES

It's never the big things that give a room its magic quality, it's the hundreds of tiny touches. Things of interest, hobbies, colorful ways of using ordinary things in unusual ways, textures, are what make a place special. One person or a couple creates all the personality of a place and then goes about the business of keeping it fresh and alive. Never lose touch. It is so vital to find personal pleasure in all that surrounds you. Your senses should be stimulated all the time by your personal surroundings.

RE-EVALUATION KEEPS SURROUNDINGS FRESH AND REAL

Keep an open mind to your changing moods and attitudes. Don't make the mistake of continuing on with a compromise or a mistake. Sense when you're in trouble and retrench.

Often we push so hard for certain things that by the time we realize our goals, we don't want what we thought we couldn't live without. A weekend retreat might be a burden, an antique Regency chair uncomfortable, and we can't find a good place for it anywhere.

The more you grow the quicker you'll go through changes in attitude which will affect your taste, your style and your needs. Keeping up with yourself is a lot of work and takes energy, but it is never dull. Make room on your bookshelves for your new interests, get rid of your dressing table in favor of a working desk. All my life I've wanted a chaise longue in my bedroom. It is a symbol of space, time, leisure. But what on earth would I ever do now, with a chaise lounge in my bedroom? Put a small refrigerator for late night wine and ice right inside your bedroom closet—wake up to cold orange juice.

Finally, when you have a vision of what you want, never compromise. You'll be miserable if you do. "If I only had" is a heartbreak to hear. If we didn't feel the difference between the real or the imitation, the elegant line or the squat proportion, the down cushion or the foam rubber, the wood or the formica, we'd probably be better off. Workmanship is the thing that has flipped normal people over the deep end. It is a curse to care at times. But don't settle when something is almost. Don't substitute when you know what you want. Plastic tulips just won't do. When you know, follow your instincts and do whatever they require. Simplify. Wait. But never compromise on things that count.

You

Insist on yourself; never imitate . . .
RALPH WALDO EMERSON

No man is free who is not master of himself.
EPICTETUS

YOU ARE UNIQUE

There isn't anyone like you in the world and there never will be. You are a product of your parents, your heredity, genetics and the environment in which you were brought up. Your personality has been molded and formed by a combination of factors and you can't do a thing to change the circumstances and conditions of this experience. Everything has left a mark on your life.

What do you want as a way of life for yourself starting right now, a way of life which will allow you maximum personal freedom and growth, as well as security and a sense of joy? How do you design for these attitudes? How do you style your living place to make it fulfill you and make you most comfortable with this mysterious unique being, you? Think about what you want, then find a way to direct your life toward that goal. Planning your place will help make it happen.

THE GUIDING PRINCIPLE BEHIND YOUR PLACE
IS THAT IT DELIGHTS YOU

Your knowledge and understanding of your past are important in planning your home design, and yet it doesn't solve any specific design problems. We should live like no one else. In fact, most of us live different lives than those we were exposed to when growing up. Your home environment is where you are a whole individual self; it is here that you connect with your family, friends, your life. This is where you're able to improve, through change, anything you want; it really is a place for you.

If you want a place you love, instill it with the things most alive in you as a person, fill it full of all that interests and excites you, and it will take on your personality, and you'll begin to love your place. Why is it so difficult to know what to do? Because what you're going to do has never been seen or done before in quite the same way; it's as unique as you.

I will try to give you the necessary building blocks, in design, to help you create your personal place and style but you're going to have to think about what you really like in order to create that place, make it totally your own.

Van Day Truex, a charming, talented designer and an artist of great personal taste, a man in his seventies now, reflects, "My apartment is a scrapbook of souvenirs." If you don't keep a diary, remind yourself, through your surroundings, of places and times when you've been happy.

People create places. We have to want to communicate good feelings about our lives through our surroundings or they will be cold and heavy. The best beginning is to fill your place with things you love. If you expose yourself to those things which uplift you you will be receptive to happy thoughts on a regular basis. Analyze the hours you spend in your own surroundings. Value the style you select and care about the quality of where you live.

WHAT IS THE QUESTION?

Perry Como sings a song called "Everybody Is Looking for the Answer." In finding your answer for your place, you have to first ask yourself the basic questions. How can you enjoy a more peaceful, calm surrounding? How much have you thought about personally identifying with your surroundings? How can you establish a place which delights your spirit and nourishes you? How can you design your interiors so they help you feel the fullness of life? How can you put yourself into where you live? Where do you begin? Where and how will you get the money to pay for all these plans? Just what is involved?

Raising the questions is an awakening in itself. Think seriously of this vital connection between your life as a whole and your surroundings. Once you've established your life needs, you're ready to plan your home design.

Establish a point of view. A client I admire won't let me forget the question I asked him when we were staring at his large empty living room. "What kind of a statement are you trying to make?" I asked. You have to set your own course and find your own rhythm and style. What seems right for you right now? Your upbringing and the upbringing of anyone you live with are certainly strong factors of influence. What usually happens is that we either follow our past completely or we question it, learn from it and find our own way. If we were brought up in a formal manner we may long for a more relaxed, freer, more comfortable way of life. The work we do, the friends we have, all enter into our thought processes.

If you are married, your style is a curious mixture of each partner's needs combined with his past. Decide how you want to live your life and be as honest and sincere with yourself as possible. Don't let any assumptions, no matter how deeply ingrained, blind your vision and make you too afraid to see the truth for you here and now. If you live alone or with a roommate, don't plan ahead for another kind of life. Build your own style.

Until you have the guts to hang mirrors all over your hall (all your life you were told mirrors were a bit vulgar) and to paint your bathroom purple (all your life bathrooms were sanitary white) and give up your stiff dining room entirely (your family may continue to ask you where is the dining room) you aren't ready to live in your own surroundings. There will be certain moments when something you've done makes you a bit embarrassed in the company of certain people, but chances are you'll love it too much to care. Remember, some people don't understand you and what makes you happy and never will. It's important to be able to laugh at yourself and what you've done, too.

Admit to yourself what you get the biggest kick out of it and you'll be amazed how that will lighten your load. An entire flavor and mood will emerge if you allow it to live.

Instead of looking for people to recognize you because you are one of them, impress them with your own appearance. Let them accept you and your design statement on your own terms. Never be afraid of being honest. You're always going to want approval. That's only human. Never expect 100 per cent. Get your approval from others on what you are doing. And when you don't, rise above it; it doesn't really matter to you and if it does, it shouldn't. If you take pride and get pleasure in doing your own things, that is all that counts.

FORMING AND DEVELOPING YOUR OWN STYLE

Every part of our lives touches the place where we live. In the words of Frank Lloyd Wright, "Space should satisfy fundamental, aesthetic, and spiritual needs of man."

We've established that our style of living is an extension of our personal values and our tastes, an expression of our exposure. A writer commented to me over lunch the other day, "Sandie, I'm only as good a writer as I am a person." This is the truth about our rooms. They can only go as far as we let them; to get to a point of satisfaction, it requires a great deal of time and thought. It requires a lot of our life too. Never forget the total concept you're trying to create.

Van Day Truex, whom I mentioned before, has spent his whole life studying the visual arts and he feels everything through his eyes. Recently he made the comment: "Looking back on my life and work I would say, it takes a long time to learn and I've learned a little." Don't be discouraged if you can't find all your answers right away. They will come, you are the only one who can put together the pieces of the mosaic in a unique and personally pleasing design. You can call in all the help you can afford in the execution and upkeep of your place, but it is essential you set up the background mood and tenor yourself. This is your life you're designing.

OUTSIDE INFLUENCES IN OUR SURROUNDINGS

There is no pleasure without company. The hidden inspiration behind our self-expression is the people in our lives. They not only help us find our inner life and inspire us toward greatness; they give meaning to our lives. Think of the varied circumstances and people you like whom you want to weave into your every day. Accept and realize the influences of your friends and family, your time and place. Your situation and setup are totally different from, for example, your mother's. Is it any wonder you don't want your living room to look just like hers? How can it, really? She did it her way because. You have to do it your way because . . . It's that simple.

GETTING TO THE HEART OF THE MATTER

It is easier to determine what we don't want than to pinpoint the precise solutions to each individual problem. To find the core, your fundamental and basic needs, you have to eliminate all excess and non-essential elements. Every artist has to pare down until he finds the heart and this elimination makes his work art. You do the same.

Be selective in everything concerning your environment. Only accept those things which hold special meaning to you, that serve a function and purpose and that are aesthetically beautiful. Edit out the excess.

LEARN TO DEVELOP AND RESPOND
TO YOUR FIVE SENSES

Let your sensitivities and your senses unlock the closed door and open up to the beauty of your thoughts. Understand that all your senses are working in tandem. Your senses are honest and all you have to do is acknowledge their potential for adding countless pleasure to your life. Why be embarrassed about the most basic pleasures? Maybe the greatest joy you had in the preparation of Thanksgiving dinner was the wonderful smells and textures. What would wine or flowers be without the bouquet? Pleasant odors are important in our rooms. It's one goal to eliminate bad smells, but it's quite another thing to create beautiful ones. Our ears need to feel too. My neighbors don't agree with me, but I gain personal satisfaction from clomping around on our quarry tile floor. Enjoy the sizzle of butter melting in a pan, the sound of running water is music. Textures. You know how vital they are. Touching is important and we should have lots of stimulating and fun things to touch and fool with. Our eyes are our windows to see outside ourselves and experience our feelings visually. We should learn to respond to the feelings we get from our eyes and what they see. Tasting is one of the great delights available. Shut your eyes when you taste and let your feelings take over.

You will gain important insights which will be helpful to you in your designing by learning to respond to your feelings through involvement with your senses.

THE ART OF LIVING WELL IS A GIFT

We all have friends who are unusually gifted at creating colorful, cheerful atmospheres for their friends and whenever you are with them you feel an uplift and sensuous joy of living and sharing. Their customary flair and ease make you feel needed and welcome. The truth is you *are* needed. Friends blessed with this treasured gift need to share it with you. It cannot be wasted. These same people have a way of making everyone they are with vividly changed by their presence and their personality. They have an energy to make life overflow with fullness. The places where they live have this same exuberance.

These people get by doing the wildest things and always with a fun-loving touch. Their self-confidence allows them to be downright corny, at times outrageous, and always creative. I've seen the most ordinary things take on inordinate importance: five Sunkist lemons in the center of a classical elegant dining table. One single daisy in a tiny vase, featured in an elegant room. The imagination and joy of self-expression are in all corners, in every surface. No one thing is necessarily a huge sucess or of any significance when you single it out. It's the over-all effect, the total experience which has such a dramatic impact. The value of each treasure is felt. Ask any one of your more clever friends the meaning behind their map or picture or table or bibelot. There is a whole story behind each funny thing and you begin to realize that everything is a symbol and has a double *entendre*. What about this semainier (a seven-drawer chest, one for each day of the week). Where did you find it? "We found it in Paris on our honeymoon and I bought it for Sara because it looks like her!" "I bought this nest of tables in Hong Kong so the children can each have one to their scale!" "I found this picture frame in New Hampshire and I hang it with nothing inside because I see Michelangelo's Sistine Chapel ceiling on the aged and craggy wood backing." These same people hang their own art, arrange their own flowers, cook their own food, and everything is amusing or beautiful or funny. They are never passive about their surroundings. That's why it is special to go to their houses and look around at the things they love. They are having a good time. You can too.

NOW YOU TRY

Start now sprinkling some personally meaningful things around. Take out that funny cut crystal vase from the cupboard. If as a child you loved it in your mother's front hall why not put your tulips in it in your hall? Unpack your grandmother's quilt and use that on your bed for a change. Notice the tulips and feel good. Enjoy making your bed with the lovely old quilt.

STAGES IN OUR LIVES

As I said earlier, sometimes we work so hard to realize our dreams that when we get to the end of the storm there is no rainbow. The perfect room you've slaved to accomplish doesn't mean as much as you anticipated it would. You have accomplished the goal you set out to achieve, having a warm room that satisfies. You love your new gorgeous room, but in some ways you actually miss the bigger-than-life dreams about it. I don't think we are ever happy or content when we have completed all our projects or realized all our goals. Then what do we do? Before you get close to that stage, begin a new project, one which is bigger than you are. The truth is that these accomplishments and niceties add joy to our lives, certainly beauty, but they in themselves aren't all consuming, all important. There has to be more.

Mentally pretend you are just starting out. You have nothing, have made no mistakes, and you are keen to get off on the right beginning. You care, where and how you live are important to you, and you want to love the results.

First, don't rush. Enjoy each step, start off small and gently build from a well-thought out, cogent beginning. When you rush you get confused, you don't last as long, you make mistakes and you can't enjoy anything fully.

Next, you must like with quality. And quality is the value of something to you. Something of quality has to be well designed, have good workmanship, be durable and be lasting. A possession, a well-designed building, an experience, all should have your standard of quality.

In the next chapter I'll discuss spatial design in detail, but I bring it up now in terms of life style as it relates to our changed society. Decoration and exterior trappings, the marshmallow and ornaments on top of the cake —the excesses we do not need today. Design has replaced decoration. What do I mean by design? Besides form, structure and style, design is *simplifying*. Design brings order to cluttered, cramped spaces, it aids in our operations, and it suits our way of living. Create your background so it suits you Monday through Sunday and when you have that flowing smoothly that's time enough to make more elaborate preparations for your boss coming to dinner or your entire family coming for Christmas.

Your designs must co-ordinate with your life style, and your life style should be well designed so it suits you. In all cases we'd be smart to face and accept our financial, time and space limitations and enjoy less more. Once you are totally practical and handle your every day with ease, it becomes a snap to add a touch of luxury here and a bit of silver polish there.

Think how well off we'd all be now if we'd given ourselves more time up front. If we started out with less, understanding and living with quality, appreciated design for design's sake and realized the refreshing pleasures of simplification in all parts of our living. The good thing is we can improve, starting now.

ESTABLISHING PERSONAL GOALS

Your individual expression must function and work for you and fill specific needs so it is satisfying to you. What will bring you the most direct results? Never lose sight of whom you're trying to please and keep working until you feel comfortable, until your design helps your life run smoothly.

The logic behind design changes is simple. Let me give you an example. You have an awkward depressing kitchen and you love to cook. Furthermore, you have three children under ten years of age and they need supervision at mealtimes. Ask yourself what is this wall doing blocking my eye contact from where the children eat? Why can't we knock it out entirely and create one open space? You don't have to be a creative genius to dream up these ideas. You have to believe in the results and have sound reasons why you want to make changes. Do this and you'll begin to envision the finished state.

Fear of the unknown has kept the most daring souls from taking steps. Focus on the probability of change and on how one thing will affect another. Realize the broad ramifications one change will bring. Take into account the finances, timing, inconveniences, and the cause and effect it will have on the other elements which make up your surroundings. Realize the chain reaction of events so you won't be too surprised if one fresh change instigates a desire to continue into other areas.

Force yourself to envision a fern print you saw in a model room as curtains, as a shower curtain in the children's bathroom. Never limit yourself to using in the same context something you've seen. The yellow you see and like as a wall color in a friend's living room might be a perfect color for you to use on your lacquered parson's table. Carry these ideas with you until a perfect place for them comes to mind. Instead of copying, you'll be creating.

Calvin Tomkins writes in *Living Well Is the Best Revenge* that Gerald

Murphy, the artist, wrote in a letter to his Sara, "Who knows," he joked, "some wretched insect which I save from your grinding heel may give you an inspired color for scarf or gown! Have you ever seen the lining of a potato bug's wings?" The origins of our imagination are limitless.

EMPLOY EVERY VISUAL AID

Professionals who work and make a living in the visual arts know how easily they can be fooled by color. Interior designers always show their clients large memorandum samples of a fabric, never a small cutting. It is difficult enough to envision without trying to play God and guess about repeats, scale and design. You can't feel the impact of a color if you don't have enough of it to see. It is far safer to buy a yard of material before you buy a bolt, or a bucket of paint before you buy a bilious room. Play it safe and gather your samples together until you're able to envision the results. Even if you have to drag a huge shopping bag around town when you look for sheets, having the samples with you from the rest of the materials in your room will be well worth it. If you're in doubt even then, buy a pair of pillow cases, try them for a week before you invest further.

When you are directed, when you know where you're going, spring into action. Don't wait until you have a total picture of every last detail. Begin and you'll gain insight as you go along. The first push is the most difficult. Kandinsky, one of my favorite artists, was paralyzed to begin a new canvas. To overcome this fear he would put a small circle on the upper corner of his white canvas. This allowed him the courage to apply his brush to color and begin. If your way of approaching a room is to buy a painting and have everything else co-ordinate around this, that's fine. If you prefer to buy a few accessories which give you your mood and work around these, that's fine too. We all need to work within a frame, a structure. It doesn't matter which approach makes you move as long as you begin.

YOU CAN TEACH YOURSELF

Le Corbusier has taught me that to respect harmony, proportion and beauty is no happy accident. There are genius minds who spend their lives working out highly technical mathematical formulas to give us inches and feet that work well together. If you've ever studied Greek architecture, you know what I mean. If you are willing to study you can benefit from these great and talented minds.

A liberal arts education can leave you blind to the visual arts. Grown men who appear to be sensitive in all fields of human experience, unless they have an artistic bent, fail badly when they are dealing with the fundamental grammar of good basic design. I've learned my lesson in exposure from "Sesame Street": STOP, LOOK, LISTEN, SMELL, TOUCH, TASTE, FEEL. Aesthetic judgments are acquired through layers and layers of accumulated observation and exploration.

Teach yourself to dissect everything until you see the truth. Question why this shape. What is it about a particular proportion that makes it so pleasing? Turn things upside down, inside out and view them from every possible angle. Be analytical and critical until you see the value. Do this to every pot, pan, painting, vase, rug, table, necktie, wall color, to entire rooms, buildings. Be a critic and review what you see. Say out loud this spoon is an ugly proportion, then tell yourself why. Comment on a door color being muddy. Notice everything. Every single facet of nature, every tiny leaf in a blooming apple tree are inspiration. Each detail should have a worth, an integrity and honesty of its own. Successful wholes have well-formed component parts. Think of Cézanne and his respect for a piece of fruit. Pull apart one of his still lifes. He devoted so much attention to an apple, a pear, a grape, looking at each piece of fruit makes you see it as a masterpiece in itself. Register on the simplest things and then study them in detail.

Michelangelo saw figures in clouds. I was looking up one day, admiring the drama of the clouds in the Caribbean sky, when my eye feasted on a perfect rainbow. Because of its extraordinary beauty and grace I couldn't take my eyes off this thrilling sight. Suddenly, out of nowhere was the precise duplicate. Can you imagine, a double rainbow? I'm so grateful I saw it; everyone else on the beach only saw one rainbow except one person, a photographer who was swimming. Our eyes should be on the lookout all the time.

It is far more important for you to learn to discriminate and feel excellence than it is to learn all the technical details that go into every part of your design planning. There are specialists who have these answers and their knowledge can help you tackle your projects with the least possible amount of frustration. Your job is to tell professionals what you want. The best way to find these sources is through friends or in the Yellow Pages if you're on your own. Design companies have all their own trade people.

Study. Become a student of the visual and decorative arts but don't go back to school. Spend the time and money you would have sunk into a course and buy some books and supplies. Developing your own style and enriching your taste can't be taught by learning old rules and facts. You need to do some work on your own.

Supplies are half the fun. Buy a notebook with side pockets for stuffing samples and odd notes. Every time I buy a spiral notebook I regret that it isn't a loose leaf because I'm forever ripping pages out; but buy whichever you prefer. No matter what you decide, keep to a standard 8 inches by 10 inches size. I've found my books invaluable for jotting down measurements, doing sketches and general note taking. Who has ever been a student without a notebook?

Use magazines as your textbooks. Instead of being awed by the glamour of the "shelter magazines," use them as your month-to-month work book. If you already get *House & Garden*, try to read *House Beautiful*. Also *Architectural Digest* or *Interiors* or *Apartment Ideas*. Check the newsstands for special half-year issues. You might want to increase your subscriptions; your investment may pay off a thousand times and save you money and mistakes. Indulge yourself in *Art in America* or *Réalités*, and if you can't rationalize the expense, put one of them on your Christmas list.

There is always a feature in each issue. Use this as your main assignment. If you feel inclined, make personal notes in your own notebook about the special information you've lifted from the text and jot down some possible uses you might have for these ideas in your current house or apartment. I'm visually oriented and even if I never refer back to my notes, the mere fact of my writing something down helps me to keep that thought in my head. Maybe this is true for you too.

Go through your magazines from cover to cover and clip out resources, shopping information and "how to" features.

After you've read all the articles and saved what seems most important, you will be amazed at how much remains in each issue. Advertising pays for the magazine. There is always the true and the false in each copy and it's good practice for you to decipher which is which. You can skim for pages and see junk and suddenly something comes up which is worth the price of the entire issue. Because taste requires discrimination on all levels it will help you to see the bad with the good.

Save the good things you find. Buy some sharp scissors and a set of scrapbooks; the best kinds are found in an art supply store. Don't cut into your beautiful art magazines, save them, but the rest can be cut up and the good ideas in them recycled into your scrapbooks. Flag the pages you plan to save as you read along, later clip them out and put them into one of your scrapbooks. Try never to get more than a month behind. Do a little as you go along and you won't get overwhelmed.

I select large scrapbooks 18 inches by 24 inches, which are actually tablets of white paper and have five different categories. I have one for exterior, nature and architecture; interiors of entire rooms; one for children (all ages); one for cooking, dining, kitchens, table settings (and anything mouth watering); the last one for details and accessories. When one gets filled up, begin a new one. Arranged chronologically, they keep a record of the interesting discoveries and trends each year and reinforce my theory that design and quality are lasting. Good shapes and forms keep reappearing issue after issue in new and old ways. Magazines spend a fortune taking these pictures and you can benefit from keeping these illustrations. You will discover you are putting together subjective picture books which will become treasures. Wait and see. You will refer to them often for ideas as well as refreshment. Our entire kitchen was created and lifted from pictures I have collected in my "food and eating" scrapbook. Besides the photograph albums of our children, I'm as proud of my scrapbooks as anything we own.

One note of warning. Don't put anything in your scrapbook which doesn't delight the eye and speak for itself. No labels please! Use your scissors to crop out what you don't like. Create your own collages with superimposed pictures. Put together your own design for the cover from odd pictures in all different scales which illustrate the content of each scrapbook. When you finish your design, varnish it so it stays fresh!

Do you keep a home file? Start one now if you haven't already. It will give you a system as you gather your information. Treat yourself to several dozen folders 8 inches by 10 inches. If manila doesn't inspire you, buy them in colors or even bright plastic ones. You need a generous quantity of divisions for all your category heads. I have labels for roof lines, color, storage information, Christmas decorations, contemporary architecture, space articles, bathrooms, lighting, environment, beauty, electricity. Always have your own records. Filing cabinets are so serious looking and difficult to hide at home. I use plastic cubes (the kind you see everywhere in bright red, blue, orange, green and yellow). You'll find you can stow away a wealth of information in one box and it can move around with you wherever you decide to work.

My mother has always kept great files. When I was thirteen I modeled for an artist-illustrator and sat hour after hour staring at a massive filing system. I had to smile and say "cheese" while gazing at those ugly files! Wondering what a creative spirit was doing with so many filing cabinets, I asked the artist. After he had showed me his precise system, which, by the way, took him twenty years to perfect, I instantly understood; his files are his livelihood. His homework is in his files and his presentation is painted with a brush. That same summer my mother helped me to set up my own files, for which I am most grateful. The headings on the folders have changed over the years but the habit is the same. Be sure you date and give sources on all your clippings. You never know when you'll need this information. Also, date and identify all photographs.

Books give us information, knowledge, truth, they become our friends. Make provisions to house your own books, have an allowance to purchase books and take time to read. All your experiences and observations can be confirmed in writing to reinforce your ideas and give them form. Who knows when we're in need of the comfort of a reference or need to look up a fact?

Although there are excellent textbooks on the subject of interior design and environment, you should not limit yourself to dry, technical information. Buy beautiful books which inspire you, you'll always learn more from books you love. The range of subjects that pertains to the art of living is endless. Novels, too, are a way to communicate reality. I complained to a friend that I hadn't enjoyed a good book in years that wasn't connected with my profession and she laughed in my face. *The Best in European Decoration*, Alexander Liberman's *The Artist in His*

Studio, Greece Gods and Art, Chateaux of the Loire Valley, The World of Children, Le Corbusier's *Modular* books, the Museum of Modern Art's *Italy: The New Domestic Landscape,* Lawrence Durrell and Henry Miller —whatever you read feeds your life, and, therefore, your design. Anyone who owns his books will take time to enjoy them, and when you're asked what you want for this present or that, ask for specific books you want to add to your library.

PROGRAMMING YOUR TIME

Don't ever say you don't have time. What you mean is "I haven't arranged my life so I can make the time to do more of the things that are meaningful to me." For the things that count, there is time. A recent survey by the Education Testing Service showed that 75 per cent of adults desire to learn more about something or how to do something better. The survey concludes, "The major obstacles, in descending order, adults cited as blocking their educational aspirations were cost, insufficient time, not able to go to school full time, home responsibilities, the amount of time required to complete the program, and the fear of being too old to begin." Don't let this happen to you.

Your design project will be a failure unless you allow yourself time. You need to program blocks of time so right this minute go get your engagement book. We all lead busy lives, but you will be amazed at how many free hours you can create and put to happy use when you provide for them in your schedule.

What will you do with an hour on Tuesday from one to two? What could you do Thursday from three-fifteen to five? You could divide your time between museums, the library, art galleries, lectures or exhibits. You need time to browse in bookstores, antique shops, art stores and boutiques. You need time to go on walks so you'll be free to be receptive to architectural details. You need time in the market place to find out what is new. You need time to fully experience things.

You are taking a course. Just like school, you're only cheating yourself when you cut too many classes. If it wouldn't occur to you not to show up at the dentist at an appointed time, why can't you treat your own time with the same respect?

Read in the paper about the Frederick Law Olmsted exhibit at the

Whitney in New York, or an exhibit at a museum near you, find an opening in your engagement book, mark it down in pen (that means it is not subject to cancellation) and go.

It may help you to work out how many hours a week you feel you can work into your schedule and then fill this time accordingly.

Often you'll want to purchase the booklets the museums put out and keep them in your library. I went to an antique quilt exhibition with a friend who bought a book on quilting, *American Pieced Quilts,* and was inspired to make her own patchwork quilt out of old neckties bought at thrift shops and from castoffs of the men in her life! This quilt exhibit at the Whitney started a whole patchwork craze which is still popular now and was in New Jersey 120 years ago. Go to whatever exhibitions are available to you.

CREATIVITY MAKES EVERY DAY A CELEBRATION

Don't be frightened by the word "creative." Everything you do with your own hands has the potential of being creative. The individual way you arrange your flowers, the clothes you make or select, the needlework you do, the rugs you hook are all accomplished through the use of your hands. Through experimentation you can create beautiful designs and work in all forms of craft, discovering new techniques in all areas and forms of self-expression.

If you decide to do the construction work yourself, put on your overalls and get busy. Pouring your own blood into your place may be one of the most satisfying experiences in your life. Most of the rewards, granted, are in the finished product and the money you've saved but there is a lot to be said for the satisfaction of building your own nest with your own two hands.

Prepare yourself for work, however. It is hard labor to do your own painting, papering, plastering and carpentry work. Labor is so expensive, it makes simple things out of the question. I'm all for never doing anything unpleasant if you can hire someone else to do it, unless you will have to go without it if you don't do it yourself. To strip your fluted columns down to the mahogany would be prohibitively expensive if you hired someone to do it, but it might be worth your time to do it yourself because it will give you such deep, lasting satisfaction and pleasure.

In many cases you have no alternative but to do the work yourself because the fortune you pay for labor only guarantees you substandard workmanship. The work that is well done is as rare and precious as gems from Ceylon. When you do something yourself you know where you are. You see, touch and feel very real things and this building toward your goals, your involvement, is reassuring. You sense a belonging and attachment, a secure and comforting feeling.

Courty Bryan, a writer friend, spent a summer building his own studio. He did all the carpentry work, the wiring, the plumbing and painting himself. I happen to know for a fact that Courty has never, until now, used his hands for anything more strenuous than typing. The one time he tried he was at my apartment helping with renovations and he came close to losing his left thumb trying to pound a nail straight into a plaster wall. I'll never forget how hopeless he was and yet he is in the process of finishing a long and difficult book, banging away on his typewriter, in the middle of his own studio, one he created all by himself. Courty said his studio breathes his life and it is real. He feels a communication and language with his surroundings which are heightened by his knowledge of every nail, every piece of wood, all the trouble and work. Courty said it is definitely a help to his ability to work well and when his work isn't going well just being there gets him over the hump.

Courty is no pioneer. Begin a project yourself. Decide what you want to accomplish and start.

Space

To take possession of space is the first gesture of the living, man and beasts, plants and clouds, the fundamental manifestation of equilibrium and permanence. The first proof of existence is to occupy space . . .

LE CORBUSIER

The Wise man looks into space and does not regard the small too little, nor the great too big; for he knows that there is no limit to dimensions.

LAO-TSE

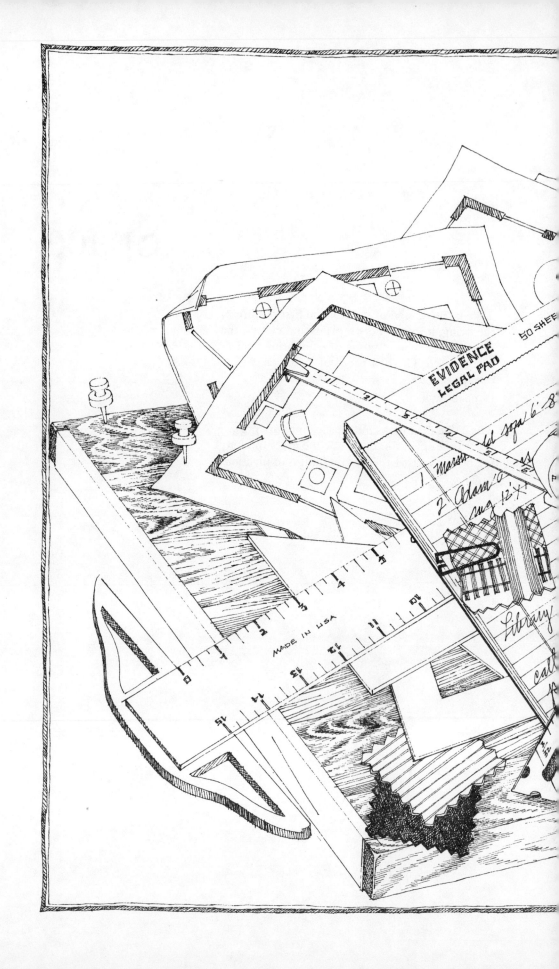

Space is where it all happens. The major reason for the total shift in living concepts is space and it is our most precious commodity besides light and air. You can never be too rich, too happy, and you can never have enough space.

Think of the studies made determining what happens to rats when they are too tightly confined. Elephants need one square mile all to themselves. Prisons are teaching us what spatial requirements man needs. The crushing problem facing us is that we don't have enough interior space to breathe in. We are cramped and have an increasing need to feel more freedom. Ceiling heights have lowered a staggering forty-nine inches in the past sixty years, yet man has grown taller, and our rooms have diminished in scale to the point of being confining. My 6-foot-6-inch friend is convinced one of the most important reasons he enjoys the country and being out of doors is the open feeling of having no ceiling overhead. Size of rooms and proportions are so vital. A bachelor moved into an apartment with one huge room and he is happier and feels better in this 14-foot ceiling room than in the huge house he left. I'm convinced we get out of the house to go to church and museums in part because it is important to expand the close environmental limitations in our own space. The first duke of Marlborough lived in Blenheim Palace in England 250 years ago with soaring ceiling heights of 68 feet. Today his descendants live in a luxurious Park Avenue apartment in New York where they feel lucky to have ceiling heights of 8 feet 6 inches. Times have changed!

There is no comparison between the amount of space we had when we were growing up and what we now occupy and provide for our children. Space designed to be lived in by two is now being used by four. We are faced with the job of opening up our minimal spaces and turning claustrophobic boxes into real places where real people live and function and feel the impact of a real living place. It is essential that we make the best possible use of every inch of available space. Design now is more important than dimension.

Never limit your thinking of space to terms of actual size. The emotional and psychic aspects of space are more important than physical dimensions and should be clearly understood. Our physical structures offer us certain restrictions and constraints which can be opened up through design and illusion. William Lyon Phelps, once a well-known professor of English literature at Yale, said, "Let the walls of your mind be filled with many beautiful pictures." It is our inner spirit which expands all our physical restrictions and allows us to work within the available framework. I will never forget the message of a leading religious leader, Dr. Ervin Seale, whose approach is metaphysical, "attitude over circumstance." George Jackson didn't waste time in his prison cell; he wrote *Soledad Brothers*. Our minds expand our spatial dimensions.

At dinner the other night my dinner partner suggested that his father needed little space. That didn't sound terribly complimentary, but I immediately got a picture of good old dad. Our space requirements are determined by our inner needs and thoughts which vary according to who we are. Any confined area can be treated with sunny colors, straight clean lines and thoughtful lighting so the space fosters uplifting, airy feelings. Emotionally, then, we can experience "up" feelings in weighty spaces, not being conscious of the limitations of four walls pressing in on us. Mirrors make a narrow hall a room, a soft-textured wall covering gives the illusion of a wall receding, and using clear colors bouncing and reflecting off of white expands and opens space. In a small unimaginative room you could place a folding screen along a wall to add interest and give the illusion of a space beyond; or hang a landscape that allows you to travel into that scene.

NEW ATTITUDES TOWARD SPACE

Think of more space. Better space. More practical space. More beautiful space. You didn't move into a larger place just to have it work and be practical. All of us follow our own needs, and our private lives are meant to comfort us and add limitless dimensions of pleasure. Dr. Alexander Comfort in his book *The Joy of Sex, a Gourmet Guide to Love Making* suggests that environmentally we should design a private place where the children can't overhear to have a proper background for a healthy sex life. This supports the design affecting behavior theory. Functionalism is never enough.

Architecture isn't going to help us out much. You should see the cages Wall Street investors use as conference rooms and offices. Where we live is probably not our own dream house. Did you know that only 1 per cent of us will ever get to hire an architect in our lifetime? There are fewer individual housing designs now than ever before because they are too expensive. Slipshod land developers are exploiting our green space with uninspired, sometimes ugly development projects. Most of us live in ordinary, often dull buildings. Few of us can feel a natural sympathy for the beauty of our physical structures. On the contrary, they often deny us any artistic protein because of their bland nothingness. All of us who live in cities know how depressing buildings can be—going into some city apartment buildings reminds me of going into a hospital. The elevator opens onto a long gray-blue corridor of doors with numbers. The only way you can tell an apartment complex from a hospital is that the smell of stale garlic replaces the smell of ether. If you live in the country you may have to buy land as far around your house as your money will permit —and even so, you will soon have neighbors close by. Your landscape may someday have cement where green pastures once were.

There has been a dramatic shift in design thinking and the emphasis now is on the inside space rather than the exterior. Think of your exterior as the silver picture frame around your life and focus on the picture you are featuring inside. Think of architecture in terms of providing you with space.

New designers see our spaces as free, fluid, simple and dynamic. Space is actually sculpted into our living and working conditions to make it easy for us to move about. Our habits and needs trigger off our particular approach to the way we deal with this space. Your ways will give an overall unifying design concept. Why should the living room be a crooked mile from the kitchen when he is here and you are there and you like him?

Don't design arbitrarily. Maybe you'd rather be together and give up your living room entirely, turning the space into a huge lived-in kitchen, one you'd get use from on all occasions.

Ask yourself, how can I manage my space so it is used and appreciated and so it ultimately answers my most important needs and feelings? Ask yourself, what comes first? What is the heart, what is the core of my life style? What aspects of your life can make your space distinctive because you are who you are? How can you live at maximum at home?

There was a board meeting in our apartment house the other evening where thirty of us gathered, and after the meeting we all stayed on for cocktails and an informal tour of the host's apartment. All the people there had only one thing in common, they lived in the same building and, with few exceptions, occupied the same basic apartment, in size and layout.

What fascinated us all, as we talked together about our different apartments, was the fact that not one of us used our apartment in the same way. Mrs. Maxwell's maid's room and bath are our dining area, her dining room is our library, her living room is our parlor, her study is the baby's room. It's no wonder, she is eighty-eight and lives alone with a cook and a house boy—a different situation entirely from our lives one floor board away. What one woman uses for a wig closet could be someone else's toy chest. Besides the structural changes, aesthetically it is day and night from apartment 9B to apartment 9C. Since that meeting we have opened our doors to each other, and I have been allowed to peek at nearly every apartment in the building. The age range of occupants is two months to ninety-two, and the apartments have as wide a range of differences.

BASIC LIVING NEEDS ARE ALIKE

With the great design freedom and possibilities open to each of us, we all have a few standard needs. We need a kitchen, a place to eat, a place to sleep and a bathroom. That is about all the needs we share in room definition. Even here we have to consider our sizes and shapes. We have a friend who is 6 feet 4 inches tall; he spent four years renovating a house and he mistakenly put a "standard" bathtub in his bathroom, so there's no way he can ever take a tub bath. We aren't all standard sizes. I pity tall men who have to stoop to a 34-inch counter height to cut a lemon or mix a drink or shave or carve or serve. Who says 34 inches is the best height for everyone? Closets need your own designs. Why have one closet bar when you can have two? Kitchen storage areas need to incorporate your particular requirements, children's rooms need different things according to the ages and interests of the children.

While there are basic needs we all share, don't ever feel you should be satisfied with anything that was designed for everyone. It was probably designed for an average person. Does such a thing exist? There is really no such thing as standard. The system is a shambles. How often have you got a flower pot to slip gracefully into a cache pot? How often have you got a ready-made curtain to fit your window? Have you ever found a towel bar to replace your broken one? Have you ever found a tile to match the ones in your bathroom? Have you ever found a door knob that adapted to your safety closet spindle? Have you ever found a replacement for your broken mirrored medicine chest?

THE WAY YOU DEVELOP YOUR OWN SPACE

List your activities Monday through Sunday. This will force you to focus on the reality of how you plan to use and live in your space. You will discover your priorities for each area of space. Jot down your physical spatial requirements so you don't crash into a table leg when you do your gym exercises or so your sewing table or tool chest doesn't miss fitting in a space by two inches. Mark down the light requirements, natural and artificial, as determined by the kinds of hours and times of day you plan to be home. If your children are home all day and your room is the sunniest, possibly you should turn your bedroom into theirs while they are young because you don't use your room until after dark. Or if your living room has northern exposure, you might consider using it as your studio.

Those of us with small children hardly consider them accessories and their needs are foremost in our minds. They guide us to no-trouble materials and keep us honest so far as our limitations are concerned.

Also friends, those you love, should always fit into your planning automatically. When you've got a good thing going your friends would walk barefoot in a snowstorm to be with you and your warmth. Whatever makes you comfortable is welcoming for them.

When you see in writing what you want to accomplish in your space you can set out to discover where those spaces are.

YOUR PLACE WITHIN YOUR PLACE

It is essential that you design into your space your sacred place. It is all right to share a bed, rooms, suitcases and an electric toothbrush as long as you have your own spot. Virginia Woolf wrote in *A Room of One's Own* that a writer needs a room of her own and money. She's right—all of us do. Just knowing it is there is a comfort and will provide you with great relief. This place you create for privacy is as basic as your soul is within your body. This spot is your place within your place. Your oasis . . . your isle of calm.

Actually you need two places, one for you and one for your things. One couple bought a town house and they are such devoted, loving people they designed every inch for sharing their love. Every desk was for him, for her. The only difficulty was the realization that the wife ended up with no space that was really hers—not his or the household's. The linen closet was "hers," the other hall closet was for him, his hobbies. The kitchen cupboards were for her, the cabinets in the library were for him, and his records, books, games and collections. Yes, the silver drawer is important to you, yes, the broom closet is essential to you, yes, you identify with your china closet and your children's toy closet, but this in no way completes your storage and space requirements. You need to create your *own* space within your own space, a space where you can have absolute privacy for yourself and your stuff, whatever that may be. The longer you deny this need the harder it will become to establish this place. Yes, it is an escape, it is for you and no one else, it is private. Build it into your life.

What will you do in your private place? You might go there to plan a dinner menu or meditate or write a note to a sick friend or read the newspaper or make an uninterrupted phone call or design needlework or correct school papers or read a book or edit a book or pay bills or wrap a present or sketch a picture or make an evening skirt or do committee work or study. Or just be still.

The place is there, the need is basic. Find it.

You may convert a hall closet into a mini office; you could turn an extra bathroom into a dark room (by "extra" I mean a bath which is not yours, let the children double up so you have a dark room). The inside of a bedroom closet can become the storage area and a comfortable chair next to the closet, the space. So many of my friends have studios where they sculpt and paint but they never get there. The reason you can't work at home is because you're not properly set up. Bill Goldsmith, a highly talented designer and artist, has his light-up drawing board in the central part of his living room. He is set up there for work.

Men need their privacy as much as women. If you are married, both articulate your needs, list them, measure what will be built in and create separate places. Don't be annoyed by his football games any more than he should be by your sewing projects. Allow each other space for rest. Have that chair so you can watch television and putter around doing your things. Have that sewing closet you always wanted.

In your planning always include a lock and key. Even if you don't anticipate the need. You will want to lock up certain things if only to ensure their safety. Have storage areas that lock, doors that lock. A bubble bath with a magazine behind a locked door at the end of a hectic day is the equivalent of a day at Elizabeth Arden without the wasted time, money and guilt! People will always barge in on a closed door but the locked door secures a moment's peace. A moment of privacy.

Explore your space until you find a sacred spot out of the main stream, away from the noise pollution of your busy life. If children and delivery boys and toys have to go through a labyrinth to get to you there will be fewer thoughtless interruptions. What you might be looking for is the worst space in your house or apartment: The ugly duckling is the sweetest of all because it is all yours. Any man or woman who does not claim his own spot is missing the whole point!

When we discuss each room specifically in the end of the book we will find your needed space. In the meantime, be looking for it yourself.

SPACE IS MADE UP OF INCHES AND FEET

You don't always need rooms to define space. I designed a house where there were no wall dividers except in the bedrooms and baths. One big space could have six or eight areas for work, relaxation and eating, and be more usable than several isolated walled areas. The ceiling and floor are necessary, but what about all those walls?

We were all brought up counting rooms and not giving much consideration to their effectiveness. Seven rooms were more (therefore better) than six rooms. It reminds me of having babies. How much did he weigh is the first question you're asked and if you say eight pounds, it is automatically assumed the child is beautifully healthy. Not true! Today, real estate value is judged on the total dimensions. Don't talk of rooms, say how many square feet you have per floor. Give the whole space figures.

When you flip this switch in your brain you are free to tear down a few dead walls and marry some rooms together. Whenever you improve your livability you increase your real estate value. I've seen couples renovate their spaces around their walls and end up building in, building in, until the scale is diminished to the point of absurdity.

Solid walls no longer should intimidate us from envisioning the same space opened up. Don't accept the prearranged use of space. It might be hopelessly unsatisfactory for your current needs. It would be to our advantage to purchase loftlike spaces where we partition the areas in flexible ways to suit our schedules and growing needs. Schools do this and we need the same functionalism. Think of the activities that go on in the school gym besides athletics and how that space is arranged to be subdivided for smaller groups. Hotels and clubs have movable walls too.

If you have one good space you'll find all your functions will work beautifully. Scale and proportion have as much to do with the success of a space as anything and it is a huge advantage to have your space accommodating. It is perfectly possible to see a client on Tuesday, have twenty for a board meeting on Wednesday, give Jimmy his sixth birthday party on Thursday, have eight for dinner on Saturday and give a brunch for thirty on Sunday, all in the same space. Sounds impossible? Just the opposite. We are all busy and if we have space which allows us this freedom we can do all these things and do them well. Think how much easier it is for us to have a run of activities, one after another. It saves time, money and flowers, but more important, we get geared up. Space properly arranged becomes our saving grace, our right arm.

Never worry about rooms being too big. I told our minister how much I loved his huge, vaulted Gothic church with its heavenly stained glass windows and ceiling reaching up to God and he said, "It's great for meditation but trying for worship. It's too big." I realized the church wasn't at fault, the attendance was.

Any open space you create can have pockets of intimacy for you and a friend, a partner or a client. It is easier to bring a space together emotionally than it is to open it up.

One of my favorite rooms is 28 feet square with a soaring ceiling, 22 majestic feet. Eating Miss Grimble's pecan pie and sipping tea in front of this room's roaring fire elevates this room to glory. Alone or with two hundred people this space is alive and excessively intimate.

If you have no intention of major alterations, consider putting in a door or an opening so you can join two spaces. If your children are away at school why can't you use one of their rooms as your sitting room, putting in a connecting door to your bedroom. When they're home you can lock the extra door to give them total privacy. Or consider closing up a door and allowing the wall to be used for storage or seating areas. Don't accept what you have unless it seems just right for your needs. Space is more flexible than a friend because you can make it over and improve its entire personality. No hurt feelings!

Analyze your rooms in use and see if you have some rooms you rarely use. Don't save a room for an occasional guest, have a great room you use every day and build in provisions for a friend. All you really need is your sofa to be a day bed and your library becomes your "secret" guest room. I say secret because it is not for just anyone who needs a sack. Dining rooms are often restrictive too. In order to have them practical for entertaining, they are often cold and dreary for dinner for two. I much prefer having tables and chairs at ends of rooms rather than in the center. It's more intimate. Where do you want to sit in a restaurant? Against a wall is a nice place to sit. If you have enough space and you'd give up anything before your dining room, consider, at least, having it an enjoyable place to be when you're not hungry! If you don't plan any entertaining for a while why not stack books on your table and enjoy having a library for a change? Remember also how easy it is to get out the folding card tables or rent tables for parties.

REDEFINE YOUR ENTIRE SPACE

The worst thing that can happen to us is to see our space as it was used by the previous occupants. I don't care how pretty Mrs. McGregor's library was, it may be terrible for your needs. Our most basic values have changed, shifting our whole attitude about design. Instead of the desire for perfection and acceptance, which drives us to extremes and excess, nurture your own human needs. Your down-to-earth, basic living values can be designed into a way of life.

Because space is more difficult to come by than things, we should punctuate our space, not fill it up. If you learn to appreciate the physical features of your space you will be able to dress it more thoughtfully.

Study your space empty. Naked space can be beautiful. Most of us have added so many layers of clothing we don't know what color our true skin tone is when it comes to our four walls and their character.

When you examine empty space the good and bad features are accentuated. Pretend you are just moving in. Allow your eye to go clockwise around your room, focusing on architectural features and details. Get a feel for your space before you are distracted by possessions which may be all wrong. Wrong for you and wrong for the space.

Examine your living-room mantel. Is it attractive? Is it in a pleasing proportion with the rest of the room? Is the height compatible with your furniture scale? Is there enough room over the mantel to hang something you love? Note all this now. Staring into a fire is a richer experience when the frame is aesthetically pleasing.

Check to see if you have all your moldings. It is possible there have been some alterations made to your space and you might be missing a piece of chair rail or crown molding. It isn't always noticeable at first, but when you have fresh yellow walls and white trim it will be woefully apparent if something is missing. Have a sound outline before you begin writing your room.

Now is the time to be critical, to experiment and to doubt. Once you make your commitment it is much harder, takes longer and costs more to make changes. We all shy away from this first stage, which is when we put mental dynamite to our places. But it is the most constructive time. To act in your own best interests requires careful examination. You should like the bones. Look for pure and clean lines now because you can always add trappings later if you wish. Take time now to economize until the simple truth is exposed.

Try to keep your space pure until you've had time to think out what you really want. It is like a partnership: You must have an understanding of how you are going to operate as a pair. Study your space until you feel the dimensions and scale. Find out the mood you can create, what needs the most work and where there are character and automatic charm. If you rush through this stage you'll end up accepting what basically is there instead of figuring out how to carry out your dreams. We all want to do something distinguished with our dwelling place and now is the time of maximum opportunity.

Study your light exposures at different times of day. Try different kinds of artificial lighting at night to see what you can do to enhance the appearance of your space. If you have a good view from some windows and a disastrous view from others, make notes so you can plan your room around the good and avoid the bad. A floor plan doesn't photograph all these projects. Plan deceptive treatment to fake the bad and study the glories so you play them up. Shutters are a wonderful help at this because when they are open they take away nothing and frame a good view, and when they are closed they hint that there's a beautiful landscape beyond. We envision in our minds shutters with nature because they are most often used in country houses where there is an abundance of natural beauty.

What are the features about your place that attracted you in the first place? There is an identification and an emotional decision that help us select our spaces. What is it that drew you to your place? Your special knowledge of how you want to live and your personality will contour your treatment and course of action within your space. However, there are specific qualities which you may like just as they are; if there is a certain character or drama this may trigger off your approach and use of the space. Let the characteristics of your space guide you along and instead of there being any limitations, see if you can discover solutions from within. A friend of mine moved into a beautiful duplex apartment which had a built-in bar in a closet in the library. He ended up using the library as an eating room and the closet bar became his china and glass closet. He didn't have to change a thing and the sink and ice maker couldn't be better located for his needs. A ceramic floor in your dining room might be the last thing on your priority list, but if you were to see one in a house you were considering, it would probably draw you to its beauty.

We fall in love with different things and are willing to make sacrifices financially and functionally in order to make them ours. One client bought a co-op which had a double-story living room. The fourteen-foot ceiling was so dramatic and unusual for New York City that we decided to articulate the height even further by carrying the bookcases up to the ceiling. The bookcases are thick and solid with books and look majestic on either side of a mammoth cathedral window. To stop them at a practical height would have made them look squat and any ordinary design would have looked like an afterthought.

Another example of a solution which came out of the apartment is a dining room overlooking the reservoir in New York City's Central Park. The conventional dining-room arrangement didn't allow anyone the privilege of looking at this rare and serene New York picture, so we rearranged the whole floor pian and centered the table and chairs in front of the window.

START FRESH

Whenever you move be sure not to fall into the trap of buying used trappings from the previous owners. It is always a mistake. Twice a day I'm asked, "What do you plan to do with the curtains I bought with the house?" Maybe you don't need curtains at all and if you did, certainly not dull worn ones. You should be totally free to make your own selections. The joy is to do it all your own way, not scrap around with yesterday's remnants. If you can't afford new bookcases which are well designed, you can wait. Why live with someone else's personality when it could never really satisfy you fully. The money you save isn't worth it. We tried to pass off some stuff when we moved and I understood completely when we were turned down. The architect and his wife who took over our old apartment completely redid it and our crystal hall fixtures got junked. To each his own.

Strip your place of everything. Remove light fixtures, ugly hardware, hinges, doors you don't want. Moldings and picture hooks. A huge radiator might be removed entirely, or replaced by a small modern one, which doesn't take up space. Rip up the wall-to-wall carpeting and examine the condition of the wooden floor. You might expose a beauty. Remove every curtain, valance, shade, blind and bracket. No one wants your old curtains either. In order to get a tax deduction you have to have them cleaned and that expense is more than its value; save them for drop cloths. Most of your hardware should probably be replaced. If you're lucky and have good brass hardware, all the more reason to remove it so it doesn't get covered with paint.

After you've stripped everything down to the veins and raw wood and you feel you know your space reasonably well, it is time to begin your concrete planning. You should be close to visionary about your ideas for your space before you go into action.

Always try to get a set of original building plans. If you're planning major construction get an architect or good interior designer to advise you of the possibilities and what your structural limitations are.

YOUR MASTER PLAN

If we had to pay the bills today for our dreams and fantasies, I'd either be in a federal prison or praying for a windfall. What we all must understand is the importance of our commitment and our forward thrust into building something extraordinary. All changes and improvements cost money but that is understood. Once we have the big picture of where we're going we can then map out our plans according to our priorities with a natural sense of timing and order. If every simple floor plan we drew were to be done according to what we could afford here and now, we would be sitting on orange crates and toy boxes. Why put yourself through such torture?

The most essential thing to understand is the importance of growing and building. Your plans should be long range and somewhat bigger than life. A little mystery and a sense of the unknown is exciting, so don't get all buttoned up. Remember, you are kinetic and your furniture is static. A bum reproduction armchair might seem harmless today but tomorrow, jarring, even depressing. Don't gamble on your aesthetic needs and visual perception for the future. You will grow more and more aware. You'll see. But you have to believe in your project or you'll never be able to wait. Long-range planning is impossible if you don't feel you'll be around six months from now. Project ahead five years. Now try to envision ten years. Because we all are living with these question marks we have to stab at what we desire the most, looking down the road into time and space.

Go back to the questions. Are you able to project your future finances? Do you intend to have another child? Will the children share a room? What about entertaining? Do you anticipate doing more entertaining as you go along and if so, will you do it simply or in a more elaborate manner? Will you ever have a helper live in? Do you want to have a studio at home eventually? Do you plan an addition?

When you have analyzed and projected into the future the dreams you want to go after, the mountains you want to climb, get out your scale ruler and make a plan. Have fun and dream of glory. You begin with a floor plan which is the least fun part of all but hang on, the beauty is in the results.

Your floor plan puts an end to trial-and-error guesswork and piece-meal decisions. An accurate plan assures a harmony in your total arrangement. No room becomes a dream easily or accidentally. It takes hard work and careful planning. I think floor plans are the most difficult part of designing. Unless you've had some architectural training, you might find them impossible to create and difficult to read accurately.

A floor plan is your skeleton, as mechanical and technical as an X ray and the most essential part of all planning and decision making. To analyze your room, solve trouble areas, design for comfort and style and understand all the relationships involved, you need a complete floor plan. Before you even begin thinking of your decorative scheme and colors, you have to plan your space. Don't let your scale plan deceive you, however. You are creating a real room on paper. Some beautiful plans create bad rooms because the scale is so hard to envision and so many other factors are involved. You have to try and project your plan into real life.

A professional is trained to read life into these pieces of paper. Because we do this all day long, after studying a given space we actually work from plans, allowing us to do jobs in far-off places. One of our draftsmen worked on plans for a law firm for six months before he ever went on location. He was able to walk through the space as though it were his own. He knew every door opening, every hinge, every outlet, every ceiling height—every inch. To make up for your lack of experience you must feel your own space as thoroughly as a three-dimensional sculpture so your plan will assure a beautifully proportioned room.

I recommend you make your plan in ½-inch scale because the ¼-inch scale used by designers is terribly small for the lay person to read.

Make a plan of your entire space instead of a separate one for each individual room. This way you will constantly be reminded of the connections. Begin with a piece of white opaque paper large enough to lay out your total space in ½-inch scale. With masking tape secure a sheet of tracing paper (architects use rolls and snap them off to any size) over your white paper. This is called an overlay. Now draw in your outlines, your walls, windows and doors. Remember, wood and plaster have thickness so you should indicate an outer wall and an inner wall. And be sure to indicate the projection of all your trims and protrusions. If you have a chair rail which extends $2\frac{1}{8}$ inches from your wall all around your room you lose $8\frac{1}{2}$ inches of visual space all around. This means that if you plan to have a wall unit it won't be flush against the wall. On your plan indicate where your doors hinge. This is important. You can pick up 36 inches of needed space simply by rehinging a door to a "dead" space on the other side of your room or, better yet, hinge it so the door swings out of your room entirely. Measure the height of all your doors as well as the height of your ceiling. I forgot to consider an exceptionally tall entry door once, much to my regret, and the chandelier ended up as shattered prisms on the floor; I should have known better!

These plans aren't for show, they're practical. You should make as many overlays on your tracing paper as you feel you need to satisfy yourself. We keep time sheets for our drafting time and spend up to thirty hours on plans until we've worked out all the problems. For example, you need to indicate all your electrical outlets in their exact location, and this should be a separate plan. Is the ceiling outlet centered? If it isn't, it becomes noticeable when a fixture hangs down off center over a table. Have you allowed enough storage space for books, games, music, TV? Do you have special places where you want to sit when you are alone? Do you feel you have created a sense of space and openness? Each piece of furniture has to breathe. The worst thing we can do is overcrowd, and we all tend to do this. If you overcrowd on your plan, your personal clutter will look like a garbage heap. Envision your rooms filled with activity and allow that life to move freely. We have friends who never use their living rooms except when they have large crowds and then half the furniture is moved out of the way and into the basement. Something isn't quite right there.

How does your sofa co-ordinate in relationship to the wall space? How can you recall shapes? Have you allowed enough space to get behind your sofa table and sit down without bruising yourself? Are your comfortable pieces placed compatibly for relaxed conversation? Are they movable or on swivels for complete flexibility? Are your end tables large enough to be a surface for objects, projects, food and drink? A desk with no electrical outlet nearby is frustrating too. Even if you close up your ceiling and wall outlets you should keep a record of where they are located. A dining-room sconce might seem undesirable to you now, but you might acquire a beautiful painting someday and want to light it. Then you could simply open up your old wall outlet for a picture light. Floor outlets should be indicated as well because if you carpet or tile over them you shouldn't have to guess at their location if you need them at a later date. Floating furniture plans, that is, furniture in the body of a room that is not so dependent on the walls, requires especially thoughtful light plans.

MEASURING

I am afraid of measurements because I am unmathematical by nature, I have no feel for numbers. If you share this failing, always deal in inches when you're physically measuring your space or your furniture. The time to transpose 74 inches into 6 feet 2 inches is when you're at your drawing board, sitting down and relaxed.

When measuring a room, try to get someone to help you. Draw a very crude sketch of the room proportion on a yellow pad and mark openings, windows, jogs and architectural details.

Move clockwise around your room indicating each area of space in inches, starting at a corner. I suggest using a six-foot folding ruler and go along the wall so you keep the ruler stiff. The metal ones are good for furniture and floor measuring. Mark the width and depth of your door trims, indicate your openings, and on a long wall add up your feet in inches. For example, starting at a corner you have a 39-inch wall, 4-inch door trim, 38-inch door opening, 4-inch door trim, etc. (indicate the door hinges). Then after you have completed all four wall elevations, measure the floor length and width. This way you have a triple check of two walls and the floor. Don't assume A and C walls will be identical. Chances are they'll have their own and different measurements. They were built by humans. Carry a folding ruler around with you and measure everything of interest. This trains your eye.

After you have all the measurements of your rooms and available furniture and have noted your technical information you can begin arranging the rooms.

Start by making scale cutouts representing your furniture. You might want to have one color represent the furniture you intend to build in, one color represent the furniture you own and want to use, and another color for things you hope to acquire. Get thick paper so it lies flat, and you might as well select colors you like because you'll have to look at your selection over and over. If you are doing a room from the beginning you need only two colors. If you put a dab of rubber cement on the back, your cutouts won't slip around.

The way you style and form your furniture arrangement is determined by your personality and how you intend to use your rooms. These things will direct you into your own ways of dealing with your space. To say there are only one or two ways of arranging a room is like implying that there are only one or two colors to wear after dark. Your unique uses for your space, coupled with the inherent characteristics of your room will guide you. Don't get burdened by your plan, just try to join yourself to your space.

Begin by determining the most ideal place, the most inviting place to sit. When you're alone you should be in the best spot. Then, develop a grouping around you. This might end up being an unusual arrangement, but experiment and see. Where do you want to sit with others? Separately in chairs or together on a love seat or sofa? If you begin by placing yourself comfortably and building a dynasty around you, I guarantee it will be a good plan. Identify with the kinds of people sharing this space so it will be personally satisfying for them too. Think specifically. It should be good for conversations. That is what "conversational groups" are meant to accomplish. A plan in action is its true test.

Once you arrange your room to satisfy your habits, if it looks funny on paper and you feel insecure, hire a designer to consult with you before you finalize your plans and make your commitments. Whatever your needs are, no matter how complicated, there are answers that will allow your space to function well. Although I have been trained to believe that there is no need to seat more than eight in a grouping (more should stand), sometimes I'm exhausted and would sit anywhere I could find a spot: you have to know how you want your groups to gather and then find out how to make this work in your space. A room might well seat eighteen people, but broken up into groups. All in one would be an encounter group!

When you make a plan, you are working and change is inevitable. Welcome it because it improves and refines your ideas. Changes are positive and constructive as well as proof of personal growth. Just remember to review everything before you begin work. One small change can trigger off a whole new set of solutions and should be carefully examined for content and form and scale. You are trying to create a room that links together like a chain.

SPACE TAKING FORM

The coming together of a space is thrilling. The longer and harder you struggle getting there somehow just adds to the joy. There are important decisions that must be determined before the space takes shape. For example, how much money can you afford to invest in the unmovable background? When you own your own space it doesn't matter so long as you improve the quality of each room, but you still have to come up with the capital. Were you ever to move you would be paid back for your labors, believe me. It is an investment, but nevertheless a big decision. When you design your background, all you have to do is stay away from bizarre designs, and do a first-class job on what you install. Do this and you'll be home free. The background is, and I repeat, the figure of your space. Pick the best proportions you can invent so no one has to come in after you at great expense and make over your efforts.

Before you enjoy the luxury of sipping Soave Bolla by a crackling fire with your feet resting on a stool, you have a war ahead of you. Demolition and destruction precede the building up of peace. Believe it is worthwhile, trust the plaster heap will diminish in time and forge swiftly ahead.

You need to determine and then hire out the work you don't plan to do yourself, and for each area of involvement you might have to get as many as four different estimates. For demolition work (tearing down walls, ripping out old plumbing, wiring, carpentry, flooring), electrical work (next because it makes a bloody mess), plastering (fixing the mess the demolition crew made, and also the electricians), plumbing and carpentry. This is your background, all of which precedes painting, papering, floor covering and refinishing. Most people are driven into nervous states by the above; it is expensive, messy, noisy, difficult and dusty. If you are willing to do the contracting, the rest of the world will be grateful and you know *you* did it yourself. Pay special attention to those you live with when you go through this because it is quite a pigsty to come home to, and unless you're there all day suffering it seems intolerable to a semi-outsider. Unless you are able to capture a bit of proportion and laugh at the daily calamity, better bite your tongue.

Never have competitive bidders come at the same time. It is rude. Tell them all frankly that you are getting comparative bids and arrange different appointments (they'll know anyway because it is the only way to do business). You then have to weigh the decision of whom you select. Weigh this from many different points of view, money being only one. You have to trust the integrity and ability of tradesmen you hire, you have to be able to deal with them personally, you need them to respect you and care about doing an exceptional piece of work, and they have to be able to work well with the other members of your "cabinet." Never underestimate the team effort.

Arrange a joint meeting once you decide whom to hire and let everyone envision the end goals. If you give your people a good understanding of the big picture they will automatically put more of themselves into their fragmented and isolated roles. Let them work out among themselves the areas of responsibility so each can take pride in helping the next guy. A carpenter can mess up a plumber, but good. Remember that. It doesn't matter if they stand behind their work and are willing to fix something that is wrong; if their doing this holds up an entire crew of men on a tight schedule and you are left with no plumbing when you have children to cook for and toilets that need flushing, you won't be grateful. Have your people tell you how long the job will take. It is ludicrous for you to tell them when it must be done if the electrician knows that your deadline is unrealistic. Few deadlines are met exactly in my experience. We were asked how long our kitchen took and I answered, "I don't know yet, so far it has been two years. When we're finished I'll let you know."

TRUST

I've been designing for years and I've never had a job go according to estimate. There are bound to be unavoidable changes and usually they add to the costs. A low bidder gets the job and pads extras everywhere he can to make up for the difference in price. A high bidder pads the estimate to protect himself from contingencies. I urge you to consider carefully your decisions regarding the selection of people you hire because trust takes on prime importance when the heat is on. The heat is always on in construction work.

From bitter experience, I suggest you do all your construction work for a given area at once and, if possible, all the construction work should be done at once throughout your space; even if you are left a bit broke, it usually is worthwhile. Because it is so nerve-racking, don't extend it into prolonged agony. This phase is no fun and should be gotten over as soon as possible so you can begin to build your castle. Once our construction work was completed, it seemed a luxury to me not to have to share our bathroom with workers. I can't emphasize enough the advisability of getting the construction part of the job over with quickly. Don't try to disappear when the work is being done, because you need to supervise, hold hands and watch the mistakes in progress! *New York* magazine had an article on renovations. The husband who was having construction done on his house would go on his lunchtime to supervise. One day he walked into his bathroom and the tiles were the wrong color. (I think they were pink and were meant to be blue.) When the owner brought this to his attention, the tile setter told him the pink were *beautiful* and he wanted to finish so he could go home!

SETTING UP YOUR OWN SYSTEM

After you've made the major space commitments you intend for each room, you have to design conveniences into these dimensions. The more your organization is integrated into your every day, the more it will free your time. Have notepaper in several different locations so you can write notes spontaneously. Have a large covered box or a trunk or a basket for favorite treasures of the children for quick pleasures and pickups. Have a shoebrush in a drawer next to your comfortable chair. What better time to buff a shoe than when you're relaxed? Have a clothesbrush on a hook in your front hall closet for the last dash out the door. Plan a file inside your bedside table. Have your sun lamp next to the telephone. Have mirrors where there's music for exercise and dance. Everywhere you turn you should have conveniences. Save time, save motion.

Store your wood next to your fireplace. Create a wood place. Have drawers in tables for matches, extra candles, coasters and a compact. Have surface space for current magazines and books. Replace your decorative dressing table with a working desk and put your make-up inside closed doors for instant access. You can create a whole mess area behind doors, so that your electric curlers, hair dryers, make-up mirror, jewelry and all those small essential personal items are right there. Have a pad and pencil handy so you can jot things down while you shave or put on make-up. Have the TV set on a swivel stand so you can catch the news while having a Vita-Bath. Have your latest magazines in your bathroom.

Group your activities by the clock. Double up. Combine several things in one space so your rooms serve twice their ordinary potential. Build in a whole workshop in one of your children's closets. Use your library by day and eat there at night. Every space should have flexibility to be used for several different purposes throughout the week. Put your working desk in the far corner of your living room so it allows you to use your beautiful space even when you are paying bills or correcting school papers.

About the telephone: I urge you to have all of them on 13-foot cords and the longest receiver cord you can get. Telephones ring at odd moments and the conversations aren't always scintillating. It is handy to be able to putter about as you order your lamb chops or your ancient auntie calls just to say hi. Why be trapped when you could mist your plants, wax a table, peel carrots, put away the groceries, clean out a messy drawer, shine a shoe or even do modest exercises? So far, the person at the other end can't see you. They might be curious about the various sounds but that adds to the fun too!

Friends of mine have their kitchen phone so high up on the wall you have to stand on your tiptoes to dial. The cord is no longer than a four-year-old's first necktie. I asked why it was placed in such an off-putting, inconvenient spot, and was told it was there to discourage Margarith the maid from long conversations!

Your primary consideration when organizing your space is practicality. Le Corbusier said, "The key to aesthetic emotion is a function of space." In order to have a well-run place, have it function efficiently and be enjoyable, everything has to work. First, make a list of all your mechanical needs. If you need to buy any household equipment such as a vacuum cleaner or an ironing board, buy the best and be done with it; the best will work and be well designed. After all, why should you put great effort into finding a beautiful chair and then choose an ugly bathroom scale. Each thing we use should be as aesthetically pleasing as possible. Can openers do have their limitations but buy the best you can find. Don't settle for ugly beige plastic garbage-can liners if you can get white or yellow or a good honest green.

Let me add here that you should keep your machines to a minimum. Gadgets and gimmicks break and repairs cause despair. Besides, they do little to add warmth and a comfortable mood. Buy only what you need because while machines save you time and effort and are freeing for us, they are noisy, cold and expensive. Did you know that any new appliance deteriorates in value approximately 300 per cent as soon as you bring it into your life and have it connected? I have a friend who has been paying storage charges on a dishwasher for five years because it is almost new and she wanted to sell it without losing her shirt. Face it, it is an old model and of little resale value.

With your well-selected machines running smoothly you'll feel organized, which will make your life a whole lot more relaxed. Now you're in the position of taking care of more human needs and personal pleasures. After all, the whole point is to have your place capable of running smoothly so it frees you to go about those things in life that interest you most. An organized domestic life is freedom. Make it the ultimate luxury for your needs.

SPACE RESPONDS TO BEING USED

When we are ingenious with the designs we build into our space we're able to use them more. Nothing is better for the spirit of a room than having it in operation. When a room is in motion it is worthy of the space it takes up and rooms that are rarely used are wasteful and uninviting. When they are brought out of the deep freeze, they take time to thaw.

Whenever we leave home we are a guest. Personally, I can think of no greater comfort or compliment than to walk right into someone else's life. All the silly things around, the clutter of activities and the vitality brought about because of their interests make a place unique. A hotel room, created for a nonperson, is clean and neat and unoccupied. Never think you are doing anyone a favor when you open up a room just for them. If you want to do something for someone else, open up champagne, not a room. A room should have the spirit of last night's fire, the scent of a candle's light and the feeling of anticipation that there is a wealth of happy hours to be spent in this room.

When we use our rooms all the time we need to have places for our belongings. To assure maximum use from every room, provide adequate storage areas. I believe we can double the usefulness of our spaces by having our hobbies and projects at arm's length. You have to determine what you want to leave exposed because many of our interests can add color and flavor to our rooms and the rest can be concealed behind doors. Why put away beautiful games and toys which are a feast to the eye and a comfort to fondle? This is the texture you need for warmth. Put away ski poles and boots, Christmas tree holders and folding work ladders, but have enjoyable, attractive things as part of every room. Hide enough of the ugly junk so your good things can be enjoyed. Exploit your space until you have stored everything you want as conveniently and gracefully as possible. This is for your pleasure and comfort. Be tough on your space so it is easy on you.

Value

He who looks for a brighter tomorrow and finds no beauty today, somehow missed the joy of living somewhere along the way.

JENNY B. DERWICH
Joy of Living

What counts perhaps is not the specific values, but the recognition by all of us that we need to reach beyond the material and concern ourselves with what makes life really worth living—and loving.

JOHN D. ROCKEFELLER III
The Second American Revolution

Fit your money to your values, instead of your values to your money. What's most important to you? What nourishes you? What fulfills you right now? Would a studio be more meaningful to you than a living room? If you have little space and you paint, it might be far more sensible to set yourself up with a working studio than to have a still-life room which restricts you from painting. Is light the most essential thing to you and would you be willing to go with less space in order to have light? Or do you prefer the English club ambience and values walnut paneling provides. A senior partner of a law firm moved into a dark-mahogany-paneled office and painted it bright white. Would a new painting make you smile or new curtains? Would you get more pleasure from an old quilt or a bed-spread? Would you prefer more bookcases in the bedroom or new kitchen cabinets? Would you prefer more closet space or expanding your bath-room size? A fresh evaluation can bring on new values and goals which might help structure your environmental thinking.

Taking the broad view, what are you trying to build in your life as a whole? By establishing long-range values you can discover purposes in your way of living, a life style. Take responsibility for your choices and make the necessary compromises and sacrifices. How we spend our time and money reveals the truest story about our lives as a whole and about our circumstances. Beyond allowing us to express our sensitivities, how we divide up our hours and funds allows us to live out our most important values and beliefs.

In all matters of living we should strive to get the most out of what we put in. In our financial matters we shouldn't concern ourselves with the cost but rather with the "cost effectiveness." Values and goals can be realized on any financial scale. Ask yourself, "What is the effectiveness of this house, this sofa, this work of art? What is it worth to me personally?" Is your house the center of your life? Is the big overstuffed sofa the one thing you crave for your library? Would you prefer to buy the painting in the gallery you saw a month ago or to invest in an entire room full of chintz upholstery? I know a musician who spends more money on his classical records than on his monthly rent. You have to determine these values according to your personal needs. You may have priorities for things that require a great proportion of your whole budget and because of their value to you the other sacrifices are worth it.

WEIGHING YOUR PRIORITIES

Compromise frequently is a necessity. Where you make your compromises is a personal choice, but the compromises should be made on the less important things in your life. If you don't care about an expensive bedroom rug, that's where you can save money. If you don't care about a paint job with the "Tiffany touch," don't spend the money. You're the only one who can determine how you should spend your money and time. An outside pressure or influence may be keeping you from finding your own way, but possibly you could give up one financial cushion in order to free the money to begin collecting art. Or maybe you want to sink roots and plant seeds, cultivating your own garden. This can be expensive. If spring arrives and you want azaleas, dogwood and forsythia in a blaze of bloom, you should budget money for this. On the other hand, you may prefer to spend a large percentage of your funds on entertaining, eating gourmet food, drinking fine wines and using hand-embroidered linen. Maybe you want to collect old rugs or old stamps or silver. I know someone who collects old clocks and buys them before anything else—because he values them highly. If you love to travel and want adventure in your life, have one modest, meaningful anchor to come home to.

The life style you put together requires selectivity in all aspects of your living, so that everything comes together for you. Don't live with a grandfather clock if you don't appreciate it; it's better to give it to someone who will. Don't accept fashionable trends as part of you unless they delight you; take what you enjoy and delete the rest. Valuable things require your belief in them or they're stealing from what's really you. You know what feels comfortable. You know what feels good.

Write down on a piece of paper the things you value most. No one is judging you, there is no right or wrong. The things you love are symbols of memories and special moments in your life. Your exposure and experience have led you to a certain keen appreciation of beauty and form. Write these human values down to be looked at privately. This exercise is for you only.

There was a provocative article recently about a man who is a time expert; he counsels his clients into realizing their personal goals. He suggests we list the thoughts that flood into our minds (three minutes to fill a big sheet of paper). Let's take three minutes to do this exercise right now. List all the things most real to you that money can't buy. They might include:

love	*joie de vivre*	designing
beauty	fulfillment	writing
happiness	contentment	nature
sharing	my surroundings	security
peace of mind	personal identity	health
knowledge	mobility	reading
truth	giving	flowers
harmony	understanding of others	beaches
roots	free time	music
change	friendships	cooking
being in touch	family	dance
with my times	privacy	exercising
serenity	art	theatre

All this requires time and understanding. We are all too busy and rushed, getting caught up in a frantic pace. If we are doing meaningful things then we're living a rich full life. Examine your calendar to see how closely related your days have been to your interests. Have you had time to read? Time alone? Family time? We should all take time. It is now that our lives are being lived. Tomorrow is today, twenty-four hours older.

Feeling all our senses fully and appreciating the harmony of forms and the rich textures around us require time. Value the miracles of our natural world. Open up your heart to the sweet smell of hyacinth and the warmth of the sun on your body. The feel of white coral under your toes, the sound of the palm leaves swaying in the gentle breezes. Are not these sensual appreciations the real pleasure of life? By training our senses to all these stimuli, we create a richer, fuller life. Lao-tse, the Chinese philosopher, said, "He who can see the small is clear-sighted." In the words of Rainer Maria Rilke ". . . cling to nature, to the simple in nature, to the little things that hardly anyone sees, and that can so unexpectedly become big and beyond measuring; if you have this love of inconsiderable things and seek quite simply . . . everything will become easier."

The decisions you'll be making about your surroundings, to accommodate your life style, require time. They will come, but it's not easy and deserves thoughtful consideration. Anytime the answers aren't in front of you it takes longer. Wait till the answers flow. They will in time. Small things and big things require intelligent solutions. Kitchen knobs might seem a small priority but when you realize that you touch them on an average of 148 times a day, it becomes important to make a selection that will please you.

"The design comes out of the problem." If you analyze your goals and accept your limitations you can find pleasant ways of answering the questions. Most often we feel bogged down because of financial restrictions. If you can't afford the expensive sofa of your dreams refer back to your priority list and maybe a modest, sturdy inexpensive sofa, well designed, with a lively fabric could make you happy. If you can't afford the paneling in your library, consider a brown-textured wall covering that will give the same rich, warm feeling. Don't despair if you can't afford the shutters for your windows. Simple casement curtains with hanging plants and a spotlight may be more exciting. Don't be upset if your bedspread estimate is too high. Rethink your needs and consider several inexpensive sheet designs for freshness and variety. If you can't afford to be a collector, rent a print or a painting from your local museum. Don't go without flowers. Buy one daisy and put it in a miniature liquor or perfume bottle.

THE SPIRIT IS WHAT COUNTS

The beauty behind any atmosphere is the spirit and vitality. In striving toward our goals and looking ahead we must pause along the way so we can assimilate the fundamental purpose of it all. What you can create in the way of charm and atmosphere through your love and caring has little to do with money. No matter how sophisticated your end results, they may lose their beauty if you lose your enthusiasm.

Each day is a miniature lifetime. All the elements that make up our lives should go into each day. Who says Saturday is more of a day than Tuesday? Why should we change our style when others are watching us? Living well is an art and requires discipline and total involvement. A friend I play tennis with describes living as "something that requires a tremendous input to get a little out."

Each day counts and should be lived joyously, enjoyed fully. No earth-shaking events need color our hours. We need not be overloaded with schedules that ulcer our stomachs or pain our backs. Quietly, in your own way, find delight in your daily rituals, whatever your celebrations may be.

Spread out the wealth of life evenly so the passing hours leave no regrets. A few sips of wine each day might give us more pleasure than a bottle that's saved for "special" times.

Home is where you should have no confinements. Here is where you can open your heart and fill it to the brim. Don't cater special luxuries to your friends that you don't indulge in yourself. Don't light candles only for company. Don't buy flowers just for guests. Don't buy presents just for friends. Don't wait until you go out to wear your new dress or suit. Don't serve drinks out of stemmed glasses only at parties. Don't save living for a rainy day.

You are the architect, designer and executor of your space. When you accept your surroundings as very real and essential extensions of your life, your rooms will glow.

Now that we've discussed you and your needs for your space, let's get on with specifics, the building blocks you'll need to create your space just the way you want it.

Part Two

Our todays and yesterdays are
the blocks with which we build.

HENRY WADSWORTH LONGFELLOW

ELEMENTS

In Part Two we'll talk about the various design and structural elements that go into creating the kind of space you want: walls and ceilings, floors, windows, furniture, lighting, fabric, color, accessories, maintenance. There is a great selection within each element, and you can choose the particular style of window, floor, etc. that works best for you, for each of your rooms. Keep in mind the functional and aesthetic aspects of each choice— is it practical, economical, purposeful, beautiful?

Walls and Ceilings

Let the walls of your mind be filled with many
beautiful pictures.

WILLIAM LYON PHELPS

Walls and ceiling determine 80 per cent of your room's scale and appearance. So how you deal with your walls determines the background mood and identity of the room and sets the aesthetic pace.

Walls separate activities and allow for variation of themes. Without these separations, individuality and privacy would be impossible in a family. Yet, today, with our shortage of space, we're finding traditionally fixed interior walls inflexible and space consuming; walls of tomorrow will be systematized so they can expand and contract according to our constantly changing space requirements. In the future we will all live with movable walls.

Space and a shift in people's basic life styles are the principal reason for the opening up of our interior partitions. The Japanese, of course, have never had solid room divisions. We've had to re-evaluate our needs because our once "cozy" space has become claustrophobic. Now it's possible to have fewer, larger spaces, make them flexible so they function for a variety of uses, and feel more expansive and free.

As our lives become busier it is important to be able to share family life and to have eye contact with others, while you are doing your work. By imaginative handling of walls, one can set the table in the dining area and be a part of the gathering in the living room. A studio can be half opened onto another room so there is a sense of being together.

There's no arguing about our need for walls (and doors to slam!) but question how yours are functioning for your current requirements. Some of us live in charming old houses or apartments that were designed to accommodate servants, when there was real separation between quarters. Newer housing automatically has fewer walls because our needs are so different today.

I'm going to discuss how you can put your walls to work so they function for you, to show how walls can be flexible, how you can borrow space from walls for your own use. We'll explore the possibilities of decorating through wall coverings and paint, how you can recontour the shape and appearance of walls, how you can open up space (through use of white and mirrors) or insulate (to buffer sound).

Walls today should be put to practical use. Many of the things you need they can provide: storage for books, TV, beds, drop-top desks, tables, folding chairs, music equipment and all varieties of hobbies and paraphernalia.

The "room divider" has come a long way now that every precious ounce of space counts. Look for flexibility in the room divider you choose. The most elaborate wall divider is a "wall system" which is a vertical storage area. These dividers come in varying heights, starting at 42 inches. Straight or curved, they are an excellent way of dividing two spaces, providing storage and creating a sense of privacy. In your bedroom, for example, you could have a 42-inch high wall system coming out into the room which would provide a little corner space for desk/dressing area. By dividing space, you can give an illusion of more space.

Certain wall divisions should not be solid divisions because your needs are constantly changing and solid divisions can cramp your space. If you don't want to invest in anything expensive to divide your space, buy burlap folding screens (they are very reasonable), and staple or glue on some book-end paper, or a favorite material. When it's not in use, a folding screen can soften a dull solid wall; then, you can move it into the room when a division is required. Screens can hide a TV, an ugly pipe or a temporary work area; then, the height will be determined according to what you are hiding.

Analyze the drawbacks of your existing layout. Are you in a financial position to make any structural changes now or in the near future, say in a year's time? Can you see any way of solving your space problem without major construction? If you were to alter your existing space by adding or removing a wall, or closing up a door, determine exactly what your requirements are and what you will gain.

MOVABLE WALLS FOR SPACE DIVISION

Now consider your total square footage. Don't cut yourself off by permanently adding another wall to further divide a room. Put up a flexible wall division so you can regain the larger space when the division isn't needed.

A family living in a city apartment did this beautifully in their children's rooms. The Millers felt they wanted the 18-foot-by-12-foot room to remain one open space for Billy and Laura to share, and yet they felt privacy for each child was important too. They used a white woven-wood flexible vertical screen which was installed on a track in the ceiling. This took up only 15 inches when stacked against the wall and opened easily to divide the space in two separate rooms.

Another approach to dividing space for children sharing a room is to have wall systems right in the middle of the room with storage access from both sides. Two girls share a room with a wall system blocking each separate area, open on one end for passage. Their drawers, desks and book storage are on either side but stem from the same source. This "system" was installed on heavy duty casters so it is movable.

STORAGE WALL—"THE BUILT-IN"

You can make a small room appear larger by building in floor to ceiling storage space. By carrying the storage space clear up to the ceiling you gain 60 per cent more capacity than you do with low cupboards, and you eliminate the need for clumsy chests of drawers and bulky furniture. None of us has enough storage space and we've outgrown our closets. Our skis are under the beds and we're climbing the walls. Here's the answer to where to put off-season clothes, suitcases, skis, tennis racquets, folding card table and chairs, Christmas ornaments, typewriters, sewing machines, movie cameras, and the mountains of apparatus that accompany us wherever we call home. The top shelf of a storage wall is a perfect place for all your paint supplies, Aunt Tillie's silver tea service and the punch bowl.

In your child's room, just think what floor space you'd gain by having one entire wall constructed for storage. You can have the plainest pinewood cabinets made with flush doors and paint them the color of the wall. (The more invisible the wall becomes, however, the more expensive.) Hidden hardware and hinges add to the labor price; nevertheless, keep your design as simple and straight on as possible. Your goal is to have a wall for storage; there is no need for decoration or trappings. Inside these doors, install adjustable shelves. Then you'll have a place for shoes, books, games, dolls, puzzles—you name it. By having doors to close, you eliminate having surfaces cluttered up with the inevitable accumulation of things.

Choose your storage wall carefully and try to square off your room.

Ideally you should put your storage on one of the two short walls (most rooms are rectangular in shape, and it will make the room a better proportion if you bring a short wall forward than if you narrow the room by building out a long wall).

Keep your doors narrow so they don't take up too much wall space when opened. Two feet are wide enough. You can use shutters as doors. Or a screen on a track; it doesn't take up any room at all.

BORROW SPACE

We all have things we'd change if we could. Too bad Elaine couldn't lop off two feet from her dining room and add it on to her bedroom where she really needed the space. But by redefining her storage needs, in effect she achieved the same result. Elaine's bedroom was tiny and she had a 12-foot-by-18-foot dining room which was much bigger than she wanted for her needs. She brought the two end walls in the dining room forward 24 inches each, and built in floor-to-ceiling storage space—ample enough for everything she owned. Then her bedroom didn't need to be bigger because she had enough space there for her current clothes, a few magazines and books, a small writing surface and a bed. When all her storage problems were solved, so were her space problems. She built these two storage walls as reasonably as possible, using inexpensive pine and ordinary hardware and hinges. She looks forward to the day she'll be able to do the exact same thing on a more "cushioned" budget so she could have "Soss" concealed hinges, "magnetic" catches, etc., but for the mileage she gained, she has no complaints. The concealed hardware and magnetic catches make the wall appear to be a solid wall. Aesthetically, it is more beautiful to have a flush wall than for the practical storage wall to be obvious. Also, the workmanship of perfectly fitted and hung doors is pleasing. This is a question merely of refinement and style.

WALL INSULATION

In our closer quarters our walls have to act as sound absorbers to pad us from the surrounding noise. If you're a young mother, you may want to soundproof the children's rooms. My friend Sara used felt that she glued on herself. She used a paste recommended to her by the store who sold her the felt and to make the seams less raw she pasted on striped grosgrain ribbon. The results are smashing in blue, red and yellow. Cork or any suede finish or cloth texture will help too. If there's a thin wall between two rooms and you're building in storage, try to do it on that thin wall if possible. Real insulation can be applied on the wall, too. Ask your lumber yard for acoustical advice. Another friend of mine carpeted her son's walls with indoor-outdoor squares; you can buy and stick them down yourself. They come in many different colors and if one gets damaged (by devils or darts) it can be easily replaced.

USE WHITE FOR SPACE EXPANSION

To increase your space without structural change, make your walls white. Liberal application of white paint or paper to your walls can increase the emotional size of your space up to 40 per cent. The most common problems facing all of us is that our rooms lack good natural light, and they are too small for our needs. Of all the tricks of the trade, nothing can do more to extend space and reflect light than the color white. It sounds too simple to be true but it's magic.

In one apartment building I know three families have the identical apartment—5D, 6D, 7D. All the families have two children. Two of the apartments are heavy and dark in feeling while the third seems huge, light and open. It's the white walls that increase the space and fool you into thinking the apartment is enormous. In fact, the rooms are quite small.

If you have a smallish room and you want to lighten it up and still use strong colors, consider using your color on the floor and ceiling and using white on the walls. It really works wonders. Don't be worried about white being antiseptic; it is what you do to it that gives it charm.

Another example of white enlarging space: A client moved into an apartment on the "F" line which was 24½ inches narrower than an apartment on the "E" line. There was an "E" apartment available on the second floor but the Kelloggs wanted to be up higher to get more light so they chose the smaller apartment. They opened up their rooms by painting the walls white, so that their 24½-inch loss seemed to disappear. You can't fake sunshine, but space, yes.

White reflects natural and artificial light. An all-white room sparkles and is as stimulating as bright yellow or shocking pink. It isn't a cold color; on the contrary, it's the greatest backdrop for color. When you use white, keep in mind what the colors in your room will do to tint the white "their" way. For example, a yellow floor with a white wall will cast a yellow tint on the wall. If you have lots of different colored accents, in art or painted surfaces, you'll get patterns of their colors reflected on your white. Without trying, you'll have "off" white but it will contain all the colors you put with it.

When white is used for space expansion it might be most dramatic to keep the space pure, with no additions. Instead of hanging something on the white wall that will close in and block your space, take another tack. Make the wall go away with lighting.

You can play up the light reflections from either your windows or your artificial lighting to highlight your walls, flooding them with subtle movements of shadow and light reflections.

For instance, a client has a piece of stained glass sculpture in front of his hall window. Without the use of any other color he has a rainbow hall, filled with moving, translucent light.

Elaina Morrow has displayed her crystal collection of animals in her window in the living room, on glass shelves. Light reflects from the animals and the whole room is a prism with millions of dancing facets of color gleaming all over her white walls. Because her walls are pure white, the colors reflected on them remain clean.

Try hanging a plant; light it with a spotlight so the wall turns into a wondrous moving scene. A mobile at the window (glass or any material) will dance on your white walls and give them an added dimension.

If you want to relieve the starkness of your white wall, use something strong, don't hang a wishy-washy "grouping" of leftover prints or paintings. White shows up everything and requires a crisp statement. One striking graphic print smack in the center of your wall will say a lot. An effective trick is to hang a perspective picture, one with depth, on your white wall; you lose yourself in the distance the picture travels. Instead of closing in the wall, the wall opens up and your eye gets adjusted to the scene and forgets the actual size of the picture or the wall.

MIRRORS: THE DOUBLE IMAGE

If you don't want to expand your space by using white on the walls, the next best trick is space-cheating mirrors. Use them strategically and you can double your space in problem areas. Use mirrors to fill an entire wall. A client with a long skinny hall did this on the wall facing her front door and it opened up the space as though there were an entrance hall. We live by illusions and mirrors create them for our space.

When using mirrors, be sure to look at your reflections. Everything shows—the floor, ceiling and opposite wall. You will catch several glimpses of yourself too, so get ready!

FILL "DEAD" SPACE WITH MIRRORS

If you have two windows next to each other, perhaps eight to twelve inches apart, consider putting mirrors between them. The solid wall disappears, and the windows appear much larger.

An interior designer friend moved into a duplex apartment where you walk right into the balcony. He decided to create an eating area in this small space so he filled the whole wall with mirror squares he had cut in 20-inch pieces with beveled edges. Bob's table and chairs butt right against the glass and the mirror allowed for useless space to become a pleasant dining area. The squares and the beveling are only a decorative element which adds elegance and interest.

A solid column that becomes a rectangle of mirror creates the illusion of space, and the solid column disappears.

Walk around your rooms and find places for mirrors. Francine Gibby has a niche with shelves where she displays her glass collection, and she mirrored the back wall so she could see everything twice. Mirror your bedroom hall wall so the children can do ballet and gym exercises. Install an exercise bar. Mirroring the back wall of a narrow bar or the back wall of a cabinet is an effective way to open up an enclosed space. Mirror the walls of your bathtub and you'll feel you're in your own swimming pool. Kathy Evans has a cupboard where she stores all her female clutter, and she has mirrored the inside of the doors so she can see her hair from all sides. The small luxuries in life are the most fun!

DO YOUR OWN MIRROR WORK

You can get mirror glass now in 12-inch squares, with a sticky backing for instant installation. Mirror cutters aren't expensive, but mirror and labor are, so if you have any mirror around you might want to experiment putting it to use. Ask at the hardware and houseware store in what sizes precut sheets of mirrored glass are available. If the standard sizes they have fit your requirements it will mean a big savings for you. When seaming a mirror (if all the sizes are too small to completely cover your space), do it in a graceful proportion. Instead of having the mirrored space split down the middle or across the center by the joining seams, have one center panel and two side half panels. When adding to the height of the mirror piece, have one panel of mirror glass cover two thirds of the area and the second piece (at the top) cover one third. Old mercury mirrors always came in smaller pieces, so yours will look intentionally seamed. When installing mirrors, always have them high enough to elevate the space. A mirror hung too low makes a tall person feel awkward.

Liz Wolcott installed a triptych of mirrors in her bathroom. She put mirrors on the back wall and at right angles coming around the sink. Visualize the mirrors you look at when trying on clothes in a store dressing room. What a great effect. When you put mirrors at right angles you can create a tunnel of images. Furthermore, Liz had the two end panels on hinges so she could adjust them in any direction (useful for checking the back of your hair).

DECORATIVE WALL OPTIONS

Before you decide how to decorate your wall, think of your options. You can have flowers, stripes, paisleys or geometrics. Your walls can be painted, papered, graphic, have a shiny or a dull finish. A wall can be bright or quiet, smooth or bumpy. You can go plain, fancy, busy, hot or cold. There's no limit. You can use fabric, paint, plaster, wallpaper, vinyl or wood. You can hang art, tapestries, rugs, bas-reliefs, sculpture, books. Or nothing. You can build entire walls of niches to display your treasures.

Remember to base your decoration decisions on an aesthetic solution that serves a functional purpose as well. A grass paper adds the warmth of texture—but it is also an aid to sound absorption. A vinyl finish is bright—but it is also scrubbable.

Look at your room and its light exposures and decide what you want the end result to look like. Whether you want a wet-look patent vinyl or a room full of flowers, there's something available that will be in your choice of color, scale and design. You have to know what you're looking for first.

Next, consider the condition of your walls. If they're a disaster, it will probably be cheaper in the long run to hang a wall covering than to prepare them properly for painting.

PAINTING AND PAPERING WALLS

You can apply the right treatment and create any mood you want by painting in color, or hanging wall coverings. What was once hand painted by artisans with pigment is now machine produced in materials available by the yard and roll. Labor is too expensive today for us to have specialized paint jobs; no one can afford quality hand workmanship, it's a thing of the past. But it's been mass reproduced for more of us to enjoy.

Back in the days when hand-painted walls were an art form, painted walls weren't flat. They had texture and, through a variety of skills, the walls were "glazed" so they had depth and transparencies. Walls were alive and beautiful unto themselves. And now machines manufacture in an hour what used to take one man two thousand hours to produce.

Of all the fabulous wall interiors I've seen, one we did a few years ago will always be my favorite: for a client who wanted her walls to be like clouds and sand, mist and sky. She wanted walls with soul, walls that lived. The assignment: organic walls on Fifty-third Street in New York.

Peter Guertler, an artist who can do anything at all with an interior wall and some paint, accomplished this difficult assignment. He experimented by mixing lead, sand and rough plaster in his paint; then he brushed on uneven swirls of texture in subtle shades of sandy tones. The walls really have that Malibu misty mood and flavor, they create a relaxed and unpretentious ambiance. Patricia added to her "beach" a small rock garden, her shell collection, lots of plants and trees and flowers. Peter's beach effect has been copied and reproduced in vinyl, so you can achieve the same effect for under ten dollars a roll. To anyone who's really a texture and pigment nut, the paper wouldn't be the same; but for most of us, this substitute is a lot better than painting a wall a color labeled "sand!"

COST OF PAINTING VS. HANGING

For a straightforward job, it's always going to be cheaper to paint. However, when you're after something special, something that gives more than color, hanging a wall covering will be cheaper than creating a special paint effect.

There is no logical scale for the cost of wall coverings, but the prices vary because of any number of factors, none having that much to do with quality. If a paper is hand printed in Hong Kong and imported, it will cost eight times as much as a domestic, machine-made print; but the "quality" could be equal. The paper hanger needs to protect himself in the event he has to replace the expensive paper, so he charges accordingly.

We can have beautiful walls today by using a textured or patterned vinyl wall covering. Vinyl papers are practical and reasonable—two necessities in our world today. Twenty years ago one used vinyl in kitchens, but now it's used everywhere.

PATTERN VS. SOLID WALLS

The advantage of a pattern on the wall is its decoration—an ugly room can be entirely transformed through the use of a patterned wall covering. The entire room can be pulled together to create a charming, inviting space.

The disadvantage of this instant decoration is that it's inflexible, and it can be expensive. Also, it's difficult to hang pictures or paintings on a patterned wall. You can move pictures around but not your wall covering.

Think of it this way: You can buy one striking, patterned dress (knowing you'll have to live with it for five to seven years) or you can buy a plainer dress in a color you like, and use eight colorful scarves to alter your costume. Which is better for you? This is the kind of decision you have to make about your room. If you're one who easily tires of things and loves changes, I suggest your walls be a less definite design.

PAPER HANGING

It's difficult to find a cheap and very good paper hanger. Talented paper hangers are getting paid whatever price they want and they always have work. If you pay twenty dollars for a single roll of printed wall vinyl (that's not unusual nowadays) your paper hanger can charge you up to twenty dollars per roll to prepare your walls (depending on their condition), line your walls and hang your vinyl. Then, you still have to paint the woodwork, doors, etc. Very often the paper hanger is not a painter.

You could hang your own paper, but it's quite a job. Paper hanging requires reading directions, being careful and being patient. Through the years I've seen professionals and novices alike make a mess of things. Look carefully at the flowers in your paper and be sure to hang it with the stems down and the blossoms up. Butterflies you can have upside down, birds maybe, but not flowers. Also, remember that all papers with any texture at all have a repeat and should be matched at the seams.

Every small error shows up in paper hanging. If you haven't matched a repeat perfectly it gets worse as you finish the strip. A wall that isn't smooth will distort the finished paper. Silver-foil papers and high-gloss vinyls show every imperfection. A glue that isn't the right kind or solution will allow the paper to lift away from the wall. In the Pan American Building, we installed two hundred single rolls of grass cloth in an office space and one week later it was all in piles on the floor. Afterward we discovered that the painted plaster wall was really a painted-over vinyl wallpaper so the glue didn't adhere.

I don't mean to discourage you, but if paper hanging were simple more of us would do it to save money.

If you plan to do your own papering start with something easy in an area where you feel free to experiment. Paper hanging is easier than working with Contac paper.

Buy a paperback book on wallpapering and read the directions very carefully. Repeat them to yourself until you fully understand the scope of your assignment. Gather all your facts ahead of time. Is your paper pretrimmed? How is it packed? What is the width of usable paper? What, if any, is the repeat? What kind of paste should you use? Do you have to line or canvas your walls? What kind of equipment is required?

Allow twice as much time as you think you'll need, so you don't feel pressured. If you're frantic your paper hanging will be a disaster. I suggest you do this job with someone else. Professionals can handle these strips of paper without wrinkling them, but beginners need help and companionship while accomplishing such a noble task. Good luck! Reserve a few extra rolls from the same running in case you make an error or just run short.

GUIDELINES IN SELECTING PATTERNS

Two things to keep in mind when selecting a paper pattern are: A design you won't outgrow and a pattern that will work well in your room. None of us can afford to change our paper every other year, so we shouldn't have too highly specialized a design that will limit us to one rigid use for the room. Consider whether the child will outgrow his room. Ginny's pink paper is no good for Johnny. Think ahead whether you might need to double up two children in one room and if in making that shift you will have to redo two rooms.

Certain rooms lend themselves to a particular type of design. For example, an odd-shaped room with a slanted roof and lots of irregular angles looks good with an all-over free-form design. All the jogs and juts and crooked walls get lost in the over-all effect. Your seams which are all peculiar won't be noticeable in an all-over print.

There are many all-over designs that have a slight direction to them such as an occasional butterfly or bird or the leaves and stems of flowers. If you decide to use this kind of pattern on the ceiling as well as on the walls, make the direction favor you as you enter the room. On the wall facing you and on the ceiling, the flowers or butterflies should be right side up as you walk into the room.

REPEATS

The size of your repeat will affect the look of a pattern on the wall. Consider your repeats as well as the scale of the design. Whether you will see the same pattern twice per length of paper or twenty times changes the look completely. I've found that it's easy to live with very small and very large repeats on the walls, it's the ones in the middle that are capable of becoming restrictive if you spend a lot of time in your room. It's a good idea to get a whole length hung on the wall so you can look at it awhile before you decide if you want it.

Nothing is more complicated to estimate than the cost of wall coverings because nothing about wall coverings is standardized. Wallpapers and paper-backed vinyls are sold by the roll (which averages five yards per single roll). Papers vary from 27 inches to 36 inches in width. Some papers come pretrimmed, which saves you or the paper hanger cutting the edges (which have to be exact), but most papers have to be trimmed.

For an average bathroom where paper is going to go above the tiles and on the ceiling, approximately six single rolls of paper will be required. When ordering your paper, specify that you want six single rolls but don't be alarmed when only two arrive. You have received your quantity but they've been packed in triple rolls, for the convenience of the manufacturer.

Canvas-backed wall vinyls are sold by the yard as well as by the roll. They are as wide as 54 inches, which means you need only 3½ yards to equal one standard single room. Check each time to be sure which you are buying. One wall vinyl sample was marked $12, and Jane Evans planned to use it for her hall which required twenty single rolls. The tragedy was that the vinyl was $12 a yard (not $12 per roll), so she needed to spend five times as much money as she had calculated. Instead of her hall costing $20 \times \$12 = \$240$, it cost $5 \times 20 = 100 \times \$12 = \$1,200$. That is a big difference.

WHERE DO YOU PUT YOUR PAPER?

By the way, even though you're using a vinyl, it's appropriate to refer to it as "paper," the man who puts it up as a "paper hanger."

Before you get your paper hanger to give you an estimate, decide where you want to paper. Do you want to paper the ceiling in your bathroom? If you are considering a papered ceiling you should have proper ventilation so the rising steam won't peel the paper. Also, your paper should be "non-directional" (one that can go up, down, or sideways and be equally appropriate). Stripes don't work well on ceilings unless you miter them in the center and that is unnecessarily complicated.

If there is good ventilation, bathroom ceilings are very effective papered because usually half the wall is taken up with tiles. I think children's rooms look cute when the ceiling is papered the same as the walls. It is practical too because a plaster ceiling often exposes cracks, which the paper hides.

LINING PAPER

Unless you line your walls, no paper hanger will guarantee his work. Every known disaster can occur and he'll blame you unless he hangs lining paper. The old paper might show through, seams open up as much as a half inch. If you don't line your walls before you hang your wallpaper, know the wall conditions well.

REMOVAL OF OLD PAPER

About 85 per cent of the time it's best to strip your walls of old paper or vinyl and start fresh. The time not to is when your walls are in poor condition and your wall covering is literally holding your plaster in place. Or when your old paper is so smooth and in such good condition you can use it as a lining. Carefully examine every inch of each seam, and if there are no problems exposed your walls are in good condition. No matter how good the walls are, if we don't like how they look we want to change them. It's a big saving of mess and labor when you can hang the new right over the old. It's a good idea to sand the seams smooth and paint over the paper with white "sealer" paint just to be sure you have a clean surface and your old paper won't distort your new by showing through.

When your walls are in bad shape you'll know it; they will repel the paper and the seams will curl and open up from the wall. Run your hand along the edge and lift up a corner to peek at your wall beneath.

To remove old wallpaper, use a steamer. You can rent one at your paint store. If there are areas of paper that are so solidly adherent to the plaster that the paper won't come off, leave it alone. You can sand and spackle your walls smooth. Be a perfectionist here because a bumpy wall before papering will look worse later. As I said earlier, the new wet-look vinyls show every imperfection; silver mylars and foils make imperfections the most obvious.

WHAT KIND OF PASTE?

Ask every time you buy paper what kind of paste you should use. There are new powdered vinyl adhesives that mix with water and these are probably good for most paper-backed vinyls. But don't guess. If you're working with something specialized like silk paper see if your paper store will recommend a paste specifically for the paper. This way you have some protection if something goes wrong.

BAD WALLS NEED COVERING

Some plaster walls are so old and cracked that you should hang a wall vinyl for medicinal purposes. Instead of paying double labor to have your bad walls canvased, then painted, kill two birds with one stone, and hang a vinyl.

WHEN NOT TO HANG WALL COVERINGS

Generally it's difficult to install wall coverings over a wood-paneled wall. Even with canvas, the covering settles and the wood seams show through.

Another time not to use a wall covering is in between moldings. Unless you have a set of rare panels or something of unusual beauty, it's an amateurish trick to stick everyday wallpaper inside moldings. The molding stops the flow of the design and cuts it up. If you have your heart set on papering your room, remove your moldings first. Textured plaster should be painted, not papered over because your wall covering won't adhere properly and it will look bumpy.

MOLDING

Any room could be improved and made to appear larger by removing the picture molding. It serves no purpose today and breaks up the harmony of your space. This molding is usually 10 inches to 12 inches down from the ceiling and it can easily be removed. (Plan to spackle and, in places, plaster your nail holes so you don't see any rough impressions when your room is finished.) If you're papering your ceiling you might want to run your paper right over the ceiling in one continuous piece with no seam or molding to interfere.

On the other hand, if you don't have a cornice molding (the turned wooden strip which separates the wall from the ceiling) and want one, that's easy to install. It should go right up to the ceiling, where the wall and ceiling meet. The depth depends on your ceiling height and on the other woodwork in your room, but on the average I'd say 3 inches are safe. Wallpapered walls and painted ceilings look more finished when they're joined by a cornice molding. Whenever you contrast your wall color and your trim color, be sure to have a cornice molding to give your room style and detail where it will be noticed.

If your room has any beautiful woodwork, I'd keep it intact because it's bound to give your room character. However, if you have ordinary applied moldings, chair rails, etc., you might want to clean up your walls by removing them entirely. Wall moldings restrict your freedom in the way you place your furniture and hang your decorations, but when they're nice, it's worthwhile to keep them.

Chair rails are optional today because they too can restrict your wall treatment. For example, Mrs. Tang brought a Japanese six-foot panel screen home from her last visit to Tokyo and it needed the whole wall as uninterrupted space. So she removed her molding. Modern pictures, fabric and rug hangings need more space than the smaller pictures we're used to hanging. Chair rails usually are between 29 inches to 38 inches high and waste a lot of wall space. A wall system might fit better against a wall if the chair molding is removed—depending on the baseboard depth. The time that chair rails are most effective is when you contrast the color below to your wall color above, separating your colors. Salmon walls, with white trim and white walls below the chair rail, for example, may be the right amount of salmon color you want in the room and the white chair rail "relieves" the room from too much salmon. The functional purpose of a chair rail is to keep your chair backs from marking and ruining your wall. Add a strip of quarter round molding at the bottom of your baseboard and it will accomplish the same objective.

MAINTAINING WALLS

After a few years a wall vinyl can look pretty gray and dingy but with soap and water you can wash it clean. One client laughed and said she had better things to do than wash her wall vinyl (her floors kept her busy enough), but when she realized how quickly her walls became dull, she was glad to have the option. Rooms with a rough-textured wall vinyl get dirt caught in the texture and washing them is more difficult. All smooth-surfaced wall vinyls are easy to clean. Experiment with mild solutions on anything printed because the design might rub off on the sponge if you're not careful. Any painted wall, if it is well done, can be washed down but I don't recommend it. They look streaky and never really as fresh. The exception to this is a glazed wall. Any textured painted wall can be touched up and cleaned.

There's no such thing as maintenance-free anything. Even formica needs care.

WOOD PANELING

Wood-paneled walls are still the easiest to care for; builders are using paneling more and more in new housing. You can't see the dirt as easily on a grained surface as on a painted wall, and also you can't chip a stained wood wall as easily as you can a painted one.

A beautifully paneled room is a rare treat in a house or apartment; but most paneling is pretty ordinary. If you've been sticking out a dark dreary brown room because you were afraid to paint your paneling, you don't have to live with it any longer. After much preparation you can paint over your stained wood using one of the new acrylic paints, and it will last beautifully. Your study can become bottle green or a rich lacquer red.

For light-colored paneling there are colored *aniline* stains so you can stain the paneling a color and still enjoy the graining of the wood. Aniline is a dye that can be colored similar to the way brown stain is used in coloring wood. Someday colored wood staining will be as common as brown staining. If your brown paneling is ordinary and drab, by all means lift it up with color.

PAINT HAS COME A LONG WAY TOO

Because there's a movement toward doing our own home improvements, manufacturers have come up with many new paints, to make it easy for a novice to be a hero. Just about any color of paint exists in sprays and a variety of finishes. Your old refrigerator can be painted cherry color in a half hour's time; better still, your purple bathroom wall tiles can be painted white. There are new paints that can be used on linoleum tiles and mosaic floors. Ask your local paint store about Swedish enamels. Even the drabbest areas can come alive with a fresh application of paint.

Painting has become the most popular "sport" in home improvement. Painting is instantly satisfying, it saves you money and is a job that isn't difficult.

COLOR IS WHAT BRINGS SPACE ALIVE

The Ryans' library was transformed from a dark, dull beige room by the application of a vibrant tomato-aspic paint. The color makes everyone look healthy and well, and the strong brilliant walls increased the size and appearance of the room boldly. The painter liked working with the color so much he hated to leave the job. He brought the excess paint home to his wife for their kitchen cabinets.

Try painting a tiny room with a blast of color, a royal blue or a crayon orange. Make your strong colors high gloss (unless your walls are in terrible shape). A little room may never be big but it will have personality to make up for the difference. A shot of color can really enliven a small passageway or a poky bathroom.

YOU CAN PAINT COLOR OVER A WALL COVERING

Most people don't realize that you can paint right over a textured wall covering. If you have a light grass cloth that has yellowed from the sun or a dark one that has faded, you can paint a fresh color right over the texture. You still get the impression of the pattern but in the color you want. This applies to a silk paper or even to a vinyl.

USE PAINT TO DISGUISE AND DRAMATIZE

You can hide ugly features by painting them "out." Anything you want to bury should be painted the same color as the wall or ceiling. Old radiators in a red room shouldn't be painted white like the trim; paint them away by painting them red. An air conditioner stuck in a white window should be painted white. If you have speakers on brackets, they too can be phased out by painting them the color of the room.

Any beautiful detail in your room, from moldings to "concave" and "convex" paneling on your doors, can be articulated through the use of a contrasting paint color. In an all-beige room, for example, you can stripe the moldings in brown. *Striping* is done with a special brush that glides along an indentation in a molding. Although it may appear to be difficult to make a straight line, it's not. A *glaze* (a smooth slippery transparent coating) is added to the color and it seems to work into the molding easily. This technique sharpens the form of details and brings them into focus. It can be as subtle or as bold as you want depending on your strength of contrasting colors.

Another trick with paint is to use the same color in varying values to heighten the effect of an angular space. For example, if your kitchen is a disaster area and completely broken up with jogs and juts, try using, say,

yellow in four different tones of the same shade. (See the chapter on
"Color.") When you can't hide something, have fun with it! You know
what intense sunlight does to articulate the angles and planes of a white
building. You can force this crispness through your use of paint. By varying the planes slightly from one to the next, not only can you dramatically
intensify what's there, but you create planes of space.

As I said earlier when talking about space expansion and the use of
white, you can blast open a small white room by painting the floor and
ceiling a strong color. To further tie the room together you can paint the
doors colorfully too, or stripe the door moldings and trim moldings the
same color as you used on the ceiling and floor. Carry this color one step
further and paint the baseboard and cornice molding and window trims
the same bright color and you will have the illusion of the white going
away.

If you have low ceilings you can lift them by elongating the vertical
element of your walls. The doors in your hallway, for example, can be
painted a strong contrasting color. Don't stop at the top of the door. Go
clear up to the ceiling with your color, completely oblivious to the door
and wall separation. You fool the eye with the strength of color.

CEILINGS

Ceilings account for as much space as the floor and they should be
given thought; they needn't be white.

For example, in a large room with high ceilings (anything over 9 feet
is considered high nowadays) where there is a "beamed" ceiling (structural supporting beams running lengthwise and possibly widthwise across
your ceiling) you might want to do more than paint the whole thing white.
If your walls are pale blue and your trim white, paint the beams white and
in the flat part of the ceiling paint the same blue, only several shades
lighter. With a white ceiling, stained beams emphasize the ceiling. A high
one soars and a low one reaches down to you.

Whenever you want your ceiling to appear the same color as your wall
or your trim, always paint it several shades lighter. You achieve this by
adding pure white to your color. The reason for this is that your ceiling is
always in shadow and it appears heavier and darker unless the color has
been lightened. You will have to experiment to determine your own pro-

portion because of your windows and lighting, but it should be lightened almost 50 per cent in order to appear the same color as the walls.

When I was discussing wallpapered ceilings, I mentioned children's rooms as a special place for colorful ceilings. Height is not important to children because they like the feeling of closeness. When you redo Johnny's room, try painting his ceiling soldier blue. It will perk up his whole little world.

COLOR

It's very difficult to make color decisions for large areas such as walls. It's not as though you were icing a birthday cake! After you read the chapter on "Color" you will have some ideas about what you want for your walls. Think of all the things that go into the room. The mahogany bookcases count for a lot when your room is settled. Compare your suggested color with the various elements and if they seem friendly together they "go" together. When you find a green you feel good about, don't worry further. If it's a bit too pale or too harsh, you can alter the final coat by adding more pigment or putting in some white which softens as well as lightens a color.

Buy a large paint-color swatch book from a paint store. Get one with as many color variations as possible so you'll have an unlimited range to choose from. Now is a good time to look through your scrapbook and see what colors you have saved.

HOW TO LOOK AT A PAINT CHIP

The most important thing to look for is clarity of color. All colors should be clean, no matter how strong or dark they are. A brown can be as delicious as chocolate or as thick as mud. Dull colors have neutralizers (brown, grays, blacks added to the pigment) that sap the strength of the color and make rooms seem heavy and somber. Public places have noncolors for noncontroversy. An airplane interior might be beige because it won't offend 160 passengers. When a color is tranquilized and calmed down so it's nondescript, it just sits there as though it needed a fresh paint job. If a color is the right tint but too strong you can lighten it with white. Test each color in bright sunlight to test its clarity, especially yellows which are the sun's color.

Usually, if you like a color chip, you'll really get excited when you see the paint in the pot. Your color begins to come alive. A good test to determine what the color will do when it's on your walls is to take the lid off the top of the can and pour out enough paint so that your paint bucket has "walls." In its own shadows you begin to get a "feel" for what your room will look like. *Remember that paint always dries darker.*

PREPAINTING PREPARATION

Some suggestions:

1. Protect all plants. Nothing can kill a plant faster than paint odor and plaster dust. Get them out of the area entirely and cover them with plastic.

2. Get a large sample of paint and examine it in all lights. It's a good idea to buy a pint of paint and make samples right on your walls.

3. Look at color with all the other colors going in the room.

4. Buy the best quality paint you can afford. Use an oil-base paint; it lasts longer and is more practical for spot cleaning.

5. When you've decided the exact color you want, don't settle for even a slight variation. When it's magnified thousands of times on the wall, you'll know and feel the difference.

6. All strong colors should be mixed by machines or they'll streak. If you find you have to change your color once you get the paint home, stop everything and have the paint machine-mixed. This avoids streaks and saves time.

7. Never trust a paint chip number. Open the paint can in the paint store. Stick your finger inside, dab a bit right on the paint chip, blow dry, and go to daylight to examine the color. You won't regret this exercise. Formulas change and once you've painted your room the wrong color blue, you're out of luck. Don't purchase something this important in a store that won't let you do this.

8. Mask off everything with drop cloths. Tape them to the floor with masking tape. Don't be heartbroken by an accidentally "spattered" floor.

9. Plan on three coats of paint. There's no such thing as one coat of paint on a wall.

10. *Always* use a primer to seal walls. If you don't, you'll apply paint endlessly and the old color will "bleed" through to haunt you.

11. Buy the best edging brush you can afford.

12. Remove all hardware. Never paint around anything. Drop your ceiling fixture and put it in a large Baggie or old pillow case to keep it clean. Paint everything and when you're finished put back clean hardware, fresh hooks and light switch plates.

Note: It is tempting to leave the hardware up and paint around it, especially curtain rods, etc. It's always a mistake to do this because if you ever decide to remove them, you've got an unpainted area to cope with; also, it makes for a messy job if you don't strip the place down. Picture hooks and nails left in the wall make drips when you're rolling on your color. A law firm renovated an old town house and spent a fortune on custom brass door hinges only to find the sloppy painter smeared them up with paint. If you can't remove your hardware, carefully cover it with masking tape to protect it from the painter.

Floors

Every artist was first an amateur.
RALPH WALDO EMERSON

Houses are built to live in, more than to look on;
therefore let use be preferred before uniformity
except where both may be had.
FRANCIS BACON

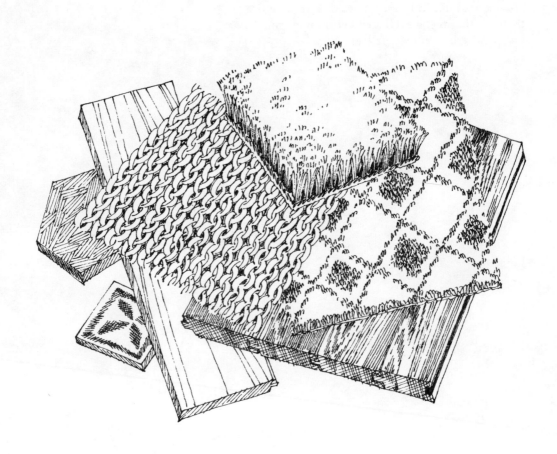

FLOORS: YOUR FIFTH WALL

Your floors connect all the design elements in your room. Think for a minute where your eyes wander when you spend any time in a room. They go down. And your feet hit the floor. Think carefully about your floors, as floors are the roots from which your design elements grow.

Practicality, cost and appearance are the three considerations that should govern all your decisions about your floors. All floors can be attractive as well as practical.

It's not unusual to find people sitting on the floor today. This break with traditional attitudes about how we should behave has allowed us to live less formal lives; we all go barefoot sometimes, and bare feet require an inviting floor.

Before you choose your floor covering, see what the floor itself is like. Because there's such a feeling of plastic in modern life, we should try whenever possible to make use of a *real* floor material, if we have it. If your floor is hard wood or tile, don't cover it with vinyl. If you have a stone floor, don't install Acrilan carpeting.

If you live in a new building, the builders may have cheated and under the wall-to-wall carpeting may be subflooring, not wood; subflooring is cheaper for the builder. Compare the cost of mud and water to wood! Subflooring is usually cement.

Most old buildings have wood floors underneath layers of vinyl. If you live in an old building and there is old vinyl floor covering in a room, pry up one of the tiles and see if there's wood underneath. Kitchens don't have wood floors usually, but be sure to find out. If under one layer of vinyl you find linoleum, keep going, you may find three or four installations of covering, one slapped on top of the other. If you find you have a wooden floor, it would probably be worthwhile to fix it up, depending on which room in the house it's in. But so many of us crave wood around us that we'd even prefer it for kitchen floors; it could be protected with a clear lacquer. Ask at your paint store for information on plastic protective coating for wooden floors. Whichever brand you buy, follow the directions word for word, pay special attention to how many hours drying time you need between coats.

If you don't want to bother maintaining the wood, but you'd enjoy having a wooden floor, have one; seal it with a carefree polyurethane protective coating and leave it alone. The floor will be very shiny and won't look as mellow as waxed wood, but it will be a lot better than a vinyl substitute.

Never scrape and stain borders, leaving the middle of the floor undone. There are times when your rugs will be up—for dancing or cleaning—and you need your floor. Anyway, it's almost more trouble to leave a patch untouched than it is to swing those heavy sanders and buffers around freely. It doesn't pay to economize here. (If you have back trouble or weigh under 150 pounds hire a sander or you may end up in traction!)

WOOD COLOR

A middle tobacco walnut is generally a good brown-stain color. It's really a matter of taste, but floors that are too dark show every speck of dirt and require a great deal of upkeep. And when floors are too dark you can't see the grain of the wood.

Many people start with a pine or an oak floor and seal it with a clear lacquer, leaving the light natural color. Bleached floors are beautiful in informal rooms but they show dirt readily. If you don't mind the "walked on" look on a light floor, get some white paint, add it to turpentine and rub it into the grain. Seal it with polyurethane or give it a waxed finish. Generous coats of a sealer will be the easiest to care for.

If you have a light floor and want it a color other than brown, try one of the aniline stains I mentioned when we were discussing paneling. You can get them now in hundreds of colors and they are as practical as a brown stain, cost no more, and they'll give your floor a whole new personality. Aniline dye is a synthetic varnish and can be brushed on easily.

If you own your property and put in a wooden or ceramic-tile floor in a room and it greatly enhances the appearance of the room, you will make money when you sell your house or apartment. People are more aware of these features now and know how costly they are, so they probably will be willing to pay for them.

TILE FLOORS—A HOUSEHOLD WORD

If you feel you can splurge on one room and invest in a natural un-glazed quarry-stone tile or glazed ceramic-tile floor, you won't regret it. Both are especially effective when you have lots of plants, creating a garden effect. They are natural and so practical. There are tiles you can buy that are textured and baked so that you never have to do a thing to them, just mop with water—a great feature when you're misting your plants and overwater. Tiles are not really much more expensive than a good vinyl, and they come in wonderful earthy textures and a wide variety of shapes, sizes, glazes and designs. Yes, it's said that Mexican women used to have miscarriages because they stood all day on these hard tiles; and if you drop a glass it will shatter; they are noisy. But, nevertheless, tiles make an exciting, beautiful floor. Before you get too excited about a tile floor, however, get a contractor to tell you if your floor can stand the weight and if you have enough depth to house the tile. Tiles are thick and need depth to lie in a mud bed, etc. If you can use tiles, then select a grout (the mixture that hardens around each tile) which can be tinted to co-ordinate in color to your tiles. Grouting doesn't have to be gray any more, but there is something organic about the natural color of regular grouting. Ordinary terra cotta clay tiles are a great deal cheaper than quarry and are thinner in gauge. They look best when they're waxed but if you don't want the headache, keep them dull and use only soap and water. Don't use a liquid plastic floor wax because, while it may shine your tiles beautifully, every scratch shows up and the floor looks terrible in no time.

VINYL FLOORS

Vinyl tiles certainly have their place in our lives, especially in rooms in great use such as bathroom, kitchen and play areas. They are less effective in more formal areas when you'd probably prefer a lovely, waxed wood. The choice of vinyl flooring available now is considerable. You can even laminate your fabric and have it made up in tiles. If your space is tiny (a 6-foot-by-3-foot bath area) you can order your own laminated floor design in one piece to avoid seams. Floor vinyls are available in colors and textures and designs to suit any mood. They are expensive however, and if you don't know how long you'll be where you are, there might be a better solution for you. If you want a fancy floor, you will have to pay a great deal for it. If you want a simple practical floor, you can save. One practical solution is to install prewaxed linoleum so you never have to wax, you only have to wipe the floor clean. No waxing—imagine how great.

Avoid beveled tiles. They pick up all the dirt and are so hard to clean. Everything gets stuck in those cracks. If you have chosen a very plain floor, choose large samples; the fewer the seams, the less difficult the floor will be to clean. In time, dirt will settle in the seams and outline each tile.

If you cannot afford to tile your bathroom floor but you also can't stand it another minute, there is now a solution for you. Use the new plastic paint which can be applied over mosaic tiles. You will need several coats and lots of drying time but it freshens up your floor and could not be more reasonable. Then you can use colored throw rugs and your floor is fresh and practical. I personally have an aversion to wall-to-wall carpeting in bathrooms. It may feel cozy under bare feet but it looks like a disaster in three weeks' time. Kitchens and bathrooms are two places one likes the floor to be really clean, and wall-to-wall bathroom carpeting almost always looks in need of a washing.

FLOOR COVERING PRIORITIES

Let's begin with the premise that you have perfectly decent wood floors, nothing to hide, and you're making your rug and carpeting decisions with an open mind. Floor coverings account for 30 per cent of all money spent on the home so we should think carefully before we buy.

First, determine your priorities for each floor and put them in order. What comes first; the cost, the appearance, the durability, the maintenance or the color?

These decisions depend on so many factors. For example, your stairs and hall might need a smashing color, something that will hold up well, and if you can achieve this for thirteen dollars a yard, more power to you.

CARPETS

Free advice when you're spending your hard-earned money is a mistake because the whole reason for seeking the advice of someone is to guarantee

results that will satisfy you. If you know what you want in the way of carpeting you can go anywhere to get it and hold out until you find the most
reasonable deal. However, the carpet industry is so competitive and loaded
with tough dealers, there is much more involved than what meets the eye.
Trust and service should be built into the price you pay, and I recommend
going to a carpet company with a good reputation.

NATURAL OR SYNTHETIC

The question is always asked as to which is better, for wear and dirt
resistance, wood or a synthetic carpeting. Any material of natural origin
(cotton, wool, linen, flax, silk, skins) is always better than an artificial,
man-made imitation. However, wool is becoming as precious as gold and
maybe someday wool rugs will be a thing of the past. I hear from rug
salesmen they now sell 90 per cent synthetics; fifteen years ago the opposite
was true. Wool prices have doubled in the past four months. It's that bad.

Whether it is obtainable or not, a natural yarn such as wool has its own
life, its own oil just like the hair on our heads. Synthetics attract dirt from
the air which stays on the surface.

Cleaning is a concern to us all. I've seen rugs wear out, but if they're
clean they aren't as depressing as a rug loaded with spots and general dirt
that won't come out. All the synthetic rugs I've seen that have been down
for a while look grayish and the color has lost its life in the heavy traffic
areas. I felt so sorry for some friends who wanted the most practical rugs
money could buy; they were sold acrilan for the carpeting throughout
their new house. Six months later, after paying huge cleaning bills, the
Williams have had to replace every carpet and rug because the spots and
dirt were so unsightly. So if you buy a synthetic carpeting it should be
in an earth color that won't show the dirt. The Williams had bought
acrilan in bright fruit colors—yellows, oranges and apple green, which
made the dirt seem much more obvious.

Too much carpeting is claustrophobic. If you love it, that's one thing,
but don't be in too much of a hurry to cover your floors. For one thing,
think of the expense. No matter how much you pay for carpeting it gets
tired after a few years. It doesn't move well; if you try reusing your carpeting from one home to another, it probably won't look great, and by the
time you've paid to have it picked up, cleaned and reinstalled, it may not

even pay to reuse it. Dyeing is expensive and with an old rug is never very successful.

If you decide on wall-to-wall carpeting, there are several things to consider. First, don't pick a very floppy pile. It will crush and show soil in traffic patterns and look sad in no time. There are "combs" one can buy for your "shag" carpeting, but who has time to do that kind of cleaning? Pick a color that is fresh but not perishable. Yellow is death on the floor, but a light beige does very well in city or country. Strangely enough, off white wears better than yellow in carpeting.

You have to have some texture in your carpeting or you're just asking for trouble, because velvet-piled carpetings show every footprint, every spot and all general soil. Disasters constantly occur, so have carpeting that has several shades of the same color and some interest in the weave that will help hide wear and tear. The only practical velvet-pile plain carpets are the color of dirt to begin with.

Remember to check all your doors to see if your carpeting will clear comfortably under them. Measure your lining and carpet together and check to see if your doors will clear them before you install them. It might save you a lot of trouble.

It's often worth your while to spend twice as much on a patterned carpet as on a plain one if it's going to save you housekeeping time. Carpeting comes in 27-inch widths, as well as in 12-foot widths, and you can have as many widths as you need sewn together to construct a carpet of whatever size will fit your space. The 27-inch widths are perfect for stairs; another advantage is that you can replace one strip in a worn area without having to replace the whole carpeting. These small-scaled geometric designs are expensive, but are machine made for wear. When used in small areas, as a runner in a hall or on stairs, they're very effective and so practical. If you use them in a wall-to-wall installation, you have to get used to the seams that will occur every 27-inches. All the patterned carpets are this width, so eventually we'll probably all get accustomed to the seams, the same way we did to the seams in 12-foot or 15-foot carpeting.

As expensive as these rugs are, they do move well. The Franckes moved their dining-room carpeting to the library in their new apartment. You can put in a border and make a new rug from an old carpet.

If you have no intention of having wall-to-wall carpeting and want to have just a pretty rug, you've really got a treat in store for yourself. My initial suggestion would be to try to stick to fairly standard sizes and shapes so they'll be easily movable and reusable.

We had clients who were building a new house and there was a curious jog in the otherwise classic rectangular living room. When we inquired, we were told it was because their present rug was that shape and it had a border that couldn't be successfully cut down.

Because rugs are so manageable, you might use several "area" rugs in a room instead of the one traditional big rug.

More and more we want flexibility in rugs. That's another reason for not choosing rugs that are big or heavy. First of all, they seem to weigh a ton and secondly, they're expensive to have cleaned. You can clean small rugs yourself, which can be a big saving. Also, if your rugs aren't too large you can feel more relaxed about the cost per square yard. In the rug business you pay for every inch, so if you're carpeting a large area you naturally have to be more cautious.

The impact of a rug is more important than its size. A beautiful woven design in lots of wonderful colors can be a small rug and make a bigger impact than a plain carpet. When you are scaling in rug sizes on your floor plan, project what kind of rug you have in mind. A small 4-foot-by-6-foot needlework rug in front of a fireplace grouping is just as appropriate as an 8-foot-by-12-foot rug that is plainer.

Artists and designers are devoting their efforts to creating beautiful rugs. Their imagination, originality and good hand workmanship make a room very special. Many of us would prefer one small beautiful rug to a dozen nondescript ones.

When you have an exceptionally good rug don't put heavy furniture on it; you will crush the pile. Use a plexiglass coffee table over an exquisite rug. This way you can see the rug through the table and it won't be crushed.

Don't forget that rugs don't have to go on the floor at all, you can hang one on your wall as a work of art. Tapestries will continue to make interesting wall art because they're beautiful and practical.

When you don't know where you'll be living tomorrow and you don't have any money to put into your floors, you've got to be inventive. Polly

Abrams painted her bedroom floor green, blue and white pin stripes and used cotton throw rugs by her bed. For $28.63 she had a great floor.

Another fun and practical floor is a spattered painted floor. Mask off your walls and spatter away—paint the floor one color and spatter with a contrasting color. Use as many colors as you like but the simpler, the better. Dip your 4-inch brush into the paint so only one inch touches the paint and flick your brush on your floor in swirls. Use your wrist and be sure to vary the direction each time so you get spatters all over. For kitchens, bedrooms, bathrooms, kids' rooms and bedroom halls, you can't beat a good spattered floor. Cleaning is like swabbing the decks of a boat; soap and water is all you need.

Windows

Style is only the frame to hold our thoughts.
It is like the sash of a window, if heavy it will
obscure the light. The object is to have as little
sash as will hold the light, that we may not think
of the former but have the latter.

NATHANIEL EMMONS

Windows provide oxygen, light and air. There's nothing like a window to open space, let in natural light and connect us with our surroundings. We can no longer take our windows for granted, they are so precious to us.

We're a country that worships the sun and yet so many of us don't get nearly enough natural light. Most of our daylight hours are spent cooped up inside where our work is; our windows are our only contact with the day out there. Even with good light exposures from our windows so much of the sun is blocked by buildings and trees that we have to supplement our rooms with additional light on the sunniest of days. This is not only a city problem; landscaping and trees block out natural light in country houses.

It has been proved that rooms with natural sunlight create uplifted feelings not comparable to rooms without sunlight exposures. There have been tests proving mice have increased their sensual responses in sunlight. We are different people in the warmth of sunlight. When we can't go to the sun we should bring it to us wherever possible.

Because of this deep need we all feel for contact with nature, out of doors and light when inside, we tend to want to sit close to our windows, especially during the daytime. The lower your windows go down toward the floor the more pleasant they are to sit in front of. If you have a bay window that looks out onto a garden you might build a window seat in the area so you can sit there and enjoy the space. Even if you live in an apartment and have ordinary windows you can utilize them for sitting. One client loves to read near her window, so she had a 13-inch-deep board secured over her radiator and had a cushion made with pillows. She sits with her back against the side wall and is in her own world. The 34-inch height didn't bother her because she had library steps to climb up onto the seat. Sarah discovered the steps came in handy for watering the hanging plants as well. If you have an exciting view but your windows start too high up the wall to comfortably see out from where you sit in your room, you can elevate the floor area by having a wooden platform made. I've seen one that looked like a boardwalk and had large recessed areas for sunken plants and trees. If you do this be sure your ceiling is high enough so you don't feel claustrophobic. Even with a low ceiling it can work though, if you want a garden effect. If you duplicate the wooden slat effect on your ceiling you can hang baskets and lights and create a greenhouse feeling which doesn't require height to be beautiful.

Examine your windows; you might not have ideal exposures. You might have to compromise light and a view for more space. Those of us in urban areas become conditioned to a less natural, artificially controlled environment. So before you dress up your windows, realize the effect they have on your time spent inside. Without windows our rooms would be virtually unlivable.

In the country where the view is still pure and private, I think it's such a shame to block out the view with window treatments; it adds so much to the rooms to have a wonderful view beyond. Not everyone agrees with me that windows are important. On a recent house tour I saw a duplex apartment, in which every window was bolted up and hermetically sealed. Bright plexiglass supergraphics were in their place. Curious, I asked, "How do you open your windows?" The owner informed me they didn't. "Windows are for looking out and we didn't like what we saw on Eighty-eighth Street and Lexington."

I couldn't wait to get outside of this "creative plaything" of a home. As my feet touched cement, I looked up at the sky: Windows never seemed more precious.

Like everything else about surroundings, windows become very personal. We have a friend who is down on windows at the moment. She can't afford to keep them clean and "cover up" curtains are expensive. She'd like windows if she had all the money in the world to keep them freshly cleaned. Katis, on the other hand, isn't the least concerned about the aesthetic considerations. She's a novelist and needs natural light in order to write. Even a dirty window is fine as long as she has daylight.

Some people are extremists about natural light. One couple who live at Ninety-eighth Street and Fifth Avenue in New York City went through long discussions with their building officials, to get permission to open up the west and south windows overlooking Central Park and the reservoir. They replaced their small conventional windows with floor-to-ceiling massive glass slabs. The sky lights their space until nine o'clock when they light candles, the perfect light for dining. It's a little bit of heaven to sit in their apartment on a beautiful night. The sky becomes the entertainment.

Not everyone can be so radical. But we can all take advantage of the windows we have and leap at any opportunity we can to improve them and the light they let into our lives. Even on cold winter days you can sunbathe if you have a working window in an exposure that allows the direct sun's rays.

WINDOWS LET IN AIR

While the most elementary function of a window is to let in light, a window also allows for the circulation of air. No room can stay fresh for long if it can't be aired. We should take full advantage of the windows we can open and shut easily so our rooms don't get "air pollution."

Although many of us use air conditioners to circulate air in our rooms, when the temperature is pleasant outside, fresh air is the nicest for our rooms and for us. Scent is such an important sense and is the most underrated one in our rooms. Any space that becomes stuffy and stale, no matter how beautiful, is a sad atmosphere.

WORKING WINDOWS

You don't have to "bring the outdoors indoors" through your windows, and you don't have to give your windows a "treatment." All you have to do is put them to use so you get your value from them. There must be 1,001 different ways to handle windows. And because windows are such a vital quality in your rooms, each set of windows frames a space and needs its own resolutions.

The personality of a window varies as much as the people who live inside it. A restaurant that pretends to be a palace will have an overdone window decor. But window treatments have lost some of their status as being representative of class and position because so many of them fake elegance. Still, to some extent, curtains and window treatments will always be a symbol of the mood and feeling of the owner, and they relate to your attitude about your life style and your way of living.

Happily there are satisfying solutions for every conceivable situation.

No longer is there an accepted way to treat the double-hung window. Louvered shutters painted white are exciting, so are blinds of bamboo or woven materials with wood slats, or shades trimmed with braid, or shaped wooden boards which surround the window (you either paint, paper or wrap them with material). There are endless possibilities. You can have vertical blinds made of strips of unconnected material, or you can use ribbons, or sheets or curtains or draperies. Curtains are usually simple and draperies are elaborate, lined, etc. A wonderful idea for a window is to hang horizontal glass shelves for trailing, green plants. Spring-roller shades (the old-fashioned kind you had in your bedroom as a child) aren't decorative. In fact, that old lace tassel hanging down your window can be depressing. These shades are functional and leave the light out, but that's about all. They can be made of pretty wallpapers and materials but they always have a rigid look somehow. Whatever blinds or shades you select, determine if they are the complete treatment, or are you planning to add curtains later? If no curtains are anticipated you should have a finished look and fit the window properly.

Space, money, light and our life styles have narrowed down our windows so they are more and more unpretentious openings. As our spaces get smaller and smaller, our ceilings lower and lower, it won't help our struggle for more breathing room to smother our windows with yards and yards of fabric. Also, old-world window treatments don't fit into our new-world finances. Before, windows had on so much clothing that our glass was suffocating; an eighteenth-century window treatment consisted of silk roman shades (to cover the glass); a padded valance, lined, interlined and trimmed; pleated and hung curtains. It would be expensive to duplicate today.

Draperies require room and need space to breathe. Depending on the number of windows and the impact of your fabric, draperies can decrease the size of your space as much as 20 per cent.

LOOK AT YOUR WINDOWS

Before planning your window design, take inventory. Go around to all your windows and have a look. If there are some that seem uninspired, strip them free of all previous installations. Remove everything—curtains, blinds, undercurtains, shades—and *all* the hardware. You can always put them back again, but if you don't get rid of your preconceptions of how to handle the window, you won't be free to visualize honestly what you're dealing with. It's hard to know how your windows look when they're concealed behind ugly cover-ups.

No bare window will ever be as bad as an ugly and dead window "hanging." Don't be afraid to remove the old before the new is ready to go in its place. Don't wait until you're "redecorating" with paint or materials, get up on a stepladder and take everything down. It's marvelous therapy for a depressed room!

You have to be able to look at your windows bare to get a feel for what you want. Anne Bushnell did this in her front hall. The transformation was so startling—sunshine pouring in her east windows—it inspired her to rip up her beige carpeting, and she ended up giving her whole hall a much needed face lift.

GETTING IN SHAPE

Once you get down to your bare windows you'll see what work is cut out for you. Analyze how much work has to be done before your windows will please you. Sketch in your notebook the basic shape of the windows and measure them in relationship to your wall elevation. If there are two windows on one wall, indicate that on your sketch. Measure and mark on your drawing the height, width and depth of your radiator as well as of your air conditioning unit, central air unit, radiant heating unit, etc. All these problems can be dealt with but they need to be thoughtfully worked out.

Begin your efforts by solving the problem windows. Paint your trims and get them in good shape so they can be more exposed. Scrape away old peeling paint and use a razor blade on the glass. If you have to use a hammer and paint remover to get your window to open, now is the time. Call in the glazier if you've got a cracked pane. You may have an ugly window facing you, but at least you've done everything you can.

WINDOW TRIM AND MULLIONS

Mullions are the wood that hold the window panes in place. White is always crisp to frame the glass around windows. Unless you have a dark-colored room and you feel white would contrast too much, paint the mullions white. Your window trim can be contrasted; usually the trim is either the color of the wall or the color of the rest of the trims in your room. When considering colors, think what other treatments you're going to add (color of blinds or shades) so the colors relate to each other.

Usually, the wood that holds your glass looks best when it is the same color as your blind, shade or undercurtain. If you intend to have a Swiss-embroidered tambour, you needn't think further—paint the mullions white. If you have pink curtains but white roll-up shades, it's best to paint the frames white. In a strong and richly colored room such as a library, white frames (not tied to anything else) would float out the window. Raise the question each time with each window because there are always new ways to approach this color question.

WINDOW INTRUSIONS

Air conditioners, radiators, exhaust pipes and window fans are always a problem and not a simple one to solve. The smaller these fixtures are the better, naturally, and keep whatever you can away from what is "eye" level when you are seated. You can put some of these necessities at the top rather than at the bottom of your window. Actually, the best place for a heater-air conditioner is *under* the window.

The Eliot Stevenses moved into a large nine-room apartment with great rooms, except that their small bedroom had only one window. Their first priority was to invest in under-the-window air-heat units so their view of Central Park wouldn't be blocked by the air conditioner. They faced a major tragedy when they submitted their request to the building's board and were turned down because their apartment was on the architectural dividing line that had an elaborate cornice, and the building wasn't about to have this cornice blasted away for the Stevenses' air-heat unit. What they did to avoid permanent depression was to install the air conditioner as high as possible on their window. When it wasn't in use, a pretty hand-painted flower shade covered it up entirely. They made use of their old clunky radiator by having the carpenter build a formica shelf the 41-inch width of their window. It's proved a delightful place for plants and late-afternoon reading.

Friends in Colorado removed the cumbersome radiators that were spoiling their windows' appearance and installed radiant heating that goes high up on the wall and hardly shows. (It looks like baseboard heating, but the advantage is that it doesn't take up space.)

One window might be full of glory and another of gloom and yet, whenever possible, windows in a room should be treated so they look alike. This isn't always possible, but if you treat each one individually you will create a room full of confusion.

VENETIAN BLINDS AND SHADES

You want, whenever possible, to be able to adjust your window treatment for light control and privacy. On some windows you will want to be able to draw shades and on others you will always want the shades up. Choose materials that allow for this kind of flexibility. The best invention for a window is still the venetian blind. Luckily, it has come a long way.

You would not recognize the modern version of the venetian blind. It's called "Riviera," has skinny one-inch slats, comes in thirty-two colors and has a clear lucite "magic" wand which tilts the slats for total privacy and opens them for complete light. The blind pulls up easily, stacks into a slim, tidy, out-of-the-way horizontal line at the top of the window.

VERTICAL BLINDS

As ceilings get lower, it's nice to hang vertical blinds that emphasize the height. They're equally as functional as the Riviera blinds and offer an endless variety of options as in materials, colors, textures, transparencies, etc. Hung like a curtain (but in strips of material), they draw to the side and stack into a few small inches, taking up no space when not needed. These blinds look best when they go to the floor, or as far down as possible. Sometimes they go to a ledge and can look fine but they should only be used when there are large expanses of glass. They are a kind of contemporary curtain—very clean and straightforward. They're complete in themselves, and if you lean toward more elaborate windows they will seem stark. Many modern buildings are using them, replacing dreary office curtains.

The old-fashioned white roller shades we used in our bedrooms have gotten zippier too. Now the roller shades come in many vinyl colors, stripes and patterns, and they can even be made out of your own fabric and laminated. Their value is they are instantly in use and can be quickly put out of the way. They don't require space. They come in wood slats, metal slats and all kinds of materials. If you need a shade to function, a roller shade is a good bet. Remember the strings that used to hang down? Now you can have a tidy plastic ring, instead.

Roller shades should always be installed inside the trim. This way you get the least amount of light leakage. Usually a window looks incomplete with only a roller shade and nothing else. In any event, if you have your shade installed with a "reverse roll" (which means the shade rolls down in the front, not in the back) it always looks better.

Blinds and decorative shades have become more and more useful to us because they function aesthetically, allow for light control and privacy, and don't take up any wall or floor space. With more built-in and under-window furniture, blinds and shades are the cleanest approach.

If you want blinds or shades as decoration, here are a few things to remember. Install your blinds or shades on the outside of your window trim if your windows are narrow. This will make the window area more complete looking and a better proportion. I suggest using pleat-up blinds (which look like an accordion) rather than roll-up blinds; they look more graceful when they pleat up (like venetian blinds), and you eliminate that big sausage roll halfway up your window.

On the top of your blind, where it's installed, is a good place to disguise the mechanics, and this can be done easily with a flap of the same material. It's called a "lamberquin" and can be as little as five inches. This gives a heading to your blind and finishes it off so you don't have to add any further cover-ups.

Bamboo and wooden slat blinds are good looking and let in light and block out the view. When your views are bad this is ideal. You can vinylize the backs if you want total privacy; you'll get less light through. Woven blinds of colorful wools and chenille yarns combined with wooden slats and dowels can create a beautiful window too. They're heavier in feeling than wooden blinds.

Wooden louvered shutters look marvelous at windows. They're expensive if your windows are odd sizes and they have to be custom made, but if you're able to get stock sizes to fit your windows, it's a big savings. Shutters can be installed on frames with magnetic catches to keep them closed or they can be installed to hang freely. I prefer the latter method of installation because it looks more natural. Experiment with paint and see if you can contrast the frame color to the shutter slats or paint one side one color and the other side another. I've seen vertical strips painted across the shutters, which was effective. In addition to shutters, wood cutouts are now available that can be inserted into wooden frames and stained or painted. Louvered shutters and these wooden cutout panels look well when they're closed so they're particularly effective when the view isn't interesting. These cutout shapes come in geometric patterns, clover leafs, circles and curves.

CURTAINS

Elaborate heavy draperies hanging from complicated valances, trimmed and swagged, seem out of step with the way we live now. But curtains, when they're simple and fresh, can make a room complete. Our dream houses of tomorrow may have hangings at the window, but they'll be light and airy and fresh. Curtains, no matter how you slice it, are a luxury.

The two things that make curtains look so marvelous are the "just right" material detailed in a subtle way so it seems to fit the room perfectly. If you've ever done any sewing yourself you know the importance of the detailing. Give your work to someone whose workmanship you trust.

To get elegant results without a major investment stick to basic curtain "headings" and uncomplicated treatments. The heading is the top of the curtain that gathers the fullness of the material on the rod.

I have a friend who is doing this in her bedroom. Tired of the gray-blue damask overcurtains and shaped hard valances, she's replacing them with billowy, white, sheer, embroidered tambour curtains. These curtains are usually quite plain except for a wide embroidered design on the edge, in a flowers-and-leaves design. By this change she is gaining a much more open room which will be fresh and lively. Her husband was instantly won over when he saw how much they saved by having informal windows.

Tambour curtains come in cotton and drip-dry materials. The cotton ones always look a little more crisp, but it's better to realize your limitations and if you don't like to iron, install permanent-press curtains that you can keep fresh. They come in several different lengths and all you have to do to them is to head the top; the front "leading" edge is embroidered and so is the bottom.

Remember how the top of a dressing-table skirt was shirred? This same shirring or smocking makes an attractive heading for tambour curtains and you can get "shirring tape" in the five-and-ten-cent store. If you prefer to have a gathered valance to match (they come in several tambour designs) you can simply loop over your tambour material and stitch it through the machine for a heading. Nothing could be simpler or more reasonable because you've done the sewing yourself.

Most people are keeping their windows exposed at night for several reasons. First, when your window is in good condition you have nothing to hide, your glass is reflective and mirrors the motions and patterns in your room. The windows sparkle with the room. Secondly, they increase the physical appearance of your space by adding depth and perspective. Hard to give this up to enclosure.

Whether curtains draw or not is totally optional. If you never close your curtains, it seems a bit extravagant to have them "to draw." You always should allow enough fullness to make them appear operative, though, and quite often that's the same yardage whether they're stationary or draw. If that's the case, you might as well enjoy the option.

Washable curtains are the ideal today. However, this isn't as easy as it sounds. First of all, no lined curtain is ever washable. Any curtain that you intend to wash must have all hardware (hooks, weights, etc.) removed each time. And there is no such thing as a guaranteed preshrunk material. Plan for shrinkage and be safe. Allow generous double 6-inch hems and, on dotted swiss or tambour linens and cottons, take several tucks on the bottom so you can let them out when the curtains do shrink.

Furniture

If the person living in it is a gentleman the
house will match him: it will be modest,
quiet, hospitable, and will have all the
necessary comforts without falling over
backwards to achieve them.

BRUNO MUNARI
Design As Art

FURNITURE SHOULD MEET OUR NEEDS

I was amused to overhear two girls at the "objects" exhibit at the Museum of Modern Art discussing the "Italian Landscape" exhibition. They were so excited about the comfort and style of the new chairs. A girl said to her friend, "Like it? I couldn't get out of it, I was so comfortable. Bill too. We're going to buy one for our bedroom, for his TV chair." And that's a chair today. Designers consider people's comfort first and the art grows from this perspective.

The best possible way to utilize space to its best advantage and to alleviate the problems of limited space is through furniture. If it functions for both privacy and interaction, it can shape the space we live in so it serves our immediate needs. Why sleep on a traditional "bed" when you share an apartment with a roommate and your room is the living room?

Louise built her own bed (with Henry's aid). She used 8-inch boards for a platform and she bought a firm hair mattress, which she covered in a printed cotton. With bolster pillows and lots of throw pillows covered in the same material she had a sofa and a bed. In front of her sofa/bed, she had a low stainless steel table that's just as flexible. It has four drawers on all sides, and a section in the top that lifts up to expose a place for records, liquor, etc. You can sit around this table on cushions and have a cozy fondue dinner because there are no legs to get in the way. The table "floats" from a center support.

We need practical, easy-to-maintain furniture. It has to work for constant use and be well constructed, tough. It has to be multipurposed and flexible for all occasions and all spaces. Comfort is key to our needs and if a piece of furniture is designed with our needs in mind, taking into consideration our scale and balance and the scale of where we live, it will be well designed. Last, but certainly not least, it should be reasonably priced. Everything is so expensive today, we need to have furniture within our economic reach.

We're having to use our furniture as a tool to make our rooms fit into our needs and activities. Louise, for example, had to find a way to fit into her roommate's living room without giving up the room as a place to entertain friends. Louise's four-poster bed would have looked absurd in the middle of the living room. Whereas her new sofa/bed is handsome, simple and in balance. There's no room for a dining table but her steel table solves that problem.

There's nothing set about our lives and circumstances. They are always changing, and furniture can only meet this mobility if we plan ahead. You can't afford to outgrow your furniture. None of us knows what size our living room will be twenty years from now, so your master furniture plan should allow for lots of question marks. Don't limit your opportunity for adventure by becoming too locked into a rigid set of standards and styles that make flexibility all but impossible. The Bennetts couldn't move into an adorable town house because their furniture was too big. Other friends have collected large furniture, from relatives and dealers, for their future dream house; meanwhile, life is going by at jet speed and they're living in a small apartment and paying an enormous storage bill each month.

We all have a dream about the perfect setup with everything settled and in place. I hate to say it, but I think we're likely to achieve this when we're too old to care much. Build your furniture repertoire with pieces you can enjoy now.

FURNITURE ROOTS

When we have our own furniture around us, we feel settled. Furniture and treasures accumulated gradually combine so many elements of your background and interests, they give your rooms their hidden dimension and personality and are a great source of comfort to you. The contrasts in the mixtures make a room interesting, keep them from being studied, contrived, dull. Furniture that is gathered slowly is always going to mean more to you. Furniture has to be far more than sentimental, though, to work for our lives. We have to make it really function and fit into the way and place we live.

REPRODUCTIONS

In my opinion, reproductions of the past are no longer meaningful. They're a contradiction in themselves. If you own reproductions and enjoy them, that's one thing, but to go out today and purchase them is a waste of money. Their resale value is nil, and generally they aren't designed to function for today's living.

DESIGNING—OLD AND NEW

Fake imitation furniture is like almost living. I'd advise you to be a purist in your furniture design selection and look for honesty and integrity in design. Stay away from manufactured reproductions whenever possible. Instead, have an original contemporary design that is a part of the times you live in. Good designs are available on any budget. You can buy an original Parson's table in a choice of four colors for as little as $16.95. If you're willing to put it together yourself, it's available for $6.95. It's expensive to be a tried and true traditionalist. Having your house filled with "fine French fakes" isn't going to give you as much satisfaction and contentment as one beautiful old piece.

ANTIQUES

Antiques are becoming so scarce, they'll soon be priceless. We're becoming increasingly sentimental about certain pieces and for good reason. When our parents started out they could find furniture at reasonable prices, but it's too late for us. When we buy or acquire an antique piece of furniture, it's an expression of our sentiment and our aesthetic appreciation, not a functional piece of living equipment. I've seen rooms where one beautiful piece made an ordinary room outstanding.

Charlene and Tom Evans' living room is radiant with one magnificently carved pine armoire. It absolutely uplifts the entire atmosphere and is a constant feast to the eye. There isn't anything else in the room that even begins to compete with this beautiful piece of workmanship and form. So if you like antiques, have a few beautiful ones or can acquire them, they can enhance your room enormously.

When you can't have good old pieces but you want the feeling of richness and strength old furniture can give a room, there are alternatives. Go to junk stores, auctions (on a rainy day, auctions have fewer bidders), even the Salvation Army, and find funky old pieces—not fine, but made of good old wood. What one person turns down or has thrown out, you may crave. For $18 you might find a used chair of uncertain style or quality that would fill a corner, at a fraction of what you would pay for any kind of new chair.

FURNITURE AS INVESTMENT

The best thing about acquiring furniture as an investment is that it is a living investment. To some of us, living with beautiful objects in attractive surroundings gives far more pleasure than having stock certificates stashed away someplace. If the old furniture serves your needs (practically and aesthetically), fits into your space restrictions, and you can afford to buy it, it's a good purchase. But if it doesn't meet one of these requirements, I question its investment value. Anything of quality, old or new, has value that will appreciate. But from a Wall Street investment point of view, there are better places to put your money, unless the furniture really meets your needs anyway.

CONTEMPORARY FURNITURE INVESTS IN LIVING

If you're in the position to add to your furniture collection, seriously consider purchasing contemporary furniture. Furniture of today fits into any room, old or new, and its simplicity of line and form integrates nicely with our living patterns and with our old furniture. Because our furniture has to function for all our lives, as well as please us, contemporary designs might serve you well. Select good craftsmanship, proportions and design, and the results will work into all the facets of your living.

Good modern designs can go both ways—contemporary furniture can be just as appropriate at a barbecue gathering as at an elegant black-tie dinner. Contemporary furniture also makes it easy to find comfort in all kinds of situations. Sofa and chair backs are low so the furniture can be anywhere in the room. Arms are thicker, more heavily padded—so the sofa and chair are good places to sit. One friend was pondering the virtues of a beautiful leather contemporary sofa; he had no business considering it because of its price, but somehow he convinced himself that the sofa was all he needed. "I'll put it in the very center of my living-room floor and my life will revolve around my beauty. And . . . (all this with a straight face) I can seat eight on my sofa at a party. Three on the seat, three on the back and two on the arms. I'll take it."

SEATING PLANS

Traditionally, we used walls to line up our furniture and if the walls were broken up with doors, etc., we were out of luck trying to get good seating for conversations and small group gatherings.

Now, a sofa goes anywhere there's floor space in order to get the necessary comfortable seating. "Floating furniture plans" referred to as "landscaping" use furniture to divide one area from another so a room can break up into a series of separate seating areas. If everything is easily moved around, you can open up a grouping so it seats more (most groupings seat four with an optimal seating for six). The chairs and sofas should be close enough together so that real conversation is possible and cushions and poufs can be pulled up by the person who wants to join the group. A pouf is a cushioned and upholstered bench, very comfortable.

But not all traditional furniture can be moved so easily. Try different arrangements using your own furniture and see what really works well and what seems to cause problems. Furniture is in a room to serve you. A chair should say, "Sit down and relax." Furniture should be inviting. Who is patient enough in our complicated lives for "show" sofas that are too delicate to sit on? Anything whose primary function is seating should be ready to hold us without fuss. Antique side chairs should be in good repair. Antique dining chairs should be strong enough and wide enough to hold men.

Sofas at right angles to each other with a pair of chairs opposite one sofa and a pair of benches opposite the other with a large low table in the middle is a very comfortable, flexible plan. Or two sofas the same length and two chairs the same design. When you have pairs of furniture you can make many different kinds of arrangements. The two sofas can be opposite each other with two chairs side by side at one end or one chair at either end. I've used two sofas back to back to separate seating groups.

Upholstered furniture is the joiner of yesterday and tomorrow. Beautiful rooms where people gather should have comfortable upholstery. You can be a traditionalist through and through but no one wants to sit on uptight old chairs any more. Upholstery allows you to have traditional furniture and comfort too. Comfort comes from the right beginning (a sturdy frame), good quality ingredients that pad it, and knowledgeable workmanship to make sure everything adds contour to the body. Remember how important the pitch of a chair back is to the seat depth. If you're short you know what can happen to your legs if the seat is too deep and too high. The pitch of a back has to be carefully integrated to the height so it supports you. A tufted seat is never as comfortable as a loose cushion seat. Loose back cushions are comfortable if you like to lounge in your chair or sofa. If you have a bad back you should have firm upholstery. It is a good idea to have at least one ottoman so you can prop up your feet. If you are tall be sure your legs rest comfortably on the floor when you are seated. You may have to have quite a deep seat and one higher than average. Above all, you have to sit and feel good. When it comes to matters of comfort, you have to determine what comfort is, personally, to you.

In the past a living room sometimes had one Lawson-type sofa (classic upholstered sofa with rolled arms). Or if the room was more formal, then it had only settees. Now, we want every piece to be comfortable. The easiest way to acquire a stiff room is to fill it with rigid furniture; this can ruin space faster than bad architecture. Architecture can be softened and warmed up but a room that's coldly assembled has a chill that's hard to defrost.

FURNITURE HAS LOST ITS FOUR LEGS

One of our designers was invited to give a friendly critique of a friend's living room. The first thing she noticed was that the room was too leggy. If you count up all the furniture in your living room and multiply the number of pieces by four, you may discover that you have as many as one hundred legs sticking up from the floor. Too many legs make a room unrestful; and they take up floor space that could be put to good use. Furniture is now made which floats on a recessed platform. Or a storage piece can be hung on a wall. Solid panels have replaced individual legs; if the panels are of clear plastic they seem to disappear entirely. For comfort, you can have chairs that are on swivel bases and have spring seats so you can actually move while sitting down, or face different directions without getting up. You can hang a basket chair from a heavy-duty hook in the ceiling, eliminating any feeling of weight at all. These tend to look better in pictures than in real life because they aren't always that comfortable.

In the future, seating will probably be organized into a "system" containing four combinable seats in a nesting arrangement. With a buckle, snap or click, presto!—three chairs become a sofa—or snap!—one sofa becomes a figure eight. Several pieces of pie-shaped polyurethane, covered in an attractive fabric, can become a "center block" for seating, and then can be separated according to your needs.

MULTIPURPOSE

The best way to utilize space is to have it exercise its potential without expanding its boundaries. The question becomes: How many activities and functions can be performed in a given space? Today's space-conscious designers are solving this for us with self-contained units, nesting, stacking and demounting furniture, wall systems, etc. Now anything is possible.

It's possible to have a round table in your living room that can be moved into your hall when you need a dining table, and when you lift up the top, there are six folding chairs, magically stored. One 9-foot wall can house a bar, a drop-down table, chairs, a record player, records, hi-fi speakers, books, magazines, a TV, it's a miracle that when it's closed up it's only 15-inches deep. And good looking.

Try to design your furniture for a specific purpose. Now we're able to choose from a vast variety of exciting designs that will fit into our lives and make our living conditions more enjoyable. Overscaling and crowding of furniture are the most common problems and no longer necessary. You have to proportion your possessions to the amount of available space.

Designers of today take into account the expenses of moving and storing by making furniture and storage units demountable. A poker card table has removable legs. Chairs and sofas can be knocked down. Tables are arranged like puzzles for space saving and storing ease. Look for flaps, leaves, hinges, anything that gives the furniture flexibility.

Think of your furniture as you do your clothing wardrobe. There should be some basic pieces which are classic and lasting. Fashionable veneers and burls have a way of coming in and out of favor. Buy basic, honest pieces which are one with you. The van should move them from here to there, from room to room, place to place without their becoming awkward or out of place.

Lighting

Truly the light is sweet and a pleasant thing it
is for the eyes to behold the sun.

ECCLESIASTES 11:7

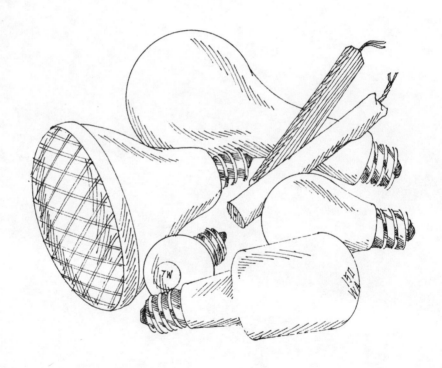

The dynamic forward thrust in lighting techniques and the availability of every conceivable kind of fixture have made lighting one of the most exciting elements in our rooms. The evolution from electrified bottles, vases and jars to an entire lighting philosophy, with a purpose, has transformed our spaces into places with imaginative illumination and a warm atmosphere that we can adjust and control to fit any mood.

Inadequate lighting in rooms can hurt your psyche as well as your eyes, can create an uneasy restless mood and disturb your sense of inner calm. The advances we've made technically, the growing scarcity of natural light and an increasing awareness of the effects artificial lighting can make in our lives, have made us aware, and we are lighting our rooms in ways never imagined before.

Compared to Europeans, we're lavish with our wattage and always have been. But, suddenly, artificial illumination has become a hot, exciting field. Lighting is coming into every nook and cranny; light is leaking out from under bookcases and shelves, inside tables, from spots on the floor and can lights hanging from the ceiling. Standing lamps and table lights are like shining sculptures. Paintings, glass collections are highlighted by shield lights or tensor spots. A long sweeping arch light, the Arco, spots onto a table or warms up a seating area. Windows are being lighted in an attempt to imitate natural daylight when there is no source available.

TWO BASIC TYPES OF LIGHT: FLUORESCENT AND INCANDESCENT

Fluorescent lighting is gas operated. The fixture comes in a tube. It requires less power and therefore is cheaper than incandescent lighting, because it doesn't need continuous electricity. It's an over-all diffused light source which doesn't bring out texture or create much excitement. Fluorescent lighting is excellent for commercial light installations because it doesn't throw off heat. Its cool, even flow has a longer span of light than an incandescent bulb can provide. The tubes are available in varying sizes and in various color tints. A combination of these tints (cool white and warm white) closely duplicates daylight. When you install fluorescent strips in a lighted table, for example, experiment with a mixture of colors. From my experience, I've found warm white (referred to as "daylight") the most pleasant because it forces the spirit of sunlight inside. There are pink lights and soft green lights, and you can have all different kinds of effects by combining a series of colors. For evening lighting you may want more tints and the easiest way to achieve this would be to have some colored plastic or heavy cellophane over the light source so you don't have to change your bulbs constantly. Ask one of your theatrical friends about colored lights and their effects on you and the mood of a space.

Incandescent lighting (the kind you get from bulbs) allows a warm natural light. Depending on the wattage and the angle, you can create warmth, drama and vigor and also bring out textures, with incandescent lighting. The drama comes through the contrasts you get from light to dark. The color of incandescent lighting has the feeling of fire and heat, although 82 per cent of the energy produced from incandescent light is heat and the remaining 18 per cent is actual light. Each of us has our own tolerance for the amount of light we wish in a given space. I study in a library where I feel the lighting inadequate and too relaxing—there are only two 40-watt incandescent bulbs in a room 8 feet by 12 feet. The amount of light your space requires is very individual. Dark colors absorb light so you would need more wattage in a paneled room than in a light-colored room. An average-size living room could take as much as 600 watts of light. That could be divided up in lots of 40-watt bulbs or 150-watt bulbs. If you have lamps with two light sockets you can have high-watt bulbs; when both are too much, cut it in half by turning off one switch.

LIGHTING AS PART OF CONSTRUCTION

New buildings are generally adequately wired for our needs, and also lighting is increasingly built into the ceilings as part of the construction costs. Instead of hanging one chandelier, we can now have the entire ceiling illuminated.

This can be done in a number of ways. Recessed "down can," or "high hats," are being built right into ceilings nowadays, for over-all light.

These should be put on low-cost dimmer controls, with separate switches for lighting specific sections. For example, you can turn off the lighting in your kitchen work area when you're finished cooking, while keeping lights on in your eating area. It's handy to have the dimmer control near your table, so you can change the lighting as needed. Entire "skylight" systems (recessed ceiling fluorescent lights with white plastic domed covers) are being used for ceilings in bathrooms and kitchens. They can be used to cover the entire space in square and rectangular panels exactly where required.

To save the expense of complicated electrical work, most of us want to deal with the electrical openings we have. All our deadly dim and dingy fixtures can easily and cheaply be transformed into today's lighting. Go around and check all your ceiling fixtures and wall outlets and measure the diameter of the cap that conceals the wires. When buying a new fixture you should be sure the plate (or cap) is as large as the one you're replacing or even a little bigger so that you won't have to plaster or paint.

An entrance hall, for example, can be changed from a traditionally wasted space to an art gallery if you simply replace your old-fashioned fixture with some lively "can" lights which spotlight your wall decorations.

"Track" lighting offers can lights (in a variety of finishes, sizes and shapes) that are attached to a metal strip and they slide back and forth on this track at the touch; you can direct the light on items of interest. The tracks can be as long or short as you want and you can have as many or as few cans as you need. For general room illumination and to highlight art and objects of interest, tracks on the ceiling with can lighting can be very functional. We installed tracks with some can lights for a little boy's room and immediately received a phone call from a nervous mother. "Johnny is going to blind himself from your hot bright lights. He lies on his back when I change him and stares into the intense light bulbs." I explained that these cans come with attachments to reduce the heat and are adjustable, so while Johnny is little it is better to have the lights directed toward the wall so he can't look directly into the light—later, when he is older, these concentrated rays of light will be a big help for desk and play areas.

Can lighting directs light very specifically and is quite dramatic. If you'd prefer more general ceiling light, there are all types of frosted glass or white plastics that can hang flush to the ceiling or down from a stem depending on your ceiling height and on where they're located. The more flush the fixture is to the ceiling the less noticeable and less concentrated the light. Hanging fixtures take up "emotional" space and even though they're high enough to walk under without ducking your head, you may feel constrained if they crowd the space. Question how you are to get to your fixture to change the bulbs too. The higher the fixture, the more inconvenient it is to change, so the fixture you select should be easy to change.

If you have some ceiling outlets in awkward places, select a simple flush fixture. Anything that hangs down into your space should have a reason for being there. A fixture centered over a table, if the table is constantly being moved around, is a mistake.

The simplest thing to do when you don't want to hang a fixture and there's an opening in the ceiling is to cap the opening with a little round disc. You can get the caps at any hardware store. They screw right on, but first be sure to paint the cap the same color as your ceiling so that it will seem to disappear. Putting a temporary cap on an opening is an excellent solution to your problem while you save money for a dreamy fixture.

DECORATIVE HANGING FIXTURES

Beauty should be the motive behind any chandelier or hanging fixture. When you deliberately drop something down into your space, it should have aesthetic purpose because today's functional lighting has taken away the non-aesthetic value we get from hanging lighting fixtures. Light your room any other way but with a compromise dangling from a chain. There are wattage restrictions to almost all fixtures and you should study the restriction before you commit yourself to any particular fixtures. I used a plastic ceiling fixture in my kitchen years ago and when I went in one night to get dinner ready, I discovered the fixture was a melted pile of plastic. It could have been serious. If you overload your wattage you can burn out your bulbs, your fixture, your fuse and, if you're not careful, your brains. Check with an electrician when in doubt. I repeat, decorative fixtures should be beautiful! They attract your attention so make them elevating.

WALL FIXTURES "SWING"

Wall openings have exciting possibilities. No longer do you have to hunt down rare globes or lanterns to cover an opening. The most common place for wall outlets has traditionally been the dining room and now that rooms have radically changed in feeling, wall lights have too. All the shapes and materials that are available for ceiling fixtures are equally appropriate for walls, especially the cylindrical shape of the can light. Wall can lights can be white, black, chrome, brass, solar bronze, clear lacquer colors or combinations of metal and frosted plastic, allowing light to spill up and down, or up or down, depending on the effect you want.

There are white plastic shells that flood light upward on the wall, beautifully simple and effective. These are especially effective in hallways and in dining rooms because they wash such a soft warm light.

Have you ever heard of the "Save the Marriage" lights? These are made by a firm in New York as a perfect solution to reading in bed without disturbing your mate. The design is so simple—a bar that hangs on the wall with two down cans, one for you and one for your mate. The light direction is concentrated so it doesn't illuminate the whole room the way a traditional lamp shade does.

The wall "swing arm" light is my favorite lighting fixture because it's the best made (the fittings are perfect, the metal is smooth and the design totally geared to operate), the best looking and the most practical. It comes in brass or chrome and has a three-way light from 50 watts to 150 watts. If you don't have a wall outlet available where you want to use this fixture, you can buy brass tubing ¼-inch wide to hold the wire inside, thus avoiding ugly dangling cords. Because of the "swing arm" you can move it near you or out of the way depending on your need. This is the best lamp for reading in bed I know of and looks just as appropriate when used in the living room on either side of a sofa. It can be used in singles (over a desk or dressing area) or in pairs (over a bed, sofa).

EXPAND SPACE THROUGH LIGHTING

One reason the shapes for lighting have changed is that lighting can now do its job without taking up space. You don't have to add another

table to your room just because you need a lamp. Instead of having
lighting that is only directed downward, "up" lighting is an effective way
to light a space. Generally, I think of up lighting as floor cans (which are
exactly the same design as ones for the ceiling but they are on the floor
instead); or small up spots which can be put on a table; or a standing
floor lamp which has a cone-shaped top, allowing the bulb to illuminate
above. Floor flood up cans can be stuck in corners to shoot light all
over; they don't fill up space but rather open it up. If you tuck them behind trees and plants, the shadows of the plants are articulated on your
ceiling and wall. Proper lighting can give an airy, spacious feeling to
your room.

DECORATIVE LAMPS

The decorative lamp, while it is only one of a dozen possible light
sources, is still an important decorative element and one with enormous
versatility. The table lamp can marry themes of old and new by combining
centuries with variety and style. For example, an old Chinese vase made
into a lamp can look superb on a simple straight-legged parson's table. Or
a very crude Greek vase can look marvelous on an old walnut table,
softened and smoothed by use and time. On the other hand, a modern
ceramic lamp or a new chalky white lamp can look fine on an old marble
or wooden table. I complain that the decorative lamp and shade take up
space and are hard to move around, but there are certain spots in a room
where nothing else works as well.

Because I consider decorative lamps "accessories," let's talk about them
further in the chapter on "Accessories."

MODERN LIGHTING MATERIALS

A contemporary version of the traditional column lamp and shade
might consist of a vinyl (looks like leather) column with an aluminum
mushroom dome for a shade. While the basic electrical charge is the same
as before, this new crisp shape and material give you something new. Now
the table lamp is a self-illuminated art form, a sculptural interpretation,
which might be made of lucite and chrome, paper over wire, or chrome
tubing.

A vase of unusual shape and beauty could be lighted from within, or it could be electrified with a harp and shade so it could be a light source for reading. A lamp isn't just a lamp, set apart from sculpture or art: Beauty can be functional.

STANDING LAMPS

Years ago standing lamps were all so ugly. They reminded me of the lamps that used to be in the post office, with the chain hanging down. Today, with so much of our furniture mobile, the floor lamp has re-shaped itself and can fit into your flexible room arrangements beautifully. If you examine contemporary rooms you will see fewer lamps and shades in the middle of the room for this very reason. Brass, chrome, glass, plexiglass, plaster, wood standing lamps are now well designed and many are adjustable in height. Instead of lamp shades, there are small metal shades in various shapes, which make the standing lamp functional, simple and unobtrusive.

Some standing lamps are so beautiful they act as architectural features in a room. My favorite decorative standing lamp is of white plaster and looks like a palm tree with a flood of light spilling toward the ceiling.

LIGHTING UP FURNITURE

Light tables are lots of fun and great for growing plants. One example: A white, round, tiered table has a circular tube of fluorescent light that floods light down onto a shelf; you can keep your African violets there, and have light good enough to read by. Light tables make excellent end tables in a bedroom; a sculptor friend uses his to display his art. Sea shells or a coin collection or a rock collection could be displayed on them; they are especially exciting when the lighted top illuminates colored objects. I have colored plastic objects which sparkle and glow from inside themselves when on my lighted cube table. You can design a lighted table as an end table, a coffee table, a sofa table behind your sofa—in any shape and any size.

Any table that has a self-contained light allows more surface room and gives a cleaner look to your room.

WINDOW LIGHTING

Because windows are our only natural light source we tend to overlook them as possible locations for artificial illumination. Whether you live in the country and want an indoor garden or you live in the city and need more light than you're getting, go to your windows. It's the natural place. You will be astounded at the positive effects this lighting technique can have on the entire mood of your room. When done well, the artificial light totally fools you and you feel the light at the window is sunlight.

Let me give you some examples. We turned a cell-like maid's room into an adorable feminine room for a little girl by installing "daylight" fluorescent strips on the top and sides of her windows. Because the view out the windows was a depressing gray shaft, we taped white vinyl over the entire window and added yards of billowy dotted swiss curtains. The result was a room flooded with twenty-four-hour sunshine.

Another trick: When overcurtains and valances are involved, install fluorescent strip lighting at the top of the window. Then line the curtains with a vinyl "no-lite" lining: It blocks out the light but don't use this light-blocking lining for the valance. The effect is so realistic; it looks like sunlight is actually spilling down from the top of the window.

Your household plants could thrive even near your darkest window if you install shelves with fluorescent strips of "plant grow" lights. None of these lights are terribly expensive to buy or difficult to install.

CANDLES TO LIGHT YOUR HEART

Give me the warmth of the sun in the day and the warmth of candles and a fire at night. Since I was a young child, I've always been thrilled by the romance of candlelight and fire in the hearth (too fascinated, I almost burned the house down once). There's a warmth and feeling of security that comes from the flickering glow of a candle and the crackling flame from the fireplace. Except in summer when it is too hot, think of all the times you can light candles to create good feeling. I don't have to enlighten you as to the change in candles and holders. Like everything else, they have moved into new shapes and should definitely be a part of your evening lighting scheme. Experiment with various scented candles too. Christmastime is cinnamon and bayberry and nutmeg, lemon can be for always, but you have to test the scent of a candle burning in your room to feel the real fragrance. Sometimes the most beautiful color has a "tutti-fruiti" scent or your nutmeg smell delights your nose and offends your eyes because of the color.

CHANGING BULBS AND CLEANING FIXTURES

When a bulb burns out it shouldn't be a complicated thing to change. When purchasing any fixture be sure you fully understand how to get at the bulb and, also, what type of bulb the fixture requires. If you have to stand on a ladder and unscrew four screws to change a bulb, that's a lot of work. I once broke a big glass globe and vowed never again to purchase anything so impractical.

Label all bulbs that are for a special purpose. There's nothing more frustrating than burning out a fixture because you used the wrong flood light. Because a light bulb doesn't give off any warning when it goes, buy in quantity, especially if you have tubular bulbs that aren't available at the supermarket.

I have thrown out my "crystal chandelier cleaner" as a symbol that time is more valuable than *that*. Because of the heat, fixtures attract all kinds of dirt and grime and need to be cleaned often to keep their sparkle. When dreaming of cut crystal prisms hanging down over your round glass table, remember that you can wipe the table clean, but you'll have to buy my jar of crystal chandelier cleaner.

Fabrics

Fabrics must provide the texture, colour,
character, scale and comfort missing in interior
architecture. They must compensate for a bland
undifferentiated architecture, make impersonal
spaces particular and personal.

JACK LENOR LARSEN

Generally, by the time you are Real, most of
your hair has been loved off, and your eyes drop
out and you get loose in the joints and very
shabby. But these things don't matter at all,
because once you are Real you can't be ugly,
except to people who don't understand.

MARGERY WILLIAMS
The Velveteen Rabbit

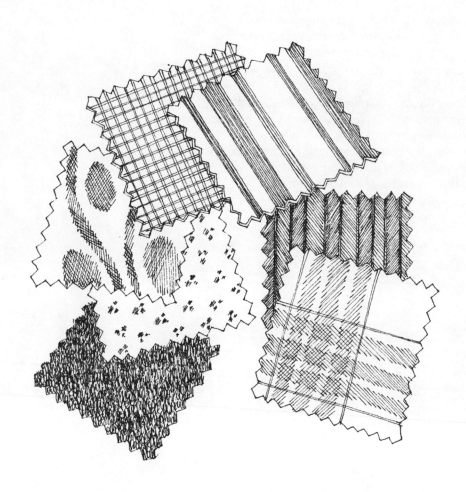

I can't imagine an eighteenth-century housewife raving about the green silk damask material on her settee and saying, "That's me, that's me." But today, we're using fabric as a means of expressing ourselves. Our less formal inclinations, our less serious, less rigid approach to life show up in the fabrics we bring into our private surroundings.

Perhaps you want an ordinary cotton in your living room. When a client recently rearranged her living room, she scattered blue, yellow and white cotton chintz all over her furniture. Can you imagine what this did to her "formal" room? A giant turnabout, with material as her vehicle! Instead of the room looking lonely unless it was filled with party people, it had a life of its own because of the crisp new printed material. Ten years ago it would have been most unusual to see an informal geometric cotton in a formal room, but things have changed. And fabrics have burst forward with a new vitality, in step with the new life tempo, style and pace.

The variety of materials available allows each of us to express whatever feelings and moods we wish. The traditional fabrics in yesterday's colors are still with us, but the designs come in totally new colors to make them more up-to-date, and they have been printed and woven on more carefree sensible materials. In addition to the traditional designs, jazzed-up, new dynamic "motion" prints are being made in all colors. Motion prints break from the static, the stylized, the staid. There are more swirls, and flames appear to grow. A motion print is full of curves and seems to swish the way the wind sways the leaves of a tree. The next time you are in a store looking at fabrics, think of movement, of flowing, harmonious directions in patterns, versus static, repetitious rigid shapes. The opposite of a motion print is a stripe or a plaid.

Another way new ideas in fabrics can enrich our lives is in patterned sheets. Who can pass up the opportunity to lie in a bed of clover, or on a bed of spring flowers, or on a blanket of pink and white clouds dancing on a blue sky, or on bamboo patterns or geometric basket weaves? Why not let the kids sleep in jungle fantasies, or on Snoopy stories, or on a country farm with horses and cows and houses with red doors? Every time you change your sheets you can have a whole new room.

Just as our attitudes towards fabrics have changed, so have our needs. Permanent-press fabrics save us time, soil-resistant fabrics save us work, and gay designs save us money (a big effect for a relatively low price). Take advantage of all these. We've changed our architectural concepts, building materials and furniture, and fabrics have to adapt accordingly. A silk damask still has a place, but not on a tubular steel chair. Comfort has come a long way and the materials appropriate for the tubular steel chair are stretched ones which are "tense," which support the body and "give" into us as we sit down. (Such a chair is not recommended for serious business decisions. It's too comfortable!)

OUR NEEDS ARE INDIVIDUAL

By the materials you select and the way you apply them to your rooms, you can have your place reflect you. You can choose between Americana documentaries and *toile de Jouys*, eighteenth-century chintz designs and crewel, silks and taffetas or "futurama" free form designs for tomorrow, bright geometric and whimsical patterns—whatever goes with your life style. Select and combine these materials in your own way.

One of the prettiest rooms I've ever seen is an English eighteenth-century living room with a twentieth-century cotton print in bright blue, green, yellow and cantaloupe. This modern geometric glazed cotton material brought the beautiful old furniture and accessories right up to date for this vibrant couple and their three young daughters. Combined with this bright printed cotton are velvets and suedes and needlework pillows in current designs and colors. Another living room with old and new furniture combined was totally transformed by the ingenious use of materials. Each fabric used was hand woven, textured and came from all over the globe, picked up in villages in Africa for pennies and in Bangkok for a few dollars. The integrity of these materials combined with the strong, lively colors made the room unique.

A man living alone chose to have all heavy earth-colored textiles of blanket weight. For color accents he used many pillows covered in African prints with symbolic designs and colors that tend to project emotions. Each pillow seems to tell a special story. All his materials are invitingly tactile.

No longer do you have to limit yourself to covering a Victorian sofa in a period fabric. Instead, bring the old clunker up-to-date by using patchwork or Bangkok plaids or an Indian batik covering. Traditionally, patterns were used to balance a room. For example, if you have a sofa at one end and two chairs opposite your fireplace at the other end, covering the pieces in the same fabric ties the room together. Now you might deliberately contrast the fabric on the sofa and that on the chairs; the furniture plan and contrasting materials create the feeling of two separate rooms because the space is divided by fabric. In large open spaces this is especially effective because there is room to make these changes without being too abrupt. One huge space can actually become two separate rooms without a dividing wall simply by the way you handle your materials. For example, the Pierponts moved into an apartment where the library and living-room wall was knocked down opening the two rooms into one. Because of finances they couldn't recover all their furniture so they simply created a library grouping at one end and a living-room grouping at another. The blessing was that there was a color co-ordination between the two fabric schemes: also, the chintz of the living room worked well with the plain textures in the library.

The Williamsons grouped their printed material around the fireplace and selected colors from the design to use for their less formal area. They chose greens and blues for textured upholstery material and used brightly colored cotton pillows to pick up yellows and reds from the print at the other end. One grouping helps the other but doesn't interfere.

Think of your materials as joining your conversation groups, not your entire space. Mrs. Brown has a room 40-foot square, and it would be ridiculous to try to tie such a grand space together with fabric. The materials she selected for the various seating separations have distinctly different feelings and yet they all have a link that ties them together— color and a sympathy for one and other. Go by your instincts in putting materials together.

Most of us want a soothing relaxed place to live, and this is only possible when we approach our rooms with sincerity. When it's not necessary to be super practical with permanent press and synthetics, it's nice to use hand-woven wools and cottons because their penetrating natural designs and textures have the colors and feelings we want to come home to.

The style of your furniture collection doesn't matter as much as what you cover it in. Friends of ours have a charming house in Connecticut and their living-room furniture is covered in one of the sweetest prints I've ever seen, a white linen with ferns and jack-in-the-pulpits. All the colors are fresh and clear; suddenly it's an August afternoon and you smell the air and hear the running water from the brook. There isn't anything pretentious or sophisticated about this print; it's charming and it makes you feel warm and good inside. It makes the house.

Another room that comes to my mind as a cozy place is a living room that has a French strawberry print on the furniture, personifying the bounties of nature. Its meandering design of leaves, berries and exposed roots makes you feel you are in a strawberry patch eating a berry or two . . .

YEAR-ROUND COLORS

Our rooms, generally speaking, need a lift and the sunnier side of the palette gives them energy and life. To assure good weather year round, incorporate yellows, oranges and reds in with your cooler blues and greens. This will take care of those bad weather days. Mrs. Eleanor Brown (founder and president of McMillen, Inc.) once said, "Every room should have a touch of yellow." I think she's right.

SEASONAL FABRICS

With some imaginative shifting of colors and textures, we can double our mileage from our basic materials and feel we've made a change. Just as nature changes at different times of year, for most of us a new season is always refreshing. As beautiful as the summer has been, fall is exciting and breaks the monotony. We begin to spend more time inside, with the change in the weather, and you may want some different materials in your rooms. If you live in the South or on the West Coast where there aren't seasonal temperature changes, a change of fabric can bring on a happy shift in pace and give you the feeling of fall in the air.

It's perfectly true that materials recall associations, and can seem inappropriate when they're out of season. Pastel ginghams look one way in the chill of February, another way in the sweltering July heat; and maroon velvet cushions on a sun-porch lounge chair aren't quite right for poolside sun bathing. We stayed at an island hotel that had leather couches and chairs in the lobby—the last feeling you want when you came so far to be in the sun.

As our life styles change and we continue to want the relaxed spirit of outdoor living year round, fall is coming later and later; the spirit of spring is lasting year round. By and large we are requiring the same life and vitality of our materials in the winter as we enjoy in the summer. The textures become warmer as we prepare for the cold bleak winter ahead. Your major furniture slipcovers can stay on year round now, allowing you to live in permanent flower gardens and spring colors.

You can make easy changes such as removing gingham and seersucker pillow covers, in favor of a nubbier, softer material underneath. You might add a heavier spread, quilt or throw to your bed to give you more warmth. You might want to put a wool throw over the back of your sofa or love seat in the cool of winter—so handy for curling up and reading. Add your fur pillows along about November. Your curtains can be returned from the cleaners and hung to add a feeling of warmth. All your earthy-colored needlework pillows can return from the closet.

IN-SEASON FABRIC COSTS

Most of us live, by and large, in one house year round, and we should plan our fabrics so they're equally enjoyable in winter and summer. Because your rooms are used non-stop twelve months of the year, your fabrics really take a beating and may just wear out in five years' time.

If seasonal change is very important to you, maybe you should consider two separate sets of slipcovers for your major furniture pieces. Two sets of slipcovers will double your cost now, but in the long run will save you money, as both slipcover sets will last longer. But if financial priorities dictate that you stick to smaller changes to give your rooms a lift, alternate the covers on your chair seats, pillows or draped table covers (round tables with fabric throws to the floor).

FABRICS SHOULD BE TACTILE

Fabrics have two basic appeals. They bring color, texture and design to our rooms, and also a tactile sense—it matters how they feel. The prettiest colors and most scrumptious textures might give your skin a rash. Always run the back of your hand over any fabric that is to go on furniture. In the past five years we've found fashions are more bare skinned so put a fabric sample under your knees and see if it feels good. Think how often you're in your living room with bare legs! Cottons usually feel good (especially after they've been softened by lots of washings). Suedes, leathers, velvets, velours feel good too. There is a new imitation suede that is washable and more touchable than suede. Some linens are fine until they've been printed and then they get stiff. The drawback of vinyl is that it feels cold and your warm body temperature makes it stick to your skin.

WHEN TO UPHOLSTER, WHEN TO SLIPCOVER

All new furniture you buy gets "tight covered" automatically. The piece of upholstery is first covered in a "muslin" (white cotton that holds the insides together), then in your "finish" fabric. This is part of the price. If a chair is $285 plus five yards of ten-dollar material, your total cost is $335. Even if you plan to slipcover your new furniture in a matter of a year's time, be sure you select a hard-wearing material for the upholstery. By doing this you can double your use by having good-wearing upholstery and the option to eventually change to a slipcover.

When you have new furniture upholstered have your cushions reversible, with zippers, and ask for extra arm protectors. The care will be almost as easy as a slipcover, particularly if you choose a practical sturdy material. Don't suffer when your family sits in your newly covered furniture. Who is it there for?

ARM PROTECTORS

Arm protectors are a smart idea. I know a couple who redid their living-room furniture and the husband was no longer allowed to read his morning paper in his chair for fear of the grime he'd cause on the arms of his chair! Arm protectors should be made out of the same material as the rest of the piece (not of lace like the ones Grandmother had). When they're made properly, they don't show at all because the pattern is matched to the pattern of the upholstery and the protectors go all the way down the side to be pinned right back in place. Don't expect your upholsterer to do this as a present. The labor is very time consuming and you should get an estimate first. Usually you'll need 1½ yards extra material; if you're at all handy you could make them yourself.

SLIPCOVERS

Slipcovers should be a real secret. A good slipcover man is as important to your furniture as a good pediatrician is to your children. He should know his craft, and care. Details can be so beautiful. Making a dress is easier than making a chair slipcover, but there are details you can instigate because of your understanding of working with a needle and thread. For example, the "skirt" or "flounce" of your chair could be gathered at the corner. This "eased" corner is softer and more graceful than an "inverted" corner pleat. This small detail can make a huge difference in the over-all look. It's no harder to do. All it is, is style. Another thing that is good looking is to drop your flounce down from under the platform, that is, directly from under your seat cushion. Check to see if you have a spring edge in the front of your sofa or chair because if you do, this styling isn't advisable because it will droop on the floor. If you have a firm front edge it can look very attractive. Try having your slipcover with no welts. It is a smooth look and those welts tend to wear out more quickly than the rest of the slipcover. Experiment with bindings and braids. Nothing has to be expensive but a simple band of color on the bottom edge of your flounce can add style. If your material is plain and you want interest, try having one row at the bottom and an additional band set up two or so inches. Experiment with various widths from ½ inch to four or more inches thick. Pin them on a sample of your material until you feel you have just the right proportion.

Look for straight lines and graceful curves when selecting furniture so you'll be free to use the fabrics you like and have them lend themselves to your furniture. All curves are difficult to fit properly when slipcovered. Avoid "show wood frames" (wood surrounding back, arms or seat of furniture) or any unusually curvaceous (wing chairs, for example) piece if you eventually plan to slipcover.

Proceed on the assumption that the person you have hired to make your slipcovers or do your upholstery cares. If he lacks talent, take the time to show him *you* care and support him while he ventures out and tries new ways. Ask him questions. Sympathize with his problems. Sometimes we expect miracles even with raveling, thick material that breaks needles and drives him crazy. Fabrics are adaptable but not acrobatic. If you don't use light weight material, check with your upholsterer before you buy too heavy a material. If you want a heavy texture, inquire if you can have the piece done with no welts, it will look thinner. (Welts are those cords that outline all the seams.) To avoid unnecessary seams, ask if your material can be railroaded (run sideways).

For more details and ideas on form and fashion, look in magazines and clip out pictures. They'll be helpful, and train your eye for what you might like.

UPHOLSTERY

Because labor is so expensive, your upholstery fabrics should be tough as nails and able to live through all kinds of disasters. All parts of the body have contact with upholstery; black shoe polish on the kick skirt or oil from your hair on the inside back shouldn't be a problem. Never pick a perishable fabric for upholstery. Even if you claim you never use the settee, all it takes is one glass of red wine to stain your white damask forever.

This brings up the question of fabric protectors. They have good and bad qualities. Any finishing process you apply to your fabric helps when you have an accident (such as a spilled cup of coffee or a drooling baby or the inevitable red wine). The soil bounces right off or wipes right up, never penetrating the fabric. Fabric protectors can be applied in the factory or you can buy a spray can of it and apply it yourself.

However, general soil is not delayed or helped by these processes. So many fabrics today come "soil retarded" but where there is use there will be soil. This is a fact of life. I have found from my own experience that my soil-treated pieces of fabric retain the soil they do acquire and never really clean very well.

Impulsive dabbing at stains can leave you with permanent spots if you're not careful. To be absolutely safe you should have a reliable cleaner advise you how to deal with stains. Cleaning services can come to you and do your furniture right in your house, but many of them claim they can do a better job if they take the furniture to their factory to be cleaned.

If you want to spot clean your furniture, use an extra piece of the material first and experiment on it with cleaning techniques before you risk failure on a sofa or chair. Get cleaning instructions from the fabric house when you buy your material and follow their advice.

The most practical upholstery materials are heavily woven and textured with enough color variation so you *can* scrub them clean when necessary. Long before fabrics wear out they get dull and dirty in places, and by spot cleaning the contact places most vulnerable (end of arms, where heads rest, where shoes kick the base) you can extend the life and freshness of your fabrics appreciably.

THE VALUE OF QUILTING

Quilting your material adds to the wearability, cuts down on wrinkling, tends not to show dirt as easily and adds a feeling of luxury. It also doubles the cost!

Quilting is practical because since your material has "wadding" (the backing) and is stitched, it is tougher, longer wearing. I think all lightweight cottons or silks used for upholstery should be quilted. Also, bedspreads if they don't get too heavy.

Usually "outline" quilting is most beautiful and appropriate for a chintz or printed material. I prefer very thin wadding so it becomes subtle stitching rather than a poof. If your design is a large open-scale one, "outline" quilting doesn't help "cover" your material. You can add "vermicelli" (looks like Japanese noodles wiggling around) stitching to the over-all background, outlining the design only. Some fabrics can have all vermicelli, others all outline. The stitching can be done in squares, diamonds, etc. Your fabric will change in feeling if you don't quilt it in relationship to the design. Talk to your workshop before you decide. Often it has to be done after the seaming to be sure the repeats can line up. This requires your getting the material to the upholsterer so he cuts it to the pattern of the furniture and seams it before it is quilted. Then it is returned to him for sewing.

FABRIC COSTS

There's no bargain in fabric or labor so you have to choose long-lasting things. On an afternoon's shopping spree in the market place in New York, a client found the perfect fabric for her living-room sofa. The fabric she fell in love with was $22.95 a yard and she needed 38 yards to slipcover her two sofas. This was three times what she had budgeted, and she just couldn't rationalize such an extravagance for her old "make-do" sofas. However, once you fall in love, how can you ever be satisfied with a substitute? The strawberry print my client loved had an impractical white background and wasn't particularly sturdy. But do you want to know what really made her say no? She realized that a bolt of the material would cost as much as a painting she also wanted—and the painting would have value forever. She made a happy compromise. She covered the sofas in an inexpensive check (cost approximately $6.50 per yard) and had her strawberry print made up in four big pillows on her sofas. The painting and the strawberries (in smaller containers) made her room alive and lovely.

When you use a design in small quantity, the impact of the design should make a complete statement. Extra large scale designs with an open feeling need room to read well and should be used on larger pieces. Smaller designs where the repeat can be framed in a pillow or a bench cover or a draped table can add just the right quantity of pattern to liven up the solids in your room.

PILLOW MATERIALS

Pillows add softness to a bed, sofa, banquette or chair, and they provide extra comfort and colorful designs. Rooms that are stripped of pillows and plants look like furniture showroom settings. If you sleep on a down pillow, you know how marvelous it is to squish it around so it gives you comfort. Down pillows are so soft and luxurious they appear to float. If you have down in your pillows, you can use soft materials and they'll contour beautifully to the shape of the pillow.

The pillows we buy today for sofas and chairs are frequently filled with dacron because down is so expensive; dacron pillows are not as soft as down but they're a good substitute. Stay away from foam because it hardens and gets lumpy.

The fabrics you use for pillows should be like a dessert after a gorgeous dinner. Don't use anything practical; for once splurge on an expensive fabric you love since you will need it in such a small quantity.

If your pillows have a snap tape or a zipper, you can easily remove the covers for cleaning, although the best-looking pillows have to be cut open to clean the covers. Indulge in trimmings, ribbons and a variety of materials used together. Reversible pillows are an instant mood changer. Have plaid on one side, plain fabric on the other. Feel free to experiment with silk scarves, napkins, old materials you have in your linen closet saved for future projects.

Refer to your magazine pictures to pick up ideas on detailing, shapes and sizes. Most pillows are much too small and get lost in a room. On an average 6- to 7-foot sofa, you could fit pillows on each end as large as 16 to 18 inches square, and if you want more pillows, scale down the next one to 15 inches square. Round pillows can be beautiful if they're supported by larger square ones. Remember to select a large needlework design so it will count for something in your room.

Falling in love with a bolt of fabric can be one of the greater thrills in our life. This is what makes our rooms.

On any budget there are materials that zing us and in most cases we should never settle for anything that is just all right. Unless you tingle at the sight, your selection isn't good enough. Not for you.

By nature, women are too practical minded because housekeeping is our responsibility. As a consequence we lean on the conservative side when it comes to fabrics. Men don't have these inhibitions.

Two examples of men stepping in and taking over the fabric selections come to my mind. Linda and Albert were getting married and their bachelor "pads" merged into a conglomeration of "early attic" furniture. Linda dutifully brought shopping bags full of memo samples home and they were all just O.K. Albert went looking with us and flipped through the racks at lightning speed. Suddenly he stopped at a wild Ken Scott geometric print in hot pinks, oranges, acid greens and yellow.

"That's it! That's our living room." You've never seen such transformation in your life. Pow. The old furniture was brought to life and their living room was alive and fun.

The very same thing happened to the Wilsons. They were moving to Charleston from New York and all their apartment-worn furniture needed recovering. Hank wasn't wild about anything Marsha brought home. He, too, joined us in the market place and we went to the new, exciting fabric houses. Everything Hank liked was splashy, huge scaled and expensive, to say nothing of all that spanking white! They ended up with a year-round spring garden; nothing I ever would have picked out for them but by far the most exciting print. Hank's rationale was "Our move to the South is a change in our life style, and we should take advantage of the warmer climate and freer mood." The fabric they chose said all that. Hank silenced us when we questioned him about dirt: "So what when it really turns you on."

So, once in a while throw all caution to the wind. A fabric design might thrill you the way an impressionist painting does. When this is the case the fabric is affordable. Some of the designs are as beautiful as superb art, so take advantage of the ones you love and find ways of bringing them into your life one way or another.

Materials can create your whole room or they can modestly fit into the rest of your elements. If you have a rug you particularly love your fabrics should work around it, the same with your pictures, or anything else you like and plan to use together. Your treasures usually set the direction your fabrics should take and you can work around them. You'll know when something's right when you see it with everything else. Textures and designs in specific fabric combinations should dictate the total color scheme you end up using. Until you find something just right, keep an open mind.

One wild print can excite you so much that you change your whole approach. A client came to me saying she wanted a green and white library. Touches of another color? No, just green and white. After agonizing over all shades of green, she found a crazy "flower storm" print in yellows, reds, blues with a touch of green and white, and she asked to take the sample home "just for fun." Naturally, that took care of the paneled library beautifully. Don't arbitrarily lock yourself into a color until you're convinced there are no other viable alternatives.

PATTERN ON PATTERN

These new prints with their straight-on colors are powerful. They can be used all over or mixed with other patterns, but whatever you combine should have the same spirit and color palette. Here's where the mix comes into play.

Pick your main design and work in others. There's not a print on the market that can't work with other patterns and most designs become more interesting when they're worked in with others.

The best technique to use when mixing materials and designs is to have one dominate your room and the rest back up your idea. There should be a recall of colors and form in your combinations but not of scale. Use your subordinate materials to tie your room together and add interest and detail to the over-all theme. Areas where you don't use your main pattern shouldn't be a letdown, rather a gentle relief that recalls the main theme and design. Consider, for example, having a wild swirling multicolored fabric for your main upholstered pieces, a plaid or check for some chair seat cushions, solid colors done in patchwork of the six colors in your print for sofa pillows and tiny check curtains. Nothing about the scale makes any sense except that the over-all effect should give your room a rhythm and flow. Don't be afraid of mixing lots of things together just so long as they relate nicely. With practice you'll get an instinctive feel for what you're trying to accomplish and you'll have the confidence to dare until you have the excitement you're after. A friend of mine fell into a smashing room because after she thought she was all finished (except incidental Victorian side chairs her grandmother left her) she found a Gauguin-ish print that excited her so much she just had to use it somewhere. Half kidding, Anne draped her sample on the seat of one of her grandmother's funny old chairs. The combination was dramatic and exciting, and to this day I can't walk into Anne's living room without getting a kick out of the afterthought that became the punch line.

You can have geometric designs dominate with an accent of flowers or vice versa. They will complement each other nicely as long as they are imbalanced in quantity. One of the prettiest bedrooms I've ever been in is mostly basket weaves (wallpaper, curtains and chaise lounge were in a pale green and white cotton print that looked like wicker) with the bed all flowers as though they were growing out of their baskets.

When mixing your patterns together, don't underestimate the itsy-bitsy. It's these tiny little designs you use as fillers that bring everything together. For example, in a patterned room, it may seem abrupt if you cover a chair and ottoman in a plain material; but a small pattern in two colors (picking up the colors of the dominant print) will flow nicely. Instead of a plain fabric for chair seats, think of a basket-weave material or a small plaid or check. On a patterned sofa you can have small designs for pillow fabrics as long as they recall the colors in the sofa itself.

When you repeat a color or pattern in a room at least once, it helps generate a feeling of harmony, just as if you move furniture around it will "fit in" if there are similar shapes.

When you have one "special" material, it should be outstanding. Use repetition of the designs and colors to make your room pull together so you can then focus on your marvelous needlework pillow or one burgundy suede poof. Pillows can all be different if they relate very closely in feeling. Usually the center pillow on a sofa becomes the focal point so it should be the most interesting.

BLENDING

Carefully matched colors and similar textures can "make" a boring room. The way to blend colors that have life and vitality is through the combination of compatible colors, not the matching exactly of any two materials.

As I said earlier, any colors, textures and patterns that are happy together are possible and when something is right, you know it because it feels good. In the showroom of fabric designer Jack Lenor Larsen was displayed his line of Thai silks and Finnish cottons, hand in hand, on wicker furniture, and they were smashing together. The silk hanging was the color of Buddhist saffron robes, and the cotton looked like the skin of an orange. Together, a symphony. Real oranges were arranged in a wicker basket as an accessory, the pure, simple approach to good design—through the sensitive combining of honest elements.

USE SOLIDS POSITIVELY

Contemporary interiors with an environmental furniture concept look best when covered in fairly solid material. Plain fabrics work well when they're repeated in variations throughout the furniture arrangement. In a less modern setting, for example, in a room filled with pattern, a solid blue chair could stick out like a sore thumb and look spotty. Solid materials impose a very definite outline of the furniture they're covering and strongly emphasize the proportions and form of the object. When individual items are brought into sharp focus, they have to be worthy of their spotlight.

Solid materials give a clean line and a restful appearance. Unless you plan on leather or vinyl, be sure to have a lot of textural interest to your woven material so it won't have a flat look and, won't show every spot. Solid textures with interesting weaves and fibers combined with interesting colors can create a great deal of excitement.

LEATHER

Leather is expensive, but it is always a welcoming material. There's nothing quite like it, and if you can see your way clear to the initial investment you'll be forever grateful you have real leather. Because it is a natural material it breathes, and dirt and oil from our bodies make it age gracefully. Choose a dark color and you won't have to worry. If you choose light leather you should have it specially treated for soil retarding first. This process is done for you by the manufacturers who distribute the leather. Inquire and get a sample to approve before you order it.

MATERIAL CHOICES

Any natural material will be more satisfying than an artificial one. Real cotton, wool, silk, linen and leather have their own life. If you buy raw Haitian cotton or an intense cotton print from Bora Bora, you'll be thrilled for good reason—the materials were made by hand and they're for real.

I believe the look of old, more mellow things will continue to give us secure, warm feelings. A friend refers to it as "the warm, used and loved look of belonging."

Synthetic fibers certainly meet many of our practical requirements, but they will never replace natural materials completely. Look for the fabric content and if the material contains both natural and synthetic fibers in combination you'll probably not even be aware of the imitation fiber. Stay away from the materials that have shine unless a fabric is real silk because they tend to look cheap.

There are heavy woven designs available now (some are even reversible so you can use them with either side showing, for a bedspread or draped table); they have a beautiful feel and look to them and they're almost totally synthetic. If you are satisfied with the appearance you're in luck.

Vinyls are especially valuable. They're tough, colorful, practical and reasonably priced. Vinyl tells the truth about our times. While I'd love to be an absolute purist and say leather should always be leather and not vinyl that looks like leather, it doesn't make any sense today. My boss's Louis XVI dining-room chairs were originally covered in a butter-yellow leather and after twenty years the leather became worn and cracked. When she re-covered them she used a vinyl that cost a fraction of the price and you couldn't possibly tell the difference.

Deep down where it counts, vinyl is a blessing. For kitchens, porch cushions, pool areas, children's rooms, playrooms, eating chair seats, consider using vinyl. It now comes in every color and there are good-looking designs in vinyl for upholstery. It's natural that we have upholstery vinyls now that vinyl wall coverings are so successful.

When selecting your vinyl, do it with honesty and don't try to have it look like something it's not. You can get away with basic leather textures, but there is a certain quality about exotic leathers that can't be duplicated in vinyl. Let your selection be a vinyl selection. This way you will have maintained the integrity of all the other real elements. We just completed a lobby where we used fake lizard in dark nut brown and it looks marvelous on big 8-foot benches and stools. It looks like vinyl too. Unfortunately it has cracked and opened up at the seams. Just because something is vinyl doesn't mean you can abuse it or that it is virtually indestructible. Be careful to select the most sturdy, heavy-duty vinyl.

SYNBAC

"Synbacing" is an inexpensive process you apply to the underneath side of your material to give it more strength. It is excellent for cottons and especially good for linen because it holds the fibers steady. Linen fibers tend to run around and this process creates less abrasion.

LAMINATING

Any fabric can be plastic laminated. This costs more than "synbacing," but is still inexpensive and well worth it for certain applications. Now you can laminate any fabric you want for a pool-side cushion, etc. The only drawback is that when you laminate a material, any dirt at all on the back shows through to the front and is hard to clean. We had place mats that I adored but as sparkling clean as I could get the front, the backs were spotted from table soil and I had to throw them out. If you can keep the underneath clean, go ahead and laminate. If you are willing to pay for a double laminating process, both sides of your material can be treated.

FADING

Fabrics still fade. If you have lots of bright sun at noon, I suggest caution regarding the materials you put right next to the window. The only other alternative, if you really want draperies, is to draw the shades, or get used to the more mellow look. Fading never bothers me nearly as much as dirt, and remember all natural things show some signs of aging.

Pastels seem to fade badly. The best vat dyes available are used for printing, but exotic colors are cannibalistic and eat into the others. Strange things happen, so if you're going to be upset when you have a sun-bleached living room, edit colors from your palette or get your room in the shade.

There is a test some fabrics undergo that allows for eighty hours of "fetameter" or sun at noon. While your material might pass the test with flying colors, no one knows just how it it will look six months from now. Good fabric houses have their fabrics undergo this test but there are no guarantees. When you buy at the five-and-ten-cent store you are on your own.

Once you've selected your materials for a room, try to make your fabric changes all at once. All of us who have had to do things piecemeal know how discouraging it is; one fresh piece of lively fabric can throw your whole room off and make the rest look tired. It's especially hard to get away with a new piece of matching fabric. If you plan two chairs in chintz, buy them together.

CUSTOM COLORS

I don't recommend having fabrics "done to color" unless you have to and then go slowly. Unless you've had lots of design experience, leave it to the designers who do this kind of thing frequently. Coloring a fabric is tricky and each single color has to work or the material will suffer.

There are contemporary firms where everything is done to order but they are really for professionals only. If you venture in to a "custom" coloring always wait for a strike-off of the actual printing prior to approval of the order.

FABRIC AS ART

Some big talents are designing textiles and many are concentrating on wall decorations. The well known architect Alexander Giard has come out with some new wall decorations that are inspiring for any space in need of a lift, and they're reasonably priced and a bargain if you compare the price to other art forms.

When you want to remove your wall "hanging" you can cover a bed or a dining table for alternate moods. Fabrics can be stretched on a rod and used as a room divider. For wall hangings, use a simple wood dowel and let the rest hang free. Use weights at the bottom if necessary. Framing fabric is something else entirely and should be stretched on all four sides.

Color

Color gives joy, it can also drive a person crazy. It can heal, in the polychromatic hospital. It is a formidable material, as indispensable to life as water or fire.

FERNAND LÉGER

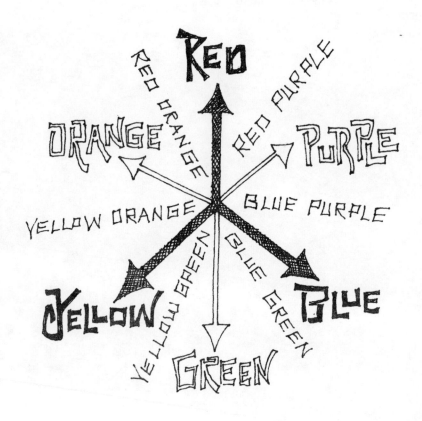

Of all the elements that make up your surroundings, nothing is so revealing or personal as the colors you choose.

There are many considerations that determine whether you'll have a pink or a blue bedroom, but after weighing them all, you'll probably have the color you like best. The thing I hope to accomplish in this chapter is an understanding of what color is, how we psychologically react to color, how we personalize color and bring it out of us and into our surroundings.

Color is so subjective, I want to try to help you find the ones that suit you best. Please excuse me if I step on your toes a few times; it's all in an attempt to help you find the color schemes that are already inside you and need to be brought out. First, a few general things about color, and then I'll illustrate the following:

1. How you can find colors that personally become you (your skin tone, etc.).

2. How color affects you in different ways and why certain people prefer certain colors.

3. Why specific colors are more appropriate for different people.

4. How you can choose colors that relate to your life style (love of nature, earth tones, outdoor living).

5. How you can integrate these colors into all rooms in your house.

Color is the quickest and cheapest way to transform your surroundings and is a natural form of communication and outlet for self-expression. Everything you could ever want can be found and is easily available in all the colors of your choice: today, over six hundred manufacturers are dealing in as many as twelve thousand colors (excluding blacks and whites) for carpeting, wall paint, fabrics, bathroom accessories, place mats and ashtrays.

WHAT IS COLOR?

Color is mysterious and complex; it is produced by light waves and reflects and changes in light. Without light there is no color. Pigment (color) absorbs some white wave lengths from white light and reflects back those remaining colors which your eye sees. Any object which absorbs nearly all wave lengths (becoming devoid of color) becomes black.

Light is the key consideration when selecting colors for your rooms because it articulates and affects the relationship of each color and the juxtaposition of one color to the other. Colors change a thousand times a day depending on the time of day and the changes in your lighting. The light has to become each color and complement the colors when they are mixed together. You shouldn't have a green rug that dies late in the afternoon when the direct sunlight fades and before you put on artificial lights.

Color is the first thing we perceive—it speaks louder than form. The aesthetic and psychological effects color plays on our lives can't be underestimated. Color has the most mood-producing effect on our senses. Because it is so powerful it can satisfy your soul. The question is how! Let's examine first what the psychological implications are behind the four most common colors: red, blue, yellow and green.

PSYCHOLOGICAL EFFECTS OF COLOR

The emotional reaction varies. The warm hues (purple, red, orange, yellow, yellow green) are exciting and let off a feeling of heat and gaiety. The cool colors (green, blue to purple) are calm, cool and can even be considered depressing. Colors next to each other on the wheel take on the same properties; for example, when I talk about red and yellow, orange is in between them, and has some properties of both. Orange gets action from red and cheer from yellow.

RED

Red is one of the three primary colors and is an aggressive, vital, warm color. Our blood rises, respiration rate increases and our pulse speeds up when we see the color red. Red stimulates our appetites (restaurants frequently are decorated in red), our cravings in all forms. Red is exciting and represents desire and action. Red like a bull is the symbol of competition and the will to win. Red is life (blood) and has the connotation of success. People are given the "red-carpet treatment." From my observation, red is the favorite color of 50 per cent "red-blooded" American men but comes on too strong for most women as a favorite color. Red is used in an entrance hall or gallery of a city apartment; green would replace it in the country.

BLUE

The other 50 per cent of American men, it seems to me, choose blue for their first choice. Blue, also a primary color, slows down the heartbeat and decreases the blood pressure and is a peaceful, soothing color. From the beginning of time, it has been a symbol of night fall and rest. While blue is quiet, calm, passive, it is also a color that gives an impression of an orderly environment. This tranquillity is relaxing and very conducive to meditation, increased sensitivity of feeling and awareness. When exhausted, sick or particularly sensitive, our need for blue increases. It's a recuperative color. The sky, the water are blue and we know their therapeutic values. Blue is tender and can be very feminine and sweet, and yet dark blue has depth and fullness. Because it has the feeling of weight, dark blue is favored by those of us who are overweight. (Is that why we feel "blue"?)

YELLOW

Yellow is the third primary color and is the brightest chromatic hue on the color wheel. Its light and cheerful effect increases our metabolic rate, so we give off greater glandular secretions, providing us with vital energy and incentive. Yellow is a stimulant, like red, but because it is lighter (and less dense) it is more of a suggestive color than a stimulating color. (Yellow says, "Be happy," while red turns you on.)

The break of day, the sun, warmth of sunlight, radiance, reflectiveness, expansiveness, deliberation and happiness are all connected with the color yellow. Yellow is hope for the future, the new and modern, the unformed. Yellow is the one color that can consistently make me happy. Yellow can do the most to uplift a space.

GREEN

Green is a secondary color (along with purple and orange) but is such a basic color that I'll give it the same importance in coloring our rooms as any of the primary colors. Somehow green is a symbol of the mysteries of life and green pastures. Green is an "astringent" color (good color for an all-purpose ammonia cleaner) and is connected with freshness. Clear water has a green color when the sun bakes it, and pistachio ice cream is fresh, mouth watering. The green in menthol cigarette commercials is so fresh you long to put smoke in your lungs. "Go" green. Green is the complement of red (it's opposite red on the color wheel). The green person is deep rooted and proud, interested in self-preservation.

WHAT IS A HUE?

A hue is an identifying name for a shade of a specific color. Red, blue, yellow. In other words, it is a way for us to communicate the precise color we are after, taking into account the tint, shade, value and chromatic intensity (degree of saturation). We give color hues names (such as Lake Como green, Riviera blue, pineapple yellow and Greek isle white); paint companies give a color hue a number, for identification.

We know that color is light and a hue is a color. Did you know that you'd produce gray if you mixed all colors (pigments) together in equal quantity? You know that complementary colors are directly opposite each other on the color wheel. Did you know that chromatic intensity is the color strength? And that a color with brilliance and high intensity advances (a wall will move forward if it's painted lemon twist)? A hue that is weaker chromatically than yellow has a low intensity and recedes. You reduce the chroma in a hue by adding to the pigment the complementary color (kill the brilliance of red by adding green) or by adding black (which "shades" a color).

You may never need to know the difference between analogous, consonant and dissonant color schemes. Brief definitions follow: 1) Analogous means harmonious and everything blends gently together. 2) Consonant is equal dimensions of warm and cool (a fabric with two blues, a purple, a pink and a red would be a consonant color combination). 3) Dissonant creates tension by an uneven color distribution with sharp contrasts (purple, red and orange with lemon twist yellow).

COLOR WHEEL

There are twenty-four basic colors. These are the colors that make up a color wheel with the primary, secondary, tertiary and quaternary colors; there are equal steps of color change between each hue. Color wheels can be much more complex but twenty-four colors are enough to illustrate how colors work together. You can purchase a color wheel at all art supply stores and art schools.

1. *Primary colors contain no other hue.*
   Red, yellow, blue

2. *Secondary colors are made of the combination of two primary colors.*
   Orange, purple, green
   EXAMPLE: Red and yellow make orange.
                   Yellow and blue make green.
                   Blue and red make purple.

3. *Tertiary colors are made by combining one primary color and one secondary color.*
   Red-orange, red-purple, blue-purple, blue-green, yellow-green, yellow-orange.
   EXAMPLE: Red plus orange make red-orange.

4. *Quaternary colors are two primary colors plus one secondary color; or one primary color and two secondary colors.*
   Orange-orange-red; red-red-orange; red-red-purple; purple-purple-red; purple-purple-blue; blue-blue-purple; blue-blue-green; green-green-blue; green-green-yellow; yellow-yellow-green; yellow-yellow-orange.
   EXAMPLE: The quaternary color orange-orange-red is made up of orange (originally mixed by combining the two primary colors red and yellow) plus the same orange repeated in equal quantity with the addition of one part red.

Before you look at the paint swatches and start planning your color scheme with the walls as the first element, think generally about the feelings you want your colors to express. Once you know what you want the room to feel like then it's easy to find colors that can achieve your goal.

Are you an outdoor person? Do you like the sun, earth colors, the sky and water? Are you happiest when you're dressed up and doing something elegant? Do you feel better in "at home" casual clothes? Shut your eyes for a second and dream of a place you'd like to be. What is the climate? Are you sun bathing on a sandy tropical island beach (lots of white with brilliant touches of pinks, oranges and yellows) or are you skiing down a slope in Switzerland? Are you alone or with people? Who?

The colors you choose to live with should be colors that help you live out your fantasies and dreams about your ideal life and the atmosphere of your physical environment. It's perfectly possible to live in a studio apartment and have it be as elegant as your dreams. No one knows these inner feelings of yours. If you feel uncertain about a color (enough so you ask your friends for their opinion) it is probably not a sure bet for a wall color or major furniture selection. When a color fits just right you won't need any reassurance from the outside because the color will work for you. It goes without saying you'll share these biases with the people you love.

An apartment or house that is used for entertaining and barely lived in except when there's a crowd is quite different from the place where you go to hide from the world while you recharge your battery and feel whole. If you live alone and realistically spend four nights a week plus weekends at home think of those times alone and what feelings you want around you. Do you feel you'd be cozier in a dark, warm brown living room on a Tuesday night? Or would a light color open up your cramped space? What is more important to you? Do you want to feel spacious (white) or pure and fresh and clean (white) or would you prefer a reduced, more restricted framework (dark) that is secure and protective? Red gives a protective feeling. Dark rich earthy colors close in a space and make it seem cozy, secure.

All too often we compensate for our inadequate shelters by saying we're never there much and we never use this room or that room unless we have friends in. Color can change all that. If your living room is somehow too serious for daytime (beige on beige on beige) how about an unserious appetizing color splashed on your walls (apricot or cantaloupe or peach). All the colors in the orange family offer excitement. If you stare too long at oranges they jump back at you, but when you're eating and talking you're not staring at your walls. If your blue living

room is deadly dull in the daylight (northern exposure), how about adding some yellow touches to warm it up. When you painted your room
blue, you were an editor for *Newsweek*, working night and day at your
office; now that you're home free-lancing and don't have a studio, maybe
you should consider repainting your room yellow so it has life during the
daytime. All northern exposures should have warm colors for daytime enjoyment. No matter how little direct sunlight a room gets, it's a shame to
use artificial light until you have to.

The key to success is to find the balance of colors that complement
both your emotions and your physical (architectural) space. In a one-
room studio you might go crazy if the walls were all painted poppy red,
no matter how much you like red, whereas the space could open up with
white walls and poppy red accents in pillows, accessories, and fresh poppies in a flower holder. A little in a confined space can go a long way.

Most of us can't dream up colors but we're deeply reactive to ones
we've seen and liked. Colors we don't enjoy leave a negative impression
and we can't remember them specifically at all. Whenever you find a
color you like, whether it's a match box, a flower, a friend's dining-room
wall or in a material, make a note of it in your book. These are the colors
you'll pull together to create your color schemes. Designers keep folders
of color samples gathered from every conceivable source. You shouldn't
have to describe a color. Have a sample. Train your eye to register and
evaluate colors. Instead of waiting until your sofa falls apart and you're
desperate to redo it but don't know what color you want, gather a stack
of colors and combinations you like. If you study Matisse you'll automatically learn about balancing colors. While it looks easy, the way he deliberately splashes red next to blue next to yellow next to pink is genius;
he's a genius colorist and you might study him for ideas. With color, as
with everything, the simple, natural, honest solutions are the ones that
have the most lasting quality.

COLOR ASSOCIATIONS

A color scheme that reminds you of the mood in a far-off place you
love will bring nostalgia into your daily living if you duplicate those
colors at home. Don't miss the opportunity for your colors to create a
double impact. Try and surround yourself with colors that represent more

to you than meets the eye. If your living room recalls a Greek experience or your bedroom scheme is lifted from a private beach in Bermuda, you'll enjoy it more.

The Whittens do this all the time. They just returned from a month in St. Croix where the sand was like white velvet under the burning blue sky. A blissful trip. The towels supplied by the beach-side hotel were bold stripes of pink, yellow and green. Soon after the vacation ended and their tans had paled, the Whittens found the exact same towel on sale at Bloomingdale's. Nothing could have delighted Sharon more than to bring the colored towels home to liven up a pale bathroom. They were a symbol that made their memories of St. Croix stay alive.

We associate colors with places we've been to; for example, colors can bring out moods of excitement, comfort, luxury, calm and adventure. While one color alone can't do much for any of us, it's the composition of colors that frames the spirit we're looking for . . . the mood we want to create for our personal environment.

OPEN UP YOUR CLOSET

I stumbled across something by accident once that has proved over and over to be very helpful in determining color solutions. My friend Shep and I were struggling to find a color scheme for her bathroom one morning and were getting nowhere. Even though we knew it would be blues and greens, it wasn't clear what we were trying to achieve. As we sat on her bed staring at the bathroom in front of us, my eye caught sight of the dress she had worn the night before. Knowing it was her fifteenth anniversary and she and her husband had gone out to dinner to celebrate, I picked up the dress and asked her if that was the feeling she was after. It was. That was the feeling and colors she wanted in her bathroom. Our minds have an image of what we're after, and it usually stems from something we can put our fingers on.

Instinctively, we choose colors we look and feel well in, colors that go well with our skin tones and coloring as well as with our personalities. I had a client once who held every fabric she thought she might like up to her face and asked, "How do I look?" She went to the extreme, but there is a lot to be learned from this. We all do this without realizing it: We select colors we look best in and that make us feel good.

Our favorite dresses can often help us select the colors and designs for our rooms. Often I go to my closet and look at color combinations and textures I like and then think how I can use the ideas in my color decisions. Do you have solid colors or many designs? Possibly this will give you a clue as to how to approach your furniture, walls, curtains, etc.

Begin then by opening up your closet and taking a close look at your clothes. There's a color and design story right there. What colors keep repeating themselves? Why are all your colors in stripes and patterns; your neutrals solid? Do you have particular things in your wardrobe you look well in (and feel well wearing)? What gives you a lift? What do you wear on a dreary day to cheer you?

Redheads have their colors, blonds with fair complexions look well in pale soft pastels. Women with dark hair and olive complexions look best in bold strong colors. Without conscious consideration, we carry these colorings into our space. What color car do you own? This is a color selection that you made which connects to the whole picture of you, your background, personality and life style.

Look at your scarves for combinations of color. A scarf could very well end up being a room's color scheme. Count how many there are and in what quantity. Look at your husband's neckties and shirts. Check to see if his suits are in a color family of earth tones or in blues and blacks. This might help you when you are determining the color selection for his library. Men are equally affected and enriched by meaningful colors in their environment. Always go back to their past experiences to extrapolate their favorite colors.

If you don't actually have a garden you have to plan your dream one. The colors of flowers can teach us everything we ever need to know about our color needs. What kinds of flowers do you want growing? How do they appear? Are they planted in formal rows or are they scattered loosely about? The way you'd design your dream garden is the way you'd like your life style to be. If you want formal English gardens, a daisy probably won't be your favorite flower. On the other hand, if you're a free spirit and totally free from society's system, elegance to you could be field flowers and jonquils in a big bunch on a sun porch. Think about these natural colors because they will be keys in triggering off the colors for your rooms.

Originally all color came from natural (organic) dyes. Now we have synthetic aniline stains and dyes which can produce Day-Glo colors of all varieties, but if we stick to natural colors when planning our rooms we'll never go wrong because we'll consider the juxtaposition and influence of one color to the next, the form and shape where the color is to go, we'll learn to differentiate subtle ways of using large doses of one color (blue like the sea and sky or green like grass and trees) and vary the shadings and patterns into a more interesting whole atmosphere.

STUDY THE TEXTURES OF COLOR

Nature is so richly textural, there is no such thing as a solid color. Everything is evolving and the interaction of all parts of a landscape make up the whole. When there are changes, whether gradual or abrupt, all elements are affected. Nothing is flat or static. Think of the contours and textures of grass. Think of a tree with its foliage. Look up at the sky and study the feelings you get from the changing colors and the clouds. Observe the delicacy of a poppy and the intense color. Smell a hot pink rose and feel how this scent and color seem to "go together," making it a perfect rose. Think about scent and how elegant some smells are while others are refreshing. Which do you prefer?

Begin to translate your craving for growing fresh flowers and vegetables into colors you want surrounding you in your rooms. You can start by examining your groceries. Slice an orange in half and compare the color of the inside to the outside. Do this with a tangy lemon and a puckering lime and with melons and berries. Take a stick of butter and hold it next to your lemon peel and compare your reaction. The butter yellow should feel softer than the lemon yellow. Does it to you?

A little picture by Nicolas de Stael entitled "Lettuce Bowl" was at his show at the Guggenheim Museum in New York; I was tempted to sit down in the middle of the ramp and eat it. His lettuce was crisp, icy cold and delicious, achieved by his translucent, gentle colorings of green. I'm sure he must have used thirty different shadings of pale bibb lettuce green to make it so realistic. Look at a piece of lettuce and study all the variations. We made a mess in our kitchen trying to paint the walls "lettuce green" because in order to get a green that was strong enough (for lettuce and not celery) it was too strong and dark a green for our kitchen. We had to give up green altogether and paint the kitchen white, because in order to satisfy ourselves we would have needed all the shadings and textures of lettuce green. There are lots of rich browns in our wooden cabinets and formica counters that make all our fresh fruits and vegetables look delicious sitting around for eye appeal.

Colors that recall food we eat are refreshing—cherry reds, lettuce or apple greens, or rich Swiss chocolate browns. Or a burgundy wine. Any colors that are eatable are always refreshing, whether they are used as a wall color for a rug or a sofa pillow. You may prefer a lemon to a squash yellow, and the squash yellow to an ordinary gold. Complement your colors with a title. Champagne, eggplant, cantaloupe, salmon, apple green, butter yellow or tomato red.

Because colors are so adaptable I can't say there are certain colors that don't go together. However, certain applications never fail. All colors from the same color family can be mixed together. All greens go together, all reds go together, all yellows and so forth. Because the colors can range from the far left and right (a green can be very yellow green or very blue green), all colors can go to their neighboring color and work together. Therefore, if you love blue you can warm up a blue room by going to the left and picking up greens and yellows. Reds can go with hot pinks and slide over to the orange family.

Think of color as making a statement of now, not as making a permanent commitment. To an extent you can change colors with your mood. Bring home a red tulip and change a white room's look. Or entirely transform the same room by painting the walls red. Whether you're after a quick spark or a complete overhaul, don't be afraid to be a little fickle about colors. When you are making a change in your life, you will want your colors to change as well. They should go with your up-to-date mood and feelings.

The sources of your color schemes are broad. Clients have sent me fresh flowers that represented the combination of colors they wanted for their house (this meant fast work for me, to get the scheme planned before the flowers could wilt and fade!), shells from the beach and even favorite neckties. I love to be taken some special place to assimilate a color mood. I've gone into gardens and horse stables and powder rooms, up hilltops, into candy stores, vegetable markets, up rocky points overlooking the sea, to jewelry boxes and other places of personal delight. Wherever you get your colors, gather them all together. Review your closets, your jewelry and scarves, flowers and fruit, vegetables and all your traveling nostalgia (post cards, etc.) that will lead to specific ways of working out your schemes. Review your notebook and scrapbooks, the work of any artist whose colors you enjoy. You've heard of decorators planning the room around a painting. I'm not recommending we decorate around art, but rather that you elevate your surroundings so *they* become an art form. The artists who show in your local museum can inspire your living-room color scheme just as easily as your favorite picture can. Save picture post cards you receive from far-off places and buy post cards at museums to study the composition and colors. For fifteen cents you can be inspired into committing yourself to a particular collection of colors for your living room.

Don't overlook your bulk mail as another color source. Top designers of men and women's clothes are hiring graphic designers to design and color their mailers and the graphic designers in turn get their inspirations from artists. For example, Love lemon cosmetics fashioned an entire advertising campaign around a Frank Stella painting. The design of the new shopping bag from your local department store might be lifted from a Matisse painting. Another wonderful source of colors and combinations is needlework shops with hundreds of shades of wool yarn you can twist and knot until you figure out the best colors to select. Save all these colors and samples. If someone sends you a note and the lining of the envelope is a pretty color you like, rip it out and save it with your other samples. Before you throw away your Christmas cards, check to see if there are any combinations you want to keep.

Look for underlying themes in your color gatherings. While everything might appear at first glance to be fairly neutral or basically three colors, study the small hot accent (the red shutters on the adobe house or the intricate pattern in a colorful costume). These are the same splashes of color we should use in our rooms to give them punch and excitement. These are the accents that liven up your scheme and make it work.

PUTTING TOGETHER COLOR SCHEMES

It is really very easy to put together your color schemes. Establish them for your rooms by arranging your favorite colors in order of priority. Next, gather some accessory colors to add to your basic colors, for zest and excitement. From studying natural scenery and the ways colors are affected by their relationship to other colors, you quickly learn that all color schemes have three basic dimensions: the background, the foreground and the focus. Color schemes also have three basic different values: light (white, off white, sand, beige, cream, onion, cabbage, mushroom, butter, etc.), medium (toast, middle greens, blues, reds, pinks, oranges, purples, yellows, greens) and dark (blacks, dark browns, rusts, earth tones, burgundy reds, forest greens). The lights and darks are the more neutral components that make up your background (can be your favorite color in varying degrees), and the medium (middle) colors are the sparkle and life to your schemes the "focus" colors, or the accents.

Think of taking a picture and focusing in tight on a garden or your child playing on the beach. The garden, for example, is on the edge of a blanket of spring grass and outlined by a shiny purple blue sky. (The green grass and blue sky are the background to your picture.) Your garden has many varieties of spring flowers (which is your foreground), but your eye focuses on the incredibly perfect red tulip. Translating this into a room, you could have white walls, a green rug (grass) and a sky blue "background" on your material which repeats the colors of your garden (yellow daffodils, pansies, green leaves and touches of this beautiful red of the tulips). You may decide to use the red for your furniture and curtains and further focus with red by adding your own red touches in pillows or fresh tulips or anemones or a red box on a table or small bench cover. Don't think for one second you have to have a "flowered" print for your material just because you got your colors from a garden. Not at all. Your fabric colors could be inspired from your friend's country garden, and your fabric can be a geometric print in the same coloring.

Let's take your child at the beach as another example of translating natural color schemes into your rooms. Your child is the point of the picture (as we are to our rooms), and yet the sandy beach and the foam from clear blue water, the sun, etc. make the picture of your little darling more interesting. The background is the off-white sand, the blue water, the blue sky and Johnny in a sailor-blue bathing suit making a sand castle. Looking further we see a yellow bucket and a red shovel in the picture.

Your living room could be a similar scheme translating the sand into a bleached floor with off-white Irish linen rugs (informal mood), light-blue walls with a blue and white print material of swirls of blues on a crisp middle-blue ground (the sky and water), and your pillows could be focusing on Johnny's swim suit, the bucket and shovel in a yellow, red and blue plaid or check. You could have a yellow coffee end table or yellow ginger jar lamps (the bucket) and tiny touches of red, possibly just a geranium on your table or a red plastic box on a brown wooden table.

Another color scheme could be inspired by a walk in the woods. A dense pine forest (deep green walls), brown floors (tree trunks and soil) with small needlework rugs in the colors of leaves and fall, rich brown and beige textured materials (birch trees and the feeling of light filtering in). Your accents could be rusts and oranges with touches of yellow for the feeling of sun.

Friends of ours love Bermuda and know the island's moods well. The sun lights up the water so it's pale green, and as far away as the eye can see the purple sea touches the warm blue sky. The seaweed is purple in Bermuda, they say, and the foam and the seaweed dance against the rhythms of the open water. Our friends have created an incredibly moving feeling in their bedroom and bathroom by using these colors bouncing off intense white walls which seem warmed by Bermuda sun. White walls, blue ceiling and seafoam green carpet below frame their private haven. The bathroom is less subtle; they selected six Bermuda colors in a free-form wallpaper design for walls and ceiling, picking up each island shade in fluffy terry-cloth towels, in the entire spectrum of the changing moods of the Bermuda water and sky. Their bathroom floor is a textured beige, and they have fluffy cotton rugs scattered about in varying shades of blues and greens.

I've found most people have difficulty mixing their favorite colors with other compatible colors that are happy together. The blue and green person doesn't know how to vary her theme. The yellow and green person doesn't know how to introduce more colors. The monochromatic (all one color in various dimensions) person can't find another color to mix with the all-gold scheme. Because of this, I am going to list several color combinations I believe work well together. From my suggestions you might get inspired to experiment on your own. Remember, color schemes are like recipes, you should try different combinations and ways of using your colors. If I list brown with a color and you hate brown, possibly you can translate brown into another dark, weighty color (dark green or red or blue or black), depending on your other colors. Remember, too, all colors that are of the same chromatic intensity can go together. This will guide you as you determine what hue and shade to pick from each color group.

In the color groupings that follow, I'm indicating value as "L" for light, "M" for medium, "D" for dark, the middle being the focus color, the light and dark being the background colors. I might indicate shocking pink as a middle value because it is a focus color. If I say "light" next to a purple and a pink, I'm indicating pastel shades.

Let me illustrate how to use the color chart. Go down the list of combinations until you find one that looks pleasing; check it. Continue on throughout all forty-one groups and check any you like. Next, study the values of each color in each group and see if you actually like a light blue or a dark blue. You may find one group of colors where you like all the values or most of them. For example, in the first grouping, you might like the light yellow (for your walls), the light white (for trims and louvers), the medium greens (for upholstery), the medium apricots (for pillows and areas in patterned rugs and for flowers) and the dark brown (wood furniture and large areas of bare floors). The chart may lead you to one or two exciting and uniquely personal color executions for your rooms.

If blue is your color and there are no two ways about it, look at all the color combinations that have blue and pinks or blue and yellows or blue and greens and reds. Check the schemes you like and then see if you can translate the combinations into your own terms. Work at warming up your blue by trying some pinks and yellows, etc. Get your blues together (in paint chips and rugs or materials) and go to the florist. Pick out all the warm colors you think pretty (one of a kind is fine). When you get home, experiment by adding one flower at a time to your blues. Keep adding and when something bothers you take out a flower or two. You'll be so shocked at the different feelings you'll get as you respond to these coloration changes. When you're all through with your experiment, you'll still have a fresh mixture of garden flowers for your delight.

If you like two crazy colors and don't find them in any scheme, don't worry. If purple and orange are your two colors, pick either the purple or the orange and use it in many varying shades with heavy doses of white to relieve it; take your other color and use that for your touches. If you don't like the imbalance, flip-flop it and compare.

Don't forget that when areas of strong intensity are contrasted with weak areas, they will seem larger. Primary colors are aggressive colors to begin with, so go easy with a comfortable quantity at first; you can always add. The focus colors are the ones that you can juggle around in the end. Your background may very well include only your light and dark "background" colors and all your medium focus colors could be in accessories. Or all of them could be used on furniture fabric. Somewhere you have to commit yourself to the color and its use.

COMPATIBLE COLOR COMBINATIONS THAT WORK

L	Yellow	M	Blue-green
M	Green	M	Green-blue
M	Apricot	M	Purple-pink
L	White	L	White
D	Brown	D	Dark brown

M	Blue	L	Off white
D	Brown	L	Beige
L	Beige	M	Rust
L	White	D	Brown
M	Yellow	D	Terra cotta
		M	Gold

L	Purple	M	Red
L	Blue	M	Blue
L	Pink	M	Yellow
D	Brown	M	Green
L	White	L	White

M	Hot pink	M	Yellow
M	Tangerine	L	White
L	White	D	Dark brown
D	Dark brown	D	Black
L	Off white	D	Chinese lacquer orange

M   Orange

M   Yellow

M   Red

M   Green

L   White

L   Pink

L   Purple

L   Apricot

L   Blue

L   Green

L   White

L   White

D   Terra cotta

D   Brown

L   Clay

M   Green

M   Blue

L   White

M   Yellow

D   Brown

L and D   Two greens

M and M   Two yellows

L   White

M   Luggage brown

M   Garden greens

M   Lemon rind

L   White

D   Brown-black

L   Silver

L   White

M   Green

D   Brown-black

M   Irish green

L   White

D   Black

D   Woody brown

M   Pink

M   Red

L   White

M   Green

D   Black

M   Yellow

L   White

D   Black

M   Red

M   Red

M   Yellow

M   Green

L   White

D   Black

D   Grape purple

L   Grape green

M   Orange orange

L   Pear green

L   White

D   Dark blue

L   Chrome

L   White

D   Woody brown

M   Red

M   Green

L   White

L   Pale blue

D   Brown

M	Blue	D	Dark brown
L	White	L	White
D	Burgundy	M	Strawberry red
M	Gold	L	Lettuce green
D	Brown		

		D	Brown
L	Pink	L	White
L	Apricot	L	Clay
L	Orange	M	Green
L	White	M	Pink
L	Beige		

L	Icing white	M	Blue
L	Nut beige	L	Beige
L	Silver	M	Green
M	Gold	L	Silver
M	Plants green	L	White
M	Flower red		

		L	Shrimp pink
L	Shiny white	D	Bordeaux
D	Dark green	M	Watercress green
D	Purple	L	Yellow (as in yellow rice)
D	Black	L	White
L	Butter-pale yellow		

		D	Eggplant
L	White	M	Tomato
D	Dark gray	L	Straw beige
D	Dark brown	M	Leaf green
L	Off white		

M	Flame	M	French blue
L	White	M	Copper
L	Wicker beige	L	White
M	August sun yellow	M	Gold
M	Cantaloupe	D	Dark-dark brown

D	Deep purple blue	M	Yellow
M	Rich goldy yellow	M	Pink
L	White	M	Green
D	Brown	L	White
L	Green	D	Brown

M	Pink	M	Blue
M	Yellow	M	Red
M	Green	M	Green
L	White	M	Pink
D	Black	L	White

M	Poppy	M	Chartreuse green
L	White	L	Chalk white
D	Dark brown	L	Bleached wood brown
L	Chrome	L	Beige
		M	Rich sun yellow

L to D Six greens
L Basket beige
L Pink blossom
L White
D Terra cotta

Shortly we're going to make definite decisions about where to put your colors, but let's review what approach we're after; we do this by committing ourselves to precise colors and combinations. Separate your colors into two groups: Group one is the over-all mood of the room, group two is the accent colors and touches.

Make your room generate a color statement. One color should dominate (in varying dimensions) so you create an unequal balance of colors in order to give a room cohesion. Your floors and walls are your biggest areas and they should be kept together by relating in color. If you have yellow walls, you can have a blue rug but there should be some yellow in the rug as well. Next, determine whether you want to continue with these basic background colors for your furniture and windows or if you want those areas to be more accented. Possibly you could have your windows go with your background and just punctuate your furniture with a new note.

Determining the distribution of color is like writing an outline for a thesis. The main idea is the whole (say, yellow and blue are your main colors). Your subordinate ideas are your accessory colors, which could be hot and wild because they're in smaller doses. How do you determine your main theme? Refer back to your mood priorities. Pick out the colors that express you and your place best, colors that seem to fit all your thoughts and feelings and space. Are your focus colors so bright that less is more or are they colors that you can see in great quantity, in which case you can use them on furniture and at the windows.

Your goal is to be able to carry this theme throughout your whole house or apartment in some form or another. Colors can change radically as long as there is a commitment to the background mood and feeling. Let's attack our colors specifically in room schemes and then we'll tie everything together room by room.

Colors in hand, the first thing to consider is the room itself. Start with the most important room to you, perhaps the living room, and work the other rooms around it. Examine your light exposures, the size, proportion, height of ceiling and the view. Review your elements and list what you've got to work with. For example:

Walls and Ceiling—open, but have to be background for art and
    books.
Floors—have to use 9-foot-by-12-foot green rug (sample glued on
    piece of white paper).
Windows—possibly use old green and yellow chintz curtains—
    view pretty good.
Furniture—all upholstered furniture re-covered.
Lighting—room darkish, need supplementary daytime lighting.
    Want to use Chinese red porcelain lamp vases.
Color—white, yellows, greens, brown, and orange-red accents.

When you commit yourself to specific colors for each area in each element, don't be afraid of your practical instincts. They're usually the best guides of all. There's no secret method to selecting and distributing your colors because there are no technical determinations. Practical solutions come from breaking down all the possibilities. Let's examine this further.

Is your room small and cramped and do you want to open it up? If so, your background should be your lightest colors. If your space is dark, this too is the case. If your room is huge, do you want to keep it spacious and open?

Color hides a multitude of sins, so if your room is dull and dreary, has awkward eaves and juts, a lively color on the wall might be necessary. Any color you use in quantity (for walls, floor or furniture and particularly at the windows) should complement and help the view unless it is so bad you want to forget about it entirely. In that case you can use (and should) bright lively colors to make up for your gloomy outlook.

In the room itself, are there any architectural features or materials that will dictate your color development? For example, a large wall of exposed old brick won't work well with oranges because the brick has a pink blush to it; reds and pinks will look better. Although you can always paint over marble (flax marble can be done by an artistic painter or you can learn to do it yourself by reading Isabelle O'Neal's excellent book *The Art of the Painted Finish*), you should have your colors lend themselves to a marble mantel or fireplace facing in order to have them integrate nicely into the rest of the room.

Suppose we have a 12-foot-by-18-foot room with northern exposure and an okay view with trees and some sky. You could use the apple-green rug you already own. Having the dark color on the floor gives the room weight. There are two reasons why you wouldn't want to take up space by using a weighty color in your furniture in this room. First, the room isn't that big and the heavy color would be bulky in feeling. Secondly, the room is fairly dark and needs a lift to create a more spacious feeling. You would do well to select a warm yellow (one with some red and orange in it to warm up your cool light exposure) for your walls and keep your furniture on the lightish side too—perhaps a heavy woven material with pale greens, yellows and whites.

On closer examination, the curtains from your old apartment don't really look well in your house. Because your old apartment had virtually no view you overcompensated with a wildly bright print at the window, but here you need a more gentle material so you bring more of your outlook into your house. I'd suggest a simple white cotton material or a linen. Or, have no curtains at all and have shutters with plants. Anytime you have plants at the window inside and trees outside, the window glass seems to disappear and your outer space becomes one with your interior.

Those apricot and lacquer-red touches you like could be brought in by your lamp vases, throw pillows and your yellowy-greeny tweedy material. And don't forget flowers. Your paintings have lots of these color highlights which tie everything together. Your books look very well in your room, but the back wall of your bookcase could use a stronger color than the pale yellow wall color. Consider bringing in another green, further tying in your rug. A strong background color behind books is always handsome.

INTEGRATING ONE ROOM'S COLOR SCHEME TO THE NEXT

If you live in a house you have more space than an apartment and you can get away with letting each room have its own distinct personality. This is especially true of the downstairs and the upstairs of the house. The carpet on the stairs and the hall-wall color are the only elements to join, and you can stop both carpet and wall color at the top step and treat the upstairs separately if you wish. To determine whether this is the right solution for you, carry your ideal scheme upstairs and examine it next to all the opened doors. Does everything go together?

In an apartment, however, you have to relate each adjoining space more carefully because not only is each right on top of another, but there is a more total space feeling in an apartment. A simple dinner party can expose every square inch of your space, whereas if you live in a house you can contain your friends in a precise area more easily. Apartments aren't likely to have powder rooms, generous hall closets, etc., so your private chambers must be entered. Integrate color through repetition of one or two basic background colors.

Gwen Carpenter tied her sun room and dining room to her living room by adding and subtracting color. She has a blue and white dining room which adjoins her blue, white, yellow, red and green living room which opens up onto her green and white sun room. There are greens or blues and whites in all three rooms, which make them go well together and still have their own distinct personality.

None of us wants to limit ourselves to one basic color scheme that gets repeated room after room. As I said earlier, color repetition can be done by adding and subtracting basic colors. You can recall color in the ways in which you treat your painted surfaces, the way you handle color for upholstery, the way you handle your color at the windows, the way you treat your floors, etc. Because I don't believe in wall-to-wall carpeting, I don't suggest a blanket of beige throughout but possibly your rugs could in some way tie in together (you could consider using the same in several rooms either in quality and color; or just color; or just quality). Two rooms, your living and dining rooms, could have off-white linen rugs even though your rooms otherwise are entirely different. Just as pairs of furniture make for visual harmony, any element you repeat in a variety of themes can tie your over-all place together, which makes it appear larger. Modern designers repeat wall colors, rug colors, lighting techniques, even materials from room to room, allowing for the use of the room to put in the individual personal touches and charm. An entire house of white walls, brown floors and straw rugs could have shots of color and texture for furniture and be a family of space.

THINK OF YOUR ROOMS AS A FAMILY

Flow of space is important because it makes you feel more comfortable in a room. Too many abrupt surprises can be startling. It's unsettling and confusing to have too much to digest too soon. That's why this recalling rhythm is so important. Not only does it help each separate room but it adds character to the over-all space.

No matter how large or small your family of rooms, they are yours and they bear your name. Your two children should have their own expression in their rooms, but they might be treated with the same technique so you don't compromise the whole. Blair likes red and blue and she has a red ceiling and floor and a blue rug with white walls. Marsha, a green and yellow girl, has a yellow ceiling and floor and a green rug, white walls. Different color schemes treated alike brings them together. A very dark cozy library may seem miles apart from your white and blue living room and yet the same vital colors make them definitely yours. I believe that each room can have its own colors if they're joined by white either in walls or trim.

Don't overlook the possibility of having every nook and cranny of space delightful. Satisfy your craving for an explosion of unrelated colors somewhere off the mainstream in a place you can close off. Consider putting a wild and silly wallpaper in your tiny entry hall (where it welcomes you and yet you don't spend any time there so you can't get sick of it). Or put a splashy wallpaper in a bedroom bath off a white hall where it gets closed off by a door. The plain white hall gives us breathing room while we digest the impact of the bathroom.

Stairs, as I said earlier, are a great breaking-off area. Your theme downstairs can radically change once you get upstairs, but the upstairs hall should be compatible with the downstairs hall. (Even when doors separate one area from the next, it takes time and space for our eyes to assimilate color changes.)

Closets should relate to your clothes, not necessarily to your room. Paint, hang contact paper or paper hang your closets with anything that is a joy to face as you select your clothes. You might want to buy posters for one dollar each or get travel posters free and paste them up in your closet. You might find this to be very lively indeed. Put mirrors on the inside of your door, for you and also for more color. Patterns and colors of our wardrobe are so mixed together, and varied, that there's no worry about adding one more.

A man's hideaway bar can be an electric charge. I've seen some with owls peeking out of trees in silver foiled forests and with geometric graphic designs that were so optically stigmatic they made you half drunk, but were great fun for a bar. Think what will go with your wine cellar, liquor and glasses. Show them off gaily, even though your solution isn't entirely co-ordinated to your room.

A laundry room can be a total shock to your color system so long as it's cheerful and functional. Indulge in elaborate drawer liners to make ordinary domestic life more colorful.

STRONG COLOR CONTRASTS IN A ROOM

Your accessories and treasures might need a strong color to contrast against theirs to show them off. I'll never forget going into a client's library (emerald walls that glistened in all lights) and being struck by one incredibly beautiful rock on a dark, dark brown table. Because of the dark green walls and dark rich brown lacquer table, this gem looked like a diamond (only more interesting).

Steuben Glass asked our company to help them display their collection of crystal; we chose dark green velvet. If you have a collection of special objects on shelves, they will show off best when there is a dramatic contrast in color between them and their enclosure. Shells, rocks, arrowheads, crystal, miniature birds and animals all require "staging" by changing their background to a strong color so the object stands alone like a jewel. You remember how difficult it is to find small shells on the beach because they blend into the sand. The same is true of treasures we live with; to bring out subtlety of color shadings and tender forms, the background should be a deep rich contrast.

Don't limit yourself to color co-ordinate anything that will be difficult or expensive to change. None of these living decisions are at all comparable to buying a dress. What we decide on for a coffee table, a headboard, dining-room chairs or a chest of drawers lives with us longer than we realize.

Your movable objects should have the flexibility not only of going from one room to another but of fitting in to future rooms and color schemes in new locations. Your basic color preferences and taste in objects should be classical enough to withstand your current craving for this season's hot pink, which might be tomorrow's horror. A stacking nest of plastic tables shouldn't be an accent color or you'll be working around that "must use in room" tired old pink for the next twenty years.

Without realizing it, colors have their rhythms and popularity, coming into and going out of favor at the drop of a hat. While an old Perry Como record could delight you forever, some singing groups have short lives and for good reasons. All your movable, portable investments should be classically colored and have the flexibility to work with you whatever your mood or wherever your place.

Choose wood furniture and lacquer and plastics that can go in any scheme. Painted furniture should be in colors you can live with forever. For example: White and off white, black, dark dark red, Chinese lacquer red, dark dark bottle green, and dark dark midnight blue are safe lasting colors for furniture finishes. Any new and up-to-date color should be avoided for purchases that are for keeps. Look at Mercedes cars to get hints as to what colors are elegant and lasting.

LIMIT YOUR COLOR FAMILIES

We all know by now what "our" colors are. Stick to them. No matter what tempts you on sale, never rationalize a "lemon" of a color in your life; you'll have no use for it once you've brought it home. Jane Crompton bought an avocado green refrigerator on sale at Macy's and I can't tell you how dreadful it looks with her apple-green wallpaper. The seventy-two dollars she saved is considerable and yet not at the expense of a beautiful kitchen. (Sure, you can spray paint or have your refrigerator sprayed but it's never as good or lasting as a factory-baked, enamel paint job.) A dirty gold chair on sale will only have to be slipcovered eventually. In an all-white room, don't spoil it by having a dark wood-grained TV. Television sets are ugly enough and difficult to make fit in. Don't make it more difficult by choosing any one that has a good picture. Be fussy and complain about the design but don't settle when you know what you want. A car color you don't like is offensive.

All your colors should be able to be thrown together and look well. Your red chair in the hall will occasionally land in the living room or in your eating area. Your ice crusher shows when you're mixing drinks.

TIPS TO AVOID COLOR MISTAKES

See all colors in their own light with their co-ordinating colors (including wood, metals, etc.). We have no true color memory and unless you have all your samples together to compare, you can't make an accurate judgment.

Never guess about color. Carry tiny swatches of your schemes with you in your purse wherever you go, and when you are out shopping for your rooms, bring along larger samples in a tote bag so you can check everything. "I can't visualize how it will look from such a tiny piece," is a familiar cry. When you are home you should then live with these samples in daylight and at night. (You'll be amazed how artificial light can completely change the coloring and you don't want to be stuck with a room that turns dead at night.)

Never rush any colors. No matter how enthusiastic you are, never make a snap judgment about color. You have to live with it; mull it over, sleep on it, come back to it and then decide.

Be suspicious of any color that doesn't look well with white and black. I don't know why this is true, but it could be because white is light and black is the absence of light, and they show up the impurities and dullness of an unclear hue. Heavy, dirty colors will look wrong against white and black and you should select a different hue. Emilio Pucci outlines every color with a fine definition of black and always has white in every design. Study your stationery boxes, your lingerie and your silk scarves. Interesting!

Your colors have to balance. One color can't pop out at you at the expense of weakening and making pale all the rest. Back to Pucci: He uses shocking, thrilling raw pigment but notice how he has the brightest color in the lesser amount and evenly distributed throughout his design. If your strong brilliant pinks and reds take over completely, use less of them and pick a stronger value of brighter intensity for your other colors so you keep them in balance.

Rely on your instincts with color. When something hits you and you have a real gut reaction, don't change what you're doing. You are the final judge, and no matter how colorful the world is getting, you may still prefer your tried and true and livable "nothing" colors. On the other hand, when you feel you want a real shot of color, hit it on the head and don't tame it down. When you feel your colors to this extent, they are "your" colors.

Accessories

Happiness is dependent on the taste, and not on things. It is by having what we like that we are made happy, not by having what others think desirable.

LA ROCHEFOUCAULD

All of us need our own personal treasures, things we like that make us feel we belong where we are. This is my place! When you return from work, a favorite clock may greet you with a gentle chime, and you know you are home. We all need the support of our surroundings.

The dictionary describes accessories as "any article or device that adds to the convenience or effectiveness of something else but is not essential." A car radio is an accessory. An ice crusher is an accessory. A painting is an accessory.

We should think of all the things in our lives that aren't absolutely essential as our accessories and try to treat practical, functional household items with the same fondness and significance as the table-top accessories we gather and show off. Lamps, shades, baskets for our plants, boxes, ashtrays, pictures, photographs and decorative throw pillows are accessories, as well as all the things you collect, your hobbies, your scrapbooks, your metals, your baubles, your statues, and the thousands of items we weave into our rooms that give them their fourth dimension.

The pen you hold to write a letter to a friend, the paper you write on counts just as much as the "accessories" that you place on top of your desk. All the things we use are real to us and important. When we enjoy touching our salad fork and spoon and enjoy keeping our family picture books and delight in the growing and flowering of our plants, these accessories might be among our most treasured possessions.

Think of accessories as items that nourish you and don't be a bit concerned about which ones "show" and which ones get "used" and which ones get put inside a drawer or bookcase, used only when needed. They're all part of you and the design, concern and care in the selection should be thoughtful since you are affected by these parts of your over-all environment. When accessories are gathered out of enthusiasm and joy, the most humble shell from a beach can be worth its weight in gold because of the memory that will flash before you of the time and place it was gathered.

Accessories are symbols of our inner feelings and thoughts. Some carry deep meanings, others simply delight our souls. They should not be small objects selected for others to recognize and become impressed by unless they're appealing to them as well. Making the right image with accessories is denying yourself the fun of self-discovery and personal expression.

We're never going to outgrow our need to have around us things that we love. As the future promises us less space we should surround ourselves with only things we truly treasure. Hoarding stuff is useless fat and it clutters up our busy lives. We should make room for things we adore because it's these personal things that make us feel attached to our surroundings.

COLLECTING THINGS REQUIRES A TASTE AND A NEED

Each of us has a collection of things that are really meaningful. These terribly important possessions, from books, to flower holders, to stone fragments from a church, to statues, games, to old scrapbooks, medals won in earlier days, to family photos, are ours alone. It would be unheard of to part with nostalgic belongings from our childhood and items inherited from our families, given us by our friends and gathered along the way. Any memorabilia that makes us feel good, no matter how sentimental, is part of us and therefore should be incorporated somewhere in our lives. I worked for a family for years on their house, and never knew anything about the man until I was called in to help him with his office. He lives in a museum of clutter and proudly said, "These are the things I care about most!"

ACCESSORIES ARE A FORM OF BIOGRAPHY

I think of treasures as I think of people. All of our things, collected and given to us through the years, tell special stories about a place visited or express our taste and appreciation for things and people we value. Our material expressions of life's pleasures range in monetary value from worthless to priceless. To us they're of equal importance. The leaf you plucked off a fruit tree in Barbados and pressed in a book may have as much meaning to you as a rare picture hanging on your wall.

The quantity of accessories and souvenirs we surround ourselves with varies enormously. It's not just a question of space and money but of vast differences in our personalities that dictate how much we want to have around us or how little we want cluttering up our lives. It's entirely up to you. Susie's stuff can be Charlie's clutter and his monastic quarters would drive her crazy. I don't think it can be traced to genetics, but environments, in order to make a totally comforting background, should have the things that each individual feels supports and pleases him.

The things we want near us *now* have so much to do with our peculiar ways and personal delights; so often they're unexplainable. All we know is we like them now and they make us feel good *now*. Tomorrow we may discover new loves because our tastes and experiences will evolve as we grow.

All of us have certain things we really love and own and other things we want to own. It's perfectly possible we've outgrown the things we have and they no longer have meaning, so we are starting out virtually from scratch. If this is the case take your time. Things accumulate so quickly and are so hard to part with; don't rush!

It doesn't matter what your budget, every one of us can afford to collect. Pleasure is created out of the small things: They will make all the difference in the long run and we have to plan ahead so we can be spontaneous when we find things we care for and want to be a part of us. You have to be ready and receptive to buy when the right time turns up. There's nothing practical about walking into a local shop and falling in love with everything you see. It doesn't matter if you collect owls or mushrooms, or American prints, or shells or paintings, or antique clocks or rare books, when you see something you fall in love with, and want to add to your collection, you have to find a way to buy it. You will never regret your extravagances, only your economies.

If you don't buy the painting when you see it, you may be out of luck. Maybe the first painting you ever considered buying was sold from under your nose because you couldn't decide fast enough. The bronze statue you saw on your way home from dinner was sold because you didn't follow up soon enough. So many of the things we see and want are either one of a kind or are limited in quantity. When you travel and find beautiful examples of local crafts you will always kick yourself if you don't buy some— these are the things that weave your life and place into one fabric. All art and accessories should be purchased from a different financial budget. It's a good idea to set goals for the amount you'll add to this "belle arte" account each year, so when you stumble across something that takes your breath away you can indulge yourself by bringing it home. Instead of only saving for a rainy day, have an account for happy finds. Don't buy things out of necessity only—but out of love. You'll be amazed how quickly you'll find yourself in beautiful surroundings because of all the wonderful things you've been able to gather through the years.

When working out your expense budget for the year or for a trip you plan to take to New England, include a separate amount (as much as you can afford even if you cheat on your food budget to get funds) for special goodies you find in those charming old antique and specialty shops. Keep building up the fund because there's no telling when something you find is going to give you that gut feeling and you'll need the ready cash. These finds are your treasures—your ways to remember your means of expression.

ACCESSORIES KEEP OUR ROOMS UP TO DATE

We're not often in the market for a new sofa and a pair of chairs but an old Indian basket or earthenware cache pot (for flowers and plants) or a rock crystal bauble brought into your room can light it up. These small things are movable and we should feel free to rotate our accessories and small objects as often as we wish.

I always love going to Mary Louise and Peter's apartment when they've just returned from a trip. Whether they've been to Colorado or Switzerland, they find something wonderful: an arrowhead, or a cowbell or a painting purchased from a Paris art gallery. They share their trip with their friends by sprinkling parts of their journey here and there. I'm fascinated with the stories behind the things people own.

BEAUTIFUL THINGS NEED TO BE TOUCHED

There's something very senuous about holding a crystal prism in your hands or caressing a piece of polished metal or picking up a precious stone or holding a delicate shell. It's a very meaningful part of the experience to touch something beautiful. Have you noticed how many adult toys there are now to play with? Lucite puzzles and balls that swing. Our objects should be out in the open for others to share. It's too bad if something is so valuable it has to be locked up. Then it becomes something else entirely.

Collections behind glass so they don't need to be dusted seem unappreciated too. Far better to have fewer, lesser things that can be shared. A bronze sculpture of a woman is far more beautiful when it is naturally polished by touching. I always think of the Hans Christian Andersen and "Alice in Wonderland" sculptures in Central Park and how they are gleaming in all the contact areas.

Is there something you've seen in *House & Garden* you really like or a graphic or a paperweight or an old walnut box or a prayer rug? If so, buy it and go meatless for the rest of the week. These finds, these extravagances, once in a while, you'll never regret. Jump in and enjoy bringing something new into your life.

Anything that really excites you becomes alive. Let your accessories stand on pedestals, follow you from room to room and be in focus. There's no difference between being proud of a person you love or a painting or a flower you tended or a clock. If you gather shells on the beach with your children, put them in a Plexiglass box or a glass bottle with a cork top and save the memory. If you love beaches the way I do, have a separate glass container (labeled underneath) for each beach you go to.

These chosen objects should have a place. Don't restrict yourself to thinking in terms of a given table in a given room. Let the things you love move with you freely and travel around. It's perfectly possible to have too many things in too small a space and by putting some things aside, others have more meaning.

Where and how we group our special treasures can make all the difference in our enjoyment. Each thing we collect has to join others in space and place. How we combine our forms and colors, how we make up our compositions, can determine their effect on us. A beauty unnoticed is a shame.

Some interior designers "tablescape." They either buy and arrange your table-top items or they take your own and rearrange them. I find it hard to think we can't all do this for ourselves with a small amount of encouragement. Our aim should be to display naturally and set off those things we love for maximum delight and stimulation. This requires giving thought to asymmetrical balance and placing our objects in interesting compositions. When we group our personal pleasures together they become friendly and human. You obviously feel strongly about these things and therefore you'll be able to instinctively feel when you like how they look and where they are.

Think of your room as a stage and your accessories as your actors. If people are the audience, how do you want them to see these characters? What is their personality and background? So much can be lost and over-looked when thoughtlessly rendered. Remember, too, not everyone is as compulsively interested in your accessories as you, so you have to make it easy for others to take part. Your sentiment and explanation of the meaning draw others toward your things. Explain them to friends.

Hang your picture at a pleasing eye level for people who are sitting so the pictures become part of the atmosphere.

Group small objects together in mass with a contrasting color for the background so they count for something.

Try three candlesticks instead of the usual two. Don't forget, people tend to remember unusual, good and bad!

Mass your pictures and photographs together in unusual ways so the beholder is captive. An intense floor-to-ceiling collection of favorites could be so much more powerful than one here and one there.

Think of colors, texture, form and scale when grouping. Your eye will help you. Add and subtract until you get combinations that delight you. A fern in an old basket, one fresh clove, a scented carnation in a bud vase, a small picture and a favorite decorative box could make a delightful grouping. Next week, try a whole new arrangement. You'll appreciate what you have so much more if you continue to experiment and try new ways.

I have a friend who uses her "good" silver every day. Silver doesn't need continual polishing when it's used each day, so it makes perfect sense. Why do we have these things we love if we don't use them and let them become a part of our daily living? We shouldn't have things put away for special occasions when we could enjoy them right now. Today is far more important than tomorrow because it is certain and it is here.

So many of the accessories we surround ourselves with are practical, functional and beautiful and should be enjoyed all the time.

Instead of hanging baskets on a wall for purely decorative purposes, use them as the occasion arises. Put your berries in a basket and let them decorate your table. Rare antique plates should leap out of the cupboard for a dinner for two or a party for twenty. Numbers shouldn't determine when we bring out the good stuff! Use your objects and accessories to add quality and joy to all your days.

Cache pots (containers for flowers and plants) can hold ice cream or a plant or Christmas cookies. Baskets can be for sewing, for popcorn or for a plant. Using our things makes them join us. Fill the box with candy, cigars or flowers. Pour brandy in your decanter and put logs in the bucket. Take your flowering plants from the upstairs bedroom and bring them to the dinner table. Your accessories should be loved and appreciated all the time and you should allow them to travel with you. I'd hate to think of the times I've brought small objects and pictures to the dinner table. What a relaxed, pleasant time to appreciate beauty and remember far-off places.

When you travel, pack a few small things you enjoy so your strange anonymous room won't be cold and unfriendly. A picture of someone you love, if nothing else. Also, when you are away and lonely for your own home, your own things, buy some flowers—one daisy will do. You'll be delighted by the instant lift you'll receive.

The true picture of us as unique personalities is our appreciations, our pride, our understanding of art and sensitivity to beauty—allow these things to enter your life. They will illustrate who you are as a person more directly than anything else.

Maintenance

Beauty commonly produces love, but cleanliness
preserves it.

JOSEPH ADDISON

My book is designed to help you set up a place to live and help keep your background surroundings current with yourself and your changing, growing needs. Maintaining this environment is a whole new topic.

I've tried to stress practical solutions to domestic living problems so we could enjoy our time at home and keep the housework chores to a minimum. But don't feel guilty unnecessarily about having a dirty house; if we went nonstop from dawn until dusk with no visitors we could redust the coffee table three times each day because it would need it. Our guilt makes us compulsive and keeps us from enjoying our time at home. Each of us has had to train himself to sit down and read *Time* magazine when the house needs picking up.

A favorite book of mine on this subject is *Keeping Up With Keeping House* by Mary Kaltman, and I highly recommend it to all kindred souls. Miss Kaltman has put it all together in a warm, practical way and helps us enjoy the running and upkeep of our nests. As a former White House housekeeper, she's most capable, highly organized and clever. Do read this as supplementary reading and you'll be on top of the dust fuzzies!

I had a garden as a child long before I had a house and I learned from my vegetables and flowers the satisfaction and pleasure I gained from the care I put into them. At nine I had something that was my own and something I could take pride in. The more involved I became the more bountiful was my garden. So often I would weed and rake each aisle just for the pleasure of seeing my garden in mint condition. My rewards were the joy of caring for my pretty garden and naturally for the fruits of my labor.

I think of household work still in this light. Surely we have lots of better things to do with our time than scrub bathroom floors, but having them clean makes life so much nicer. There are times when it is nourishing to scrub a tub until it sparkles or wax and polish the floors until the smell of wax takes over. Polishing your brass scale until it comes up to a pale yellow shine or caring for your plants or washing a lovely piece of crystal can be a delightful exercise. Even getting ice out of a tray can be rewarding if you're receptive to the beauty of the crystal clear cubes, more interesting than lucite because they're alive.

It's no fun to sit back and watch your surroundings go to seed. Furthermore, digging in the soil with your hands and scrubbing a door trim clean and polishing your door knocker can have rewards in the process of work as well as the pride and joy in the results. Look at maintenance from both sides. Rooms need to be cared for in order to smile.

SIMPLIFY

Our standards of cleanliness should be balanced by our ability to cope. Anything is possible and it's up to us to analyze what we care most about. Instead of feeling burdened by trying to keep up with our unrealistic "dream style" we should liberate ourselves by getting out from under the drudgeries of nothing but housework and get it in balance with our "life style."

Gloria Steinem says women are a maintenance class. This certainly is changing, but the best way for men and women to improve the quality of their time is to economize on housekeeping, so we're not bogged down with triviality. It is perfectly possible to cut down on 50 per cent of your work load and end up with a more sparkling series of rooms. Here's how:

First, hook up with the industrial age. Modern technology is making living very practical and on days when we're not with it, it can take over for us entirely. Today, everything in our lives can be practical, durable, non-fade, non-shrink, smudge proof, easy care, drip dry and permanent press. No longer do any colors have to be impractical—there's vinyl.

We have to have things that work. No longer do we have to maintain old furniture we can't afford to repair or that is a chore to keep up; there are too many options. We can have plastics or formica or simple natural wood. A totally functional oriented life that minimizes labor is a way to give us greater joy. While it alone won't give us inner satisfaction, the things we can do with our spare time will. The thousands of artistic and creative hobbies we can do that relate to our home delight and satisfy us. Hooking a rug, making decorative candles, weaving fabric on your own loom, making a sampler with your daughter, making a model airplane with your son, spending virtually an entire day in the kitchen preparing dinner for two, decorating your kitchen cabinets with fruit and flowers, canning peaches, making a needlepoint pillow cover, making a patchwork quilt from your father's old ties, "instant" framing the most recent family photographs you blew up in your own dark room or making a giant production of Christmas cooky baking—we have to work hard to find time to do these things. It takes time to bake your own bread. The best ice cream I've ever eaten was peach made by a friend from her own peaches. She does this each June as a family tradition.

I believe we should push all the buttons we need in order to get our work done and gain more free time. Whenever possible, have a machine save you steps. The touches that personalize your home have nothing to do with washing machines and dishwashers. The warmth you can add to your rooms with flowers, plants, a needlepoint pillow, or anything at all you create with your hands is what you should be freed to do. Let your machines do your dirty work. Get the self-cleaning oven, the self-defrosting refrigerator and no-iron contour sheets so you can create beauty which will feed all your senses. Cutting up fruit with someone you like is more fun than scraping egg off breakfast plates!

It's perfectly true that a house that is enjoyed is going to get dirty and show signs of wear. My friend Richard said he loves summer because everything is done outside and there's no housework to be done. Even the bathtub has fewer rings because of all the swimming. It's great to take the summer off and forget the house, but when people use it again, it's going to get cluttered up.

Sandra loves everything and everybody. Her life, friends, hobbies and all her disjointed activities cause a frenzy in the house. Every room Sandra gets near becomes action packed; something current is going on everywhere you look. Committee work, needlework, schoolwork, piles of this and that, something is always being read, reviewed, repaired, packed, wrapped, or cooked in the oven. Sandra and her energy tend to get her place looking on the messy side. (You begin to trip over Christmas boxes just after Labor Day.) When things get out of hand, she closes doors and that's when she knows enough is enough. Time to sort things out.

We all get buried under from time to time and instead of feeling warm and good from all our treasures, we feel choked and uneasy. Even things we desperately love to look at and do can grow thin on us at times when they're junked up and out of order. When this happens, we need a fresh look at all our things. Get ready for a weekend project.

AN AESTHETIC HOUSE CLEANING

Periodically, give your rooms a clean sweep. Gather every movable decorative item you own, including the things inside your cupboards and drawers. Put the breakable things together in one safe place and begin making them sparkle. Things become dull and heavy with dirt you don't notice day to day. Dusty, faded strawflowers should be thrown out. When everything is fresh and clean and in good repair, place things about at random, but look at each item with fresh eyes. Move everything around and try new groupings. Put less around this time and allow each thing to breathe more freely. A coffee table that is crowded before drinks, ashtrays and nibbles are added isn't practical.

The items you have left behind might be the ones you don't favor now and they can go inside a cupboard. Eventually, if you don't miss them and never really want them out or you find you never really use them, you should find a way to phase them out of your life.

Try mixing your early things with your more recent ones. Gather a whole bunch of small things (brass weights, silver cigarette box, carriage clocks, ashtrays, your rock collection) and put them together on your coffee table. Change the scale with something else entirely, like a lacquer box. As you play around, walk out of the room and do something else for a while so you can get a fresh look at what you've done. Take down a selection of George Bernard Shaw's plays you have leather bound in your bookcase to reread and enjoy.

The less stuff you have cluttering and confusing your rooms, the better. Bring fresh accessories out of storage cupboards for various occasions. If you have everything in good repair and well organized, you can take a few minutes to bring out new surprises. This way you won't take your rooms for granted and crowd them with meaningless stuff.

We can all be practical up to a certain point and then we have to throw caution to the wind and indulge in some luxuries. Mrs. Gilbert keeps her vacuum cleaner under her bed because her mist-green rug is her extravagance; it is most fragile and every morning she gives it a two-minute once-over to keep it spanking fresh.

You should be able to scrub down most of your place with soap and water. If you had a "specialized solution" for each chair and table you'd go mad in no time. Your Formica counter tops and bathroom floor should be cleanable with a sponge. They're no big deal when they're clean. However, a gleaming brass bowl filled with fruit for your centerpiece requires elbow grease, and a wooden hallway floor needs someone to put on the paste wax and run the buffer. Brass door knobs need care too.

None of us can afford to send everything out to be professionally cleaned. Think three times before purchasing anything that can't be wiped with a sponge, thrown in the machine or spot cleaned at home.

ORGANIZING CLEANING SUPPLIES

Instead of having one central place for all cleaning supplies, have many mini totes so you're never more than a room away from Ajax, a sponge, paper towels, a jiffy cleaner. In the five-and-ten or the hardware store, buy several plastic caddies with handles. Equip each with a set of basic bathroom supplies and put it in each bathroom, or in a linen closet or some central place. Daily touch-ups can be spontaneous and over within minutes if you have the supplies handy.

Don't feel peculiar putting dusting cloths in end-table drawers and lemon wax in the drawer of your desk. Be prepared! You never know when the urge to wax your desk will hit you and you shouldn't pass up the opportunity.

After a party use a shopping bag to do a fast clean-up—collect dead flowers and cocktail napkins, empty ashtrays.

PLANTS AND FLOWERS

For two dollars you can get a plastic container with an adjustable nozzle at the end which is a perfect plant "mister"; or find a pretty brass one. Have one filled with water in every room where there are plants. If you mist your plants each day you needn't dust them, and they will look and feel so much healthier. Hide the "mister" behind a potted palm.

A florist friend let me in on her secret for long-lasting fresh-cut flowers: Put one or two drops of ammonia into every quart of water. This keeps the flowers smelling fresh and helps keep the water from getting dirty.

HOME REPAIRS

Section off a whole shelf, either in the linen closet, the laundry area, under a kitchen cabinet or a drawer of a chest, for a repair bin. If it's empty it will feed your soul and if it's got wounded treasures inside, they'll get attended to when time permits. Label the bin "Broken Objects I Love." The tail of the Steuben whale you won in a paddle tennis tournament needs gluing on and the string to the Greek worry beads broke, the piece of veneer fell off the dresser (Scotch tape it on a large piece of colorful paper so it doesn't get lost), the antique etched globe, the broken ashtray—all of these odds and ends can be fixed as a rainy Saturday project if they're gathered in one place. "Broken Objects I Love" doesn't mean mend something that is shattered when it might be good riddance to old rubbish.

TAKE A LOT OF NOTES

If you try to remember to buy mayonnaise and that the window measurement for the blinds is 46 inches wide by 57 inches deep, and that you need to replace one burgundy glass and that you're getting low on toilet paper . . . you can do it, but your mind may be cluttered with the wrong thoughts. Remember that time expert I mentioned earlier? He is a great advocate of note taking. All that stuff should be written on various lists.

Cleaning instructions should be written in your household book for permanent reference. One thing I've found very timesaving is to have a household book which I keep in the kitchen with my cookbooks. In it I have a general list of household supplies (what size garbage liner and other tidbits of information), of foods and brand names I use, an index of all sources of supply with telephone numbers, a room-by-room résumé of cleaning requirements, and instructions on the care and watering of my plants. If you do this before you suddenly go to the hospital with appendicitis, you'll be most grateful. It's especially handy when you take trips or have a baby sitter. Who knows if she wouldn't love a little bonus for doing some ironing or polishing some silver?

I don't have the space in this book to tell you all the inside trade secrets on how to remove the gouges from your end table or repair your damaged hardwood floor or clean your wooden shutters or repair a cigarette burn in your Indian rug or lift up stains left by household pets. All I can tell you is there are answers and solutions to all these and thousands more daily headaches that seem hopeless at the time. Carol Eisen wrote a book entitled *Nobody Said You Have to Eat Off the Floor*, which is witty and full of practical advice. The point is to keep a sense of humor about domestic chores.

Mrs. Brown keeps reminding us at McMillen that anything that goes wrong in our decorating or designing or maintaining of our space is repairable. Our problems have solutions. I suggest you basically trust Mrs. Brown's advice and if your disasters *seem* unsolvable, don't believe it until you've been proved wrong. I received a hysterical phone call from a client whose mover had dropped her safe off the dolly onto her entrance hall's marble floor. The cracks in the marble were sanded down and filled in and to this day I can't remember exactly where the tragedy occurred.

Another time, Mrs. X demanded we go out to her house to see how our painters had ruined her floors; her house was two hundred years old and she had no intention of scraping the old patina off her floors, and therefore she felt her entire house was destroyed. We were able to get her out of the house for a day, and restored her floors to their old luster. Our floor men used a dark stain, mixed in some wax and with superfine steel wool rubbed with the grain; any plaster dust, scratches or paint specks disappeared, and after a generous application of wax the problem was solved.

At Christmastime a client's needlework rug got damaged when a candle burned a three-inch square hole right in the most noticeable traffic area. We were able to match the yarn exactly and a "little old lady" who specializes in just such things came to the rescue.

An old family vegetable platter drops and looks like powder . . . this too can be put back together again.

Before panic sets in, be certain you contact experts who can advise you. Sometimes the biggest messes are the easiest to repair.

If you have a new lacquer coffee table it is going to scratch. Count on it scratching so you won't be fooled. Your table will chip too. Plan ahead for this by having a small jar of "touch up" lacquer on hand, and one night (instead of polishing your fingernails) touch up your coffee table.

Basically, it boils down to this. If you love your possessions you're going to want to care for them and you should intelligently find individual solutions to the care and upkeep of all your treasured possessions. Worry not . . . somewhere, somehow, there is a solution and cure.

Finally, do everything you can to keep your surroundings lively and fresh but remember nothing stays new forever. As things are used they age and mellow, and scratches form on furniture just as lines form on people. Learn to accept a little worn spot and a few scratches. They're completely natural and appealing. It's the rooms that get used and are lived in that are the ones we find most comforting and satisfying.

Develop the concept of going from room to room always neatening up. My mother never let us go empty-handed. This saves you the horror of unattractive messes to face when all you really want is to relax. A picked-up room that is lived in and enjoyed is far better than a barren spotless room. Have the children bring in shopping bags to gather all their stuff.

Part Three

Now that you've thought about what you want from your living space and have some knowledge of the design elements with which you'll build your environment, you can begin to put your rooms together. In this chapter, we'll put your personal design priorities into practical use. These chapters are the nuts and bolts of how to come to grips with your physical space, room by room.

My approach is the same one I use professionally, what I've found over the years to be effective in assembling a room. No matter how confident you are about your tastes and needs, it is always frightening at first to envision how to transform a space into your own unique design.

We'll go through each element, step by step, so you'll know how to design each room and each design in that room; the same basic design steps apply to all interior space.

For purposes of illustrating what you might do in each room, I'll give you examples and suggestions of how others have made *their* design decisions. Your choices will be different, naturally, but your procedure will be the same, and you may find some appealing practical ideas you can work into your spaces. Refer back to Part Two for more suggestions in deciding on, for instance, your kitchen windows or bedroom walls. Tie it all together.

Begin in one room and break the design down into the nine separate elements discussed in Part Two, in the same order: walls and ceiling, floors, windows, lighting, furniture, fabrics, color, accessories, maintenance. Make a chart for each room, like the one on the following page, and leave space to fill in your design choices.

Use the chart in two ways. First, fill in the existing physical conditions you have to deal with. Then, make a second chart on which you fill in what preferences suit you for your new design. As you work on each room, referring to this chart may help you think about your separate design elements and organize them into a unified design.

Stand at the doorway to your kitchen and ask yourself, "Where do I

ROOM:								
Walls and Ceiling	Floors	Windows	Furniture	Lighting	Fabrics	Color	Accessories	Maintenance

begin?" The first element in your chart is walls and ceilings, because if the walls are changed they automatically change the floor, the whole space. Does your structure require physical changes? Do you have enough storage? Are you satisfied with the function and appearance of your built-in cabinets? Make notes on your chart.

After you've written down all the existing conditions and features of your room, then jot down on your fresh chart your preferences and ideas for your new design.

Measure each room carefully and make your floor plan. All your questions can be analyzed on paper.

Now you can explore all the various possibilities, understand your priorities, and make intelligent decisions about each design element.

Kitchen

When the objects we use every day and the
surroundings we live in have become in
themselves a work of art then we shall be able
to say that we have achieved a balanced life.

BRUNO MUNARI
Design As Art

Kitchens are busy looking by nature, and the walls are usually broken up into odd shapes which may not be big enough to carry a patterned wallpaper. I recommend plain walls. You can either paint with high-gloss enamel paint so they are scrubbable or you can hang a paper- or canvas-backed vinyl. The wet-look vinyls are the easiest to clean. Most people want scrubbable walls. But if you're like me, and a lazy house cleaner, perhaps you'd prefer to redecorate more frequently and scrub less; a day with a bucket of paint can be more fun than a day with Spic and Span. Rough plaster walls in a kitchen provide a romantic atmosphere. They seem to age naturally; it is not difficult to put lime on them every two years to keep them looking fresh.

Wall coverings are more clinical than paint or plaster but, as I mentioned earlier, wallpaper is an imitation. If you want a pattern, pick a wallpaper with a small repeat, one which can be cut up and still have the intended impact. If you don't feel you need a pattern at all decide between vinyl or paint. If your walls are in good shape paint is the most economical. But shiny walls show everything, so take a good look at the condition of your walls.

Your kitchen cabinets count for a large percentage of your total wall area and their color and style should be tied together with your walls. You can do this by contrasting colors dramatically or by having them closely related. For example: Dark wood cabinets look more beautiful if they are surrounded by white walls. Contrasting textures help, dull cabinets set off against wet white walls, or highly lacquered wood cabinets set off against chalky white walls.

If you will have a contrast between the cabinets and the wall, the ceiling probably should be the same as the wall. The exceptions to this would be if you chose a busy paper for the walls which you don't want overhead; or if your ceiling is very low and your wall is dark. You might need a light-colored ceiling in this case. But generally you are safe if you tie the ceiling and walls together. Consider the plane of counters as a second floor. Harmony is produced by having the ceiling and walls flow together.

Work areas should be considered separately. The wall behind your stove is the most vulnerable spot in your kitchen. I recommend you install a chrome sheet there so you can scour it when necessary.

The wall behind your counters can get messy too, so you might consider having it covered in the same material as your counter top. I don't think "splash backs" count for much. (Splash backs are those 4-inch-high strips of counter-top material repeated where the counter and wall join.) If you splash your soup in the blender it isn't going to help to have a 4-inch-high spash back. I think it only breaks up the wall one more time. Inquire about molded formica counter pieces so you have no dirt-encouraging cracks where the counter and wall join. If you can afford beautiful, glazed tiles this is an excellent place to install them, because they are so central to the total kitchen design, they will be fully appreciated. Begin directly under the cabinet and go right down to the counter with decorative tiles. When measuring, allow space for grouting in between each tile. If this idea appeals to you, plan your kitchen with this in mind and if you can't afford to do it right away, it doesn't matter. Paint the back wall until you have the money for tiles. If you have collected old tiles from your travels, you can insert them attractively, with plainer tiles to frame them.

I believe in simple kitchen walls because they are such a good place to hang posters and pictures. Kitchens in city apartments don't always have windows, and if they do the view is often questionable. If this is your problem hang a beautiful ecology poster, which you can have pressed with clear plastic so it is washable. A relaxing perspective of a lake with trees and sunshine can bring New Hampshire into 14B or bring summer to the suburbs in February. Your solid walls can become the window of your dreams.

Other wall ideas for your kitchen: a basket collection hung in a group. Use small nails with no heads (referred to as brads) and insert them on an angle. A nest of baskets might be hung vertically, the biggest one at the top, the next biggest underneath, etc. Odd baskets should be grouped at random, possibly having a favorite brass horn or a sentimental cowbell mixed in with your basket collection for color. They won't be dust collectors if you use them. Any decorative wall candleholder will add a glow to your eating area. If you have a table against a wall, a mirror will open up the wall. Instant frames (picture holders which are easily movable, inexpensive and come in a variety of sizes) with lovely, appetizing magazine photographs of food can be fun and flexible. I've seen menus from famous restaurants framed. Or a gallery of family photographs. Enjoy the use of your kitchen walls. Don't take them too seriously!

Kitchens are full of cupboard doors, and I believe the dead walls on the inside doors should be utilized. Instead of having your cluttered reminder board exposed, hang this behind your cupboard doors. Have a cup with pencils at hand so you can jot things down. You'll be amazed how handy it is to have this on the inside.

There is no greater test of a floor's performance than in a kitchen. The two considerations in making your kitchen floor selection are beauty and practicality.

Notice I mention beauty first. Because the kitchen is the heart of domestic life and it is where most of us are spending more and more time, bringing our parties closer and closer to our everyday life. So your floor should look nice. Use this large area to bring romance and atmosphere into a potentially clinical area. Truly beautiful floors are the most practical too. Examine any restaurant, coffee shop or public place where food is prepared. What is on the floor? Almost always a real material. The most beautiful floors are stone or brick or quarry tile, ceramic tiles, slate or wood. When you aren't planning to hide your kitchen floor with massive furniture and rugs, it becomes a key decision. All other kitchen plans and schemes should be worked around your floor decision.

The easiest floor to clean is a real tile floor because it is glazed in a cement bed and grouted hard so there are no cracks where dirt can get embedded. Dirt doesn't show up as much on natural tiles or on vinyl either. Quarry tiles are hard on your feet, but you can always throw down small mats in front of your work area for comfort. You don't have to wax these tiles if you don't want to; soap and water are all you need.

A beautiful tile floor can create your whole kitchen flavor. Look into the expense and study it carefully. Tile is more work and mess to get installed than vinyl, but it may be worth it.

Vinyl is not inexpensive. Asbestos vinyl is the cheapest, but it is difficult to clean. Vinyl costs will approach those of a real quarry tile floor.

Designed kitchen floors with fancy borders and complicated, intricate patterns are corny and expensive. Why attract attention to a vinyl kitchen floor? Select the least ugly tile and lay it on the square or diagonal, depending on how your room is shaped. Never have beveled tiles (tile with diagonal, slanted edges); they may disguise the dirt in the seams but you need a nailbrush to get out the dirt. All travertines and tiles with pockmarks in them hide the dirt; dirt gets caught in the holes. You have to determine whether you want your floor to look reasonably clean when it's not, or whether you want to see the dirt so you can be clean.

A wood floor is also good in a kitchen. You can finish it so it can be mopped, or you can paint and spatter it so it doesn't show the dirt. If you have a depressing floor and you can't afford to change it, paint. You have nothing to lose: Paint over your ugliness with a bright deck paint, use several coats. It won't last forever but it will tide you over.

Maintenance is constant in kitchens. You might want to invest in a cove baseboard, which is rounded and curves up from the floor to the wall so you don't have the dirt build up in the corners. It comes in vinyl or tile.

If your kitchen doesn't have a window, be sure you have a good exhaust fan. It is as important as your stove, for ventilation is necessary for creative cooking. All cooks make smoke; fire and cooking smells are inevitable.

If you do have a window you are lucky. Windows allow for fresh air, let in natural light; they're a place for an air conditioner and/or exhaust fan; they are a great place to grow plants and herbs, and they make your kitchen a real space, not just a closet with a hot stove. Be sure your window goes up and down so you can use it and clean it easily.

You might want to paint your windows and trim with a high-gloss white enamel paint to allow every ray of light to come into your life, and they can be easily washed. Install hooks on the trim or on the top of your window for hanging baskets of greenery. Install white glass or clear glass shelves twelve inches apart for more plants, avocados, tomatoes, pears, anything pretty you want to look at. Have a box at the bottom of your window for herbs. If you feel ambitious, install a window box outside as well; you'll believe you're in a garden. Look into those prefabricated greenhouses which are reasonable in price and easy to install. Inquire at your local nursery or flower store for catalogues and prices. Install plant-grow lights at the window to ensure progressive greenery.

If you are fortunate enough to have to design a window for your kitchen, think about knocking out wall space and have your window go down to your counter top. If you do this you can sink a planter into your counter top so your greenery actually appears to be growing from the good earth. Look into pivot windows with sheets of glass that are so easy to clean and beautifully simple. Consider installing a valance light at the top which will shoot light up and down.

Riviera blinds are practical in kitchens for simplicity, light control and the ability to hide an ugly fan or air conditioner when not in use. Shutters are good, too, for similar reasons. You don't need anything if you decorate with hanging plants. Curtains in kitchens are impractical. They look limp and dirty in no time and get gray from the smoke and grease. They should never draw because your window is too precious to cover up.

LIGHTING

I was in a modern kitchen that had interesting lighting, none of which came from the obvious kitchen light source, the ceiling. Lights shot up from the top of the upper cabinets, lights were under all the cabinets, and bands of lights were over the stove and sink area. All the variables were separately controlled for complete variety; this bachelor likes his lights more than his cooking! The lighting seems to get him into the kitchen so they're a big success.

Most of us want the kitchen to be for dining, as space permits. Two requirements when you have a kitchen space for both working and dining: Your lighting must come on very strong and also disappear instantly. For cooking you need to see; for serving and dining you need mood lighting.

Install sufficient lights over your table area; even though you may not use them for entertaining or dining, your table is a work area too, and you'll need good light for any project. Then you won't have to drag in a standing lamp with a cord to trip over, and you'll save yourself all the fuss of dragging things from room to room each time you want to do a puzzle or mend a vase or plan a menu. Kitchens can be terribly dark on gray days.

Ceiling fluorescent lights are practical for general illumination. They certainly don't add much charm, however. If your ceiling is high enough (anything over nine feet) no one will notice the lights, especially if you only use them when you're working, not when you're entertaining! They should be used like your apron . . .

There are attractive frosted plastic fixtures which give the impression of a skylight. If you are doing construction work you could look into recessed can lights. They are out of the way and provide good light. If you have a large space to cover, they would be too expensive and it would be better to stick to fluorescent units.

There are plenty of things you can do without going to great electrical expense. On your existing outlets, you can hang a down can (those ceiling lights which direct light down in concentrated areas). Or screen in a 300-watt frosted ball light you can get at the hardware store which goes right into your present socket. A track with down cans can be installed easily. I think under-cabinet fluorescent lights are handy. Be sure each one has its own on/off switch. You need a stove light and will find it gives enough light when you are serving. Lights at your window are good for the plants and give the illusion of more daylight. Spotlights on the floor around your eating area are dramatic and warm, especially when they are hidden behind plants. Swing arm lights mounted on the wall can serve for desk area by day and disappear when you are dining by candlelight at night. Have a dimmer switch for your lighting. If you don't have your lights on a dimmer and you feel your kitchen seems stark or cold, you may have an overdose of fluorescent light. Delete one or two strips and notice the difference. You'll have to experiment until you feel you have the right amount of light, for each occasion.

FURNITURE

Kitchens have few movable or portable pieces of furniture. Just as on a boat, most kitchen furniture is built in. There is nothing warm about storage cabinets and broom closets, but we need as much storage space in the kitchen as possible. How can you create a warm, inviting atmosphere in your kitchen through furniture?

The cabinets should be beautiful and cleanable; nothing beats wood for these qualities. If you have old painted cabinets and have no intention of replacing them, paint them an exciting way. However, if you have the choice, select a wooden cabinet. I've never understood why so many people trouble themselves with expensive formica cabinets. Counter tops are one thing, but built-in cabinets in the kitchen are furniture, and wood is best.

A kitchen is no place for fancy moldings or hardware. Select the simplest cabinets, try to have all the hinges concealed or unobtrusive, select the plainest knobs. Clear lucite knobs are good because they disappear.

If you have glass doors on some of your old cabinets there are two things I suggest. First, consolidate all your prettiest crystal, glass and china and display them. They'll add depth, sparkle and color to the room. Hang Mylar silver-foil paper on the back of your cupboards for an added dimension; art supply stores sell it by the yard, sticky-backed. If you prefer to conceal the cabinets, paint the inside backs of the glass panels. If you do this think of contrasting the colors, and have some fun brightening up the kitchen this way. The frame could be one color and the glass another. If you feel like having more fun, paint the glass sections in one or two alternating colors.

Your counter tops are vitally important because these are where you are closest to your kitchen materials. No matter what mood you're after, you will in all probability select formica for the counters because it is the most practical. I love wooden counter tops and when they are treated, they are very cleanable. Tile counter tops are beautiful but noisy and expensive; and I've heard complaints that grease gets stuck in the grouting. But if you decide against formica, counters of either wood or tile would be fine.

When selecting your kitchen formica counter tops, one with a slight texture won't show as many scratches as a smooth surface. Also I'd stay away from fake woods: A plain formica in a beautiful color looks better. For kitchen counters, the colors that seem best include white, yellow, fresh green, dark blue or dark brown. (We'll discuss this further when we get to the color section.) To give your counters some architectural distinction, give them a thick apron (the term "apron" refers to the thickness of the side; it doesn't have to be solid). Instead of the usual one-inch apron, have the carpenter put in a two and one half-inch apron. Measure first to be certain your drawers open, though!

After your cabinets are planned, you have to consider your refrigerator, sink and stove. Space permitting, you may have a dishwasher, a clothes washer and dryer. These have to have a relationship to the other elements because they are necessary pieces of equipment and will dominate your space. To simplify life integrate white into your plans so all your major appliances go together.

Your table and chairs should be romantic. Why have an ugly banquette and table when they can so easily be charming? Why treat your space thoughtlessly when it is so important? Even if you claim you only eat breakfast there, why suffer through *petit déjeuner?* Examine your space to see what works out best for you, a table with chairs or a table and a banquette. The advantage of a banquette is the coziness of it, and, also, you can have the table up close to the wall. For anyone who uses the kitchen as the main eating place, a country, friendly atmosphere will tie in nicely for all occasions. Remember, with candles and an elegant table setting you can transform a casual room into an elegant dining space. Wicker side chairs would be nice. Or bamboo. As comfortable as armchairs are, I don't think any of us should be so ambitious in our kitchens as to use them unless we have endless space. Narrow side chairs are functional. When you have a second, more elegant eating area, I think the white Saarinen pedestal chairs are great for kitchens. They're good looking and comfortable, and there is a well-designed pedestal table to go with them, too.

Counters and carts on casters are wonderful aids. A movable counter can break up galley space and dining space, and can be moved out of your kitchen entirely if you need more room. A serving cart can do the same. I've designed kitchens where there were movable counters which became dining tables for parties. Build in what you must, but think about having some movable items too.

MATERIALS

Except for a few decorative throw pillows or a few movable chair covers, I don't believe in fabrics for kitchens. They get dirty too quickly.

We covered our banquette cushion in a natural linen and it looked marvelous. For one week! It is now re-covered in a chocolate-brown patent-leather vinyl and looks fabulous—and can be sponged clean after each meal. Since no one can keep up with perishable materials in kitchens, vinyls are a necessity. For special occasions, you might have cotton chair covers to tie on the seats. These can be stored with your linens. For fun, have napkins or mats made to match the "company covers." You can make these yourself.

COLORS

The fewer colors you have in your kitchen the more outstanding it can become. The background colors, after all, should relate to each other and set up the accessories you use; they should play up the table you set and make you feel you are in a natural setting. This is essential in countering the clinical, sterile atmosphere kitchens can have.

If you have painted cabinets, you'll probably want more color. Pick one color for your walls and one for your cabinets. As I said, I'd keep your inflexible items non-colorful because color can tie you down. That is, paint your walls a strong raspberry if you want to, but don't invest in raspberry formica.

Tie your colors together. Have as few drastic color changes as you can. A light cabinet with dark counter tops looks terrible unless the floor relates to the counter tops too. I think the strength should be at the ground, with an earthy floor color (practical for dirt); then go up to a lighter cabinet, counter top, upper cabinet; and light walls. Although I know lots of exceptions to the rule, most of us want light walls in our kitchens because they are often such dark rooms.

Yellow is one of the most pleasant kitchen colors. Don't be fooled into gold—choose a chiffon or lemon yellow. It is spring fresh, and food looks wonderful on and against yellow. White is excellent, especially white mixed in with stained wood. We selected dark-brown counter tops for our kitchen because we wanted a strong contrast against our rough plaster walls. On the other hand, we didn't want to depart in color from the brown of our walnut cabinets.

If your formica is a depressing color, paint it. Your paint store can tell you what paint to use. Be sure to clean your formica thoroughly first. Or use large areas of butcher block maple over your formica to warm it up and lessen the sting of a dull formica you can't change.

By now you know that I prefer pure designs. The kitchen is where you can select functional equipment and accessories which are simple and beautiful.

ACCESSORIES AND HARDWARE

Before you spend your money on another room in your house, invest in an intelligent gathering of necessary and beautiful kitchen equipment. You should be nourished by beautifully designed equipment throughout your kitchen space.

Look at the inside of your cupboards. Do you have a beautiful cooky jar? How is the design of your spice rack? What do you cook in? Take inventory and list what you need to purchase; what unattractive equipment you need to replace. If our cooking pots and pans are beautiful, they can come to the table or server. Isn't it easier to have half the dishes and half the items to store, and half the work? Examine your can opener, toaster, clock and tea kettle. These are items you use every day and you deserve to have them be attractive.

Open your ice box. Too few people use pretty food and drink containers for storage; so whenever they serve, they have to transfer the goods. Use your beautiful pyrex containers to store drinks and food. Pour your leftover wine into a large decanter and store it in the refrigerator. Have a pretty basket filled with fruit for instant use. Don't have ugly refrigerator storage containers, have one quality for all uses. Glass is so pretty, practical, cleans to a sparkle and doesn't wear out.

It is no fun to eat off the same plates meal after meal. It's dull. Have a variety of plates and glasses, and if you only have one set of flatware, it's best if it's a simple design. There are certain meals that call for earthy accessories and a too fussy silver pattern doesn't co-ordinate. If you already have a terribly dressy pattern, you might invest in some rustic utensils for informal suppers.

Natural accessories in a kitchen give it flavor. Cookbooks, your Chinese wok, plants, your basket collection, your spices, your wooden spoons, copper pots—all add texture.

Because most of us can't make a complete inventory of each plate, napkin or glass we select, learn to purchase things that will mix together. If you have two of a kind of any item you can pair that with another pair of items and do this up to fifty pairs, if you wish.

Break down your thinking into two categories. Think of one notion as rustic, country and casual and the other as more sophisticated and elegant. Everything you buy should fit into one of these two groups. It's a good idea to select your casual equipment in one group of colors, your more formal equipment in another, complementary color. If you follow this simple rule you'll always have enough equipment for large groups because all your small quantities will blend together nicely. Eventually, you should be able to mix plates, napkins, glasses and demitasse cups to feed twenty-eight friends without borrowing. Once your basic colors have been established, you can enjoy building your collections. Don't deviate from your basic co-ordinating colors and patterns or you'll find you have little use for what you buy. For this reason, it's best to stay away from definite patterns as much as possible except in small flexible items such as dessert plates or candleholders. Your goal should be to set up an open-stock system where things co-ordinate in color and mood and have as many varying uses as possible. Mix all your things together and experiment until you come up with a new combination.

Dining Room/Library

Reason should direct and appetite obey.
MARCUS TULLIUS CICERO

'Tis not the meat, but 'tis the appetite
Makes eating a delight.
SIR JOHN SUCKLING

WALLS AND CEILING

Any of us who live in old houses or buildings may find that one of the prettiest rooms we have is wasted. The dining room frequently doesn't get the use it deserves.

It is significant to begin this chapter with the subheading "Walls and Ceiling," because it might be that you should either break open a wall and join your dining room with part of your kitchen or divide it and create a living-sitting place. The Duncan Phyfe pedestal table with ten Chippendale side chairs, standing in the middle of this large space, may not use the space well enough, for a modern family's needs.

Examine your walls and determine what will work best for you and your space. You may have to close up a door opening in order to be able to put furniture against a solid wall. Dining rooms once had many doors that you may not need now. You need space for books, art and general wall-storage units. Removing a door trim and closing up an opening is a relatively small undertaking. If you need all your doors but don't want your space to look like a gallery of openings, consider having a concealed door installed. This is done with Soss hinges and looks like part of the wall when closed.

If you want to marry your kitchen to your dining room but not completely, possibly an arched opening would be a success, with arched doors to close when you want privacy.

The way you decide to use the dining-room space will guide your wall decisions and color scheme. I suggest you use this space as an all-purpose room. It will create an exciting atmosphere, be used more and become a fun room in which to entertain.

Dining-room wallpapers used to be, typically, a "tree of life" design. Now, instead, I suggest covering the walls in a more solid, richly colored wall covering, one that is a good background for books. The ceiling and trim can be white to tie into the next room and add light. Your pattern comes from the activities, the things you hang on your walls, and from your books. These will give you plenty of pattern.

FLOORS

If you convert your dining room into an activity center, you may decide to carpet the floor. This is an excellent place to use wall-to-wall carpeting because it helps cut down on noise, it is easy to maintain, it ties a space together, and you can easily drag your furniture around on carpeting. For home movies, for birthday parties, for game playing and for guests spending the night, carpet is a good solution. Also, when you have buffet suppers, it becomes a place to sit.

The 27-inch-wide all-wool patterned carpets are good for dining rooms; they are good looking, don't show the dirt as much as a plain carpeting, and they will wear beautifully—they were designed for abuse. Pick one you won't mind spending your life with because if you move, they can be relocated easily. Patterned carpets are one more reason not to have heavily patterned walls. Remember, seams in the carpeting occur every 27 inches. As I said before, you might be someone who would be bothered by them. Best to look at someone else's installation before you invest.

WINDOWS

Frequently, the worst windows get relegated to dining rooms. I find most of the ones I've worked on have no view and the rooms are dark. All the more reason to create a rich, strong room with a library atmosphere.

Create a garden at your window. Just like in your kitchen, you can install a small window greenhouse with lights and all those moist smells of nature at work. A curtain drawn across an unattractive window day and night is like wearing a Band-Aid over an ugly finger. Attack your window until you can give it a lift. Plants and lights inside or out, or both places, fool the eye and soul.

If you have a situation that calls for window seats here is a good place for them. This room should have many interesting places to sit. Near a window garden is a nice place to be. Anytime you have a good view be sure to group furniture around your windows. We all like to look out.

Think twenty times before you hang curtains. Shutters, blinds, plants . . . nothing.

LIGHTING

A chandelier hanging down over nothing is no lighting solution. If you're actually going to use this room at all times of the day and night, you'll need more and better lights.

Recessed can lights on the ceiling, on a dimmer, provide good out-of-the-way light, but they are expensive. You can hook up some good-looking wall lights in your sconce outlets to give off some light and, depending on your floor plan, you can use table lamps and standing lamps. For dark corners, you can spotlight up from cans in the floor or you can use standing lamps which shoot light up.

Again, be sure to have good concentrated light over your table, for non-dining activities. If your plan calls for a modern touch, an Arco light sweeping over a table would be beautiful. Don't consider it unless you have a spacious room though, because it needs breathing space.

FURNITURE

The most important thing to remember when planning your dining-room furniture is that it should be very flexible. When you are free to move and rearrange your furniture so it works for six, eight or fifty, you'll find your life is simplified. While a 72-inch round glass table top may be perfect for some occasions, it is far from flexible and it weighs a ton. As you move from one event to the next, your room has to have furniture that adapts.

If you already have furniture you want to use, this will direct your thinking, of course. Place the furniture you have so it fits in to the best advantage and work from there.

Your eating table can be used equally well for games and a general work area. I have a client who is having a wood table made up with brass inlays to indicate the boundaries for Ping-pong! A small (15-inch diameter) end table has a nest of three more tables inside, and they are ideal for buffet dinners. Some nests of tables have reversible laminated tops so when the white side gets dirty, you can flip it over to the clean black side. The tops, because they are movable, can become trays as well.

Think of having a large square coffee table which houses four leather pads underneath; this can give you another eating area. You don't need to be a hippie, or Japanese, to enjoy sitting close to the ground.

There is no reason why your sofas can't be excellent spots for a Sunday nap or for a friend to spend the night on. Make sure your sofa measures 70 inches inside the arms, or has no arms at all, and you'll be in business. There are good sofa designs now with removable arm cushions, to give the length you need.

I think the chairs should be lightweight and graceful because you may need to drag them from room to room. If you do lots of entertaining, have big parties and use several rooms for eating, it may be worth your while to invest in some simple stacking or folding chairs. They can cost as little as $9.95 each, and you should create storage space for them.

A key to the success of this space is your ability to provide a charming spot for two. This special place should have the most comfortable chairs. Perhaps a simple upholstered side chair, a swivel pedestal armchair.

No chair should belong to one room and one room only. When making your selection, envision your chair traveling around and see how it works in other rooms. For example, I think it a great idea to have the side chairs in this room match a pair of armchairs in your living room or complement them.

Keep your furniture to a minimum. Here may be an excellent spot to install a wall system. Imagine having a wall fifteen inches deep containing a drop-down desk, eight folding chairs and places for all your para-phernalia. Silver, glasses, a bar, hi-fi and records, scrapbooks, music equipment and games, all could have their place. The joy of these systems is the growth potential. A three-sectioned piece is perfect for now and you can add as you gain money and space.

FABRICS

The materials that seem appropriate for libraries are rich, nubby, cozy materials and are comfortable to curl up in and relax on. When you combine your dining, library and guest room all in one, I can think of no greater mood you could create than that of a library. For all occasions and purposes, this warmth and heavily textured feeling will do the most to tie in all your varying needs and elements.

A soft, dark brown leather might be nice; it is sensuous and romantic.

Have real leather or a lovely woven material. Chair seats could be vinyl, but needleworked chair seats for your old dining chairs would be stunning. Do one a year and replace the vinyl.

Materials gathered from all over the world combined with suede and leather and heavy woven fabrics create a wonderful feel. Needlework pillows might look great on your sofas. Fur pillows ("fun" fur) are soft and cozy. (Fun furs are totally synthetic and scrubbable. McMillen has a beige fur material on the banquettes in one of their showrooms and it is soft to the touch, warm and lovely. There are imitation suedes, too, which are beautiful and easy to wipe clean.)

The feel of your dining-library materials is important. They should be gentle to the touch. Twenty-seven-inch-wide wool carpets are beautiful and hard wearing if not as soft as you might prefer. Your fabrics should soften the room by their feel. No matter how warm your colors are, if you select a scratchy, itchy material, you will regret your selection.

Natural fibers get better with age, just as leather softens with the oil from our skin. Think how wonderfully soft your shirts are when they're six years old and fraying, just about to go; sheets are the same. Natural heavy cottons take on this same aging. While they are practical and well designed, no synthetic material is as sensual as a natural fiber. When a real material wears, it never gets depressing-looking the way a synthetic that is dingy and worn does.

COLOR

Dining in a strongly colored room can be elegant. White trim in a dark rooms keeps it from being gloomy, is a welcome contrast and sets off the wall color beautifully. The strong wall color gives a background for all the wood furniture and creates a cozy mood.

When selecting your dining-room color, be sure it is alive in candle-light. Test your paint sample at home with a candle before you settle on it. Keep your colors to a minimum here because you will have so many colors and textures in your table arrangements and eating accessories. The all-green-and-white room comes alive with pink napkins and lily of the valley plates, pink hyacinths sitting in clay pots. Your color scheme should be carried down to the ashtrays you intend to use and your place mats. Don't attempt to have the colors completed in the background; if you do the room will seem cluttered and confusing when you're using it for dining.

Try not to limit yourself by using the same table cover at every meal. You can set the mood and pace of an evening meal by your selection of plates, napkins and glasses. The fun part is arranging your accessories together so they have special meaning and all fit well together.

We have friends who love to entertain and do it often and well. I've never had the same menu repeated, but if I sit down to that beige table setting for one more meal, I'm going to lose my appetite. Beige place mats, beige napkins, beige plates, beige salad plates. Beige dessert plates. Beige demitasse cups and saucers.

Our accessories aren't things we have out of need or have to keep static. Build up a collection of things you like and move them around for variety.

Books are so beautiful mixed in with plants and special objects. Your assortment of flower holders will add interest to your room, as will your plant containers. It is all these personally selected things you love that distinguish your room from the room of a friend.

Living Room

Each artist writes his own autobiography.
HAVELOCK ELLIS

Elsie de Wolfe, the founder of residential interior decoration in this country, wrote in her book *The House in Good Taste*, in 1915, "A Drawing-Room is the logical place for the elegancies of family life." She goes on to say, "the keynote must be elegant simplicity and aristocratic reserve." We are all so lucky because not one of us will ever be saddled with a "Drawing-Room!"

Elsie de Wolfe's very next chapter makes good sense. In her words: "The Living-Room! Shut your eyes a minute and think what that means: A room to *live* in; to be sick or sorry or glad in, as the day's happenings may be; . . . Big and restful, making for comfort first and always; a little shabby here and there, perhaps, but all the more satisfactory for that—like an old shoe that goes on easily . . . A big fire blazing in the open hearth . . . flame blue and rose and green. He must indeed be of a poor spirit who cannot call all sorts of visions from such a flame! There should be a certain amount of order, because you cannot really rest in a disorderly place, but there should be none of the formality of the drawing-room . . . there should be nothing in the room too good for all moods and all weather. . . . I wonder if half the fathers and mothers in creation know just what it means later on to the boys and girls going out from their roof-tree to have the memory of such a living-room?" Think how good these words are! She goes on to say, "A living-room may be a simple place used for all the purposes of living . . . an official clearing house for family moods . . . it must offer comfort, order, and beauty to be worth living in."

Elsie de Wolfe knew how to live well. One room she designed received the compliment: "It makes us feel that it had been loved and lived in for years."

There is nothing but common sense in her words. She commented, "You can judge people pretty well by their books, and the wear and tear of them. Going one step further, you can judge people by the realness of their living-room." Elsie de Wolfe said, "Your living room should grow out of the needs of your daily life . . . The room will gradually find itself, if you use it, so be careful of the life you live in it!" All this sound advice in 1915! Bruno Munari in *Design As Art* said the things which make a gentleman's residence will match him: "It will be modest, quiet, hospitable and will have all the necessary comforts without falling over backwards to achieve them."

WALLS AND CEILING

The most welcoming, inviting living rooms all over the world are light and sunny. You enter these living rooms and immediately feel you've gotten closer to the family life and people who live in the house. A real living room makes everyone feel comfortable, not just a chosen few. Any living room that doesn't comfortably connect to the rest of your rooms in your house had misled values. Think of it as the focal point to your daily life.

Begin by determining if you are satisfied structurally with your room. Think of your walls as the horizon in your landscape and make them clear and refreshing. The wall color you select should be a pleasant neutral background.

If your doors are in the right place and you are merely cosmetically sprucing up, study the condition of your existing walls. If they are in good condition without too many large cracks and rough surfaces, you can count on paint being your best solution. If, however, they are in bad repair and you feel a wall vinyl will make a nicer surface, select one with a canvas backing so it actually acts as a support to keep the plaster in place. This is certainly cheaper than canvasing your walls and then painting, and you benefit from the texture of the covering.

Determine where you will end your color and where you will begin your trim and ceiling color. You should remove any picture molding that doesn't function to hang your pictures. If you plan a modern room and intend hanging large canvases, you may want to remove the chair rail to give you more wall space. If you remove moldings and need to do a great deal of plastering (sometimes moldings come right off and sometimes part of your wall comes with them), you may have to consider a wall covering to disguise the area in question. After the plaster settles, the paint may show some cracks. When this happens you should allow the plaster to settle completely, spackle and repaint. A wall covering would guarantee hiding it completely.

The ceiling and trim look well when contrasted in some way with your wall color. If you have a soft green wall, for example, you can paint the ceiling and trim white. If, however, you have a white chair rail and trim and you want more wall color in your room (without darkening your ideal color tone), you could paint your ceiling 50 percent lighter than your wall color. It will actually appear to be the same color as your wall and will look particularly good if there is a cornice or crown molding separating the two surfaces. When you have lots of ceiling beams, paint them trim color (white) and the ceiling and walls can be treated alike. If you have a white ceiling, put a drop of the wall color in your paint to turn it toward the wall color.

To me, nothing is fresher than white woodwork. It is like puffy clouds in the sky. I prefer a contrast most often between trim and wall unless you have all white walls. You can have semigloss or high-gloss trims and flat walls. If you have shiny walls you may want flat trims, although they aren't as easy to maintain as semigloss.

FLOORS

There is nothing so beautiful as bare, freshly waxed brown hardwood floors. Not only does the wood breathe, but it is as rich as soil and has textures that add a new dimension to your room. Beautiful wood floors are like the good earth and make you feel good.

To add to their beauty, you can spread beautiful rugs in key areas to articulate a seating arrangement and create intimacy. Your rugs might define a given area and bring a furniture group together.

No ordinary rugs will do, however, because when you have lots of wood showing, it becomes a showcase for your rugs. Because your wood floor has so much depth in its grain and texture, so too should your rugs. No solid carpet cut and bound for specific areas will do this. You need a real rug. One approach to take is to use old Asian or oriental rugs, or new Tibetan, Dhurrie, Greek, Portuguese, Spanish or Irish rugs. Another is to buy a modern rug with a texture and some interest so it won't look ordinary on your floor. Do some research and compare. Look into prices. Hand-made, interesting modern rugs are often as expensive as some old ones; it is simply a matter of preference. Do you want pattern on your floor? Do you want texture? Do you want strong colors? Beautiful rugs can be a minimum size because of the impact of their quality. Old rugs mix well in large rooms as long as you allow space in between for them to breathe. Patterned rugs look wonderful with patterned materials just as textured rugs look fine with textured materials. And vice versa! Look until you find something you love. Until then enjoy your hardwood floors. The basic thing to remember in choosing a color for your living-room rug is to select a color that ties in well with all your favorite colors. The color of your rug is what everything else rests on.

If your wood floors are in poor condition, consider painting them with rich dark-brown paint. Or you might prefer wall-to-wall carpeting; it can be beautiful and will cut down on noise. Be sure to choose a neutral color and one with a tight pile. The wrong color floor is a bad flower container for the color you add. In my experience, I've found that shaggy wall-to-wall carpeting quickly gets to look worn out where you walk, and the vacuum cleaner leaves tracks on it like a lawn mower cutting tall grass. Even cement floors can be painted and end up looking quite respectable. Never be discouraged with an unfinished floor. A charming penthouse apartment I saw once had shiny black floors; I really thought they were marble but it was many coats of black paint over subflooring.

WINDOWS

Probably you'll want your living room to have as much light and sunshine as your windows will allow. Study the quality of your natural light and judge how much light your windows provide. What are your light exposures? How many windows do you have? How big are they?

Look at your windows and determine their basic character, nature of their architecture, proportion. Double-hung windows with solid sheets of glass give a different appearance to a room than windows with wood or leaded mullions. Size is important and so are arches and heights. Modern windows with metal trims are the worst to deal with because they have little charm.

Now, look outside. What do you have in the way of a view? One of the most dramatic rooms I've ever been in was a dark-brown lacquered room with french doors leading out to a terrace overlooking the East

River. The windows were left bare, the trims were painted white and they framed the river with its movement and sparkle.

Some windows are good, some fair, and some are dreadful. What single window treatment can work for all three degrees of good, average and poor in one room? Shutters! The mid-nineteenth-century houses built them into the reveals (the recessed area around the window), and if you're fortunate enough to live in one of those old houses check to see if you have shutters in your reveals. Often they are covered over with layers of paint and hidden completely. I'm working on a house now for a bachelor who has stripped all the shutters throughout his house, exposing the most beautiful old mellow wood. Shutters are practical, allow light to come in and provide privacy. Shutters take up no space, add architectural interest lacking in most of our rooms and go with old and new, rustic and elegant.

You love curtains? Then have beautiful windows warmed by materials you like. My only suggestion is that you keep them simple. Elaborate window dressings seem outdated in most rooms today.

When deciding which style curtain to choose, ask yourself what you want them to do for the room. If you want them to add color, life, warmth and pattern to an ugly window situation, try straight-hanging panels. Beautifully made, lined and trimmed panels with ample fullness so they look generous, with an interesting heading (the detail which gathers the material together at the top to give it the fullness) can look marvelous. The most common heading (and one you perhaps should avoid) is the *French heading*, also known as pinch pleats. This is the one you see in most ready-made curtains, but it isn't good enough, unless you can hide it with a valance. It is the easiest to make, but it looks ordinary. Examine all kinds of headings before you settle on one.

If you select a woven white or off-white fabric you won't need decorative trimming. A pattern or a solid fabric should have a trimming to finish it off. One attractive trim is braid set in the inside edge of the pair of curtains, and across the bottom (referred to in the trade as "down the leading edge and across the bottom"). Set the braid in the width of the braid away from the edge on the inside leading edge of each panel of material. For example, a 2-inch-wide braid is sewn two inches from the edge, and is set in and sewn from the bottom of your curtain as much as four inches. When doing this, you give the curtains style and also hide your hemstitches. If you plan two rows of a braid, set them apart in a pleasing proportion. Stand at a distance with the braid pinned to your curtain to see how it will look. Keep the colors of the trim closely related to the material if you just want a finished look. Contrast the braid if you want an accent. It is the same principle as the monogram on a shirt, a towel or on stationery.

In a charming living room in an old Long Island house we wanted the curtains to be understated. The heading we came up with was a five-inch "bunch" of material (a cross between a typical french heading and a casual shirring), which looked relaxed and just right.

The longer that sunlight streams into your living room, the more beautiful your room will seem. Never make the mistake of thinking of your living room as a night room. This is your home, not a night club. Any good living room should be designed for daytime use and if it is wonderful in the brightness of noon, it is sure to be a smash in the glow of a fire and candles. Lighting your living room comes from outside and in.

To light your room in the evening, it is better to have many different sources of light coming from all over rather than a few that have more wattage. An average-size living room can easily have as many as fourteen lights.

There is nothing romantic or beautiful about ceiling lighting in a living room. It is a way to get your room lighted but that's about all; it should never be regarded as decorative. If you have one three-way can fixture which spots down on a seating group and two paintings, it is serving a valid purpose. You might prefer low light in your living room. Living rooms should have dozens of different lighting arrangements, so that the mood of your place can continuously change as you adjust your lights. Have three-way lights whenever possible. Also, an "on-off" button on your cords so it is easy to flick lights on and off. Use dimmers. Get floor buttons installed so you don't have to stoop over. Use cans and spots to emphasize your plants and art. Corners lighted softly add perspective, whereas furniture in corners adds clutter.

A light box (a square-or rectangular-shaped cube with light tubes inside and a tinted glass or plexiglass top so light grows out of furniture) would enable you to have thriving African violets and lovely objects lighted up so they glow. Standing lamps with brass and chrome shades take up no room and are wonderful for reading. When you are entertaining, the brass or chrome shade can be turned so it spots on a painting.

Lamps can be thought of as sculpture. Take your time as you gather your living-room table lamps. You probably need only four or five in your lifetime, so get ones you love. They might be expensive but fill in with tensor lamps in the meantime.

After dark use candles and floor flood-lights. Let your quince blossoms cast beautiful designs on your ceiling, let your room gear down to the flicker of candles. The French "regor" candle (difficult to get here) comes in a glass and is beautifully designed. It should be lighted at cocktail time because it permeates your place with a memorable scent. They come in red or green and both are lovely.

What is a more wonderful source of light than a roaring, crackling fire? On a gloomy Saturday, instead of using 100-watt bulbs, light a fire.

FURNITURE

The Romans used to say that "In matters of taste, there is no argument." Select your living-room furniture carefully. Build your collection slowly and with thoughtful consideration toward a growing need to feel and be relaxed and comfortable. Upholstered pieces should be the most comfortable. The rest of the furniture should be aesthetically pleasing.

The simple lines of contemporary upholstery go in all rooms in all settings. They set off that funny old rocker and that fine faiance. In matters of upholstery, smooth, straight and simple lines make the most inviting places to lounge. Check your seat, arm and back heights and repeat them often. Everything is lower now (except prices of course), so measure to be sure your sofa back is low enough to "float" in your room and not have to be stuck against a wall.

Chairs that aren't upholstered are more than just an extra seat. They should be beautifully designed and inviting. Never buy anything just to fill space or for additional seating. Regular store-bought furniture has a way of dissatisfying you eventually unless it is an original designer's piece. Value the old, value the new and custom-made but avoid imitations.

When each single piece of furniture is superb in style and character and your eye has made the selection, all pieces will automatically go together and give the room a harmony of form and co-ordination. It is the pieces you don't really like, but own, that make awkward rooms. Edit out all of these pieces, gradually if necessary, and your living room will be yours.

Furniture is only one way of seating. Environmental designers are using platforms and architectural forms to do away with the clutter of furniture. While you wait for your Le Corbusier armchairs or your Saarinen or your Eames, use cushions, use the floor. If we can only get as modern as the 1930s, that is better than being buried in the eighteenth century.

FABRICS

The best way to bring people and life into your living room is to have warm, soft, practical textures and materials. With these you will end up living in your living room. Jack Lenor Larsen understands this and has fabrics which have real feel, real life. Going to his 59th Street showroom in New York gives a delightful lift. The other day when I took a couple there who live in an adobe house in New Mexico, they commented, "These materials long to be touched."

Fragile fabrics create rigidity. To assure comfort and pleasure for you and your friends, have materials that will only get better-looking with wear.

Just as you probably feel something special about a custom-made piece of furniture which has been made by the hands of one man (rather than by a machine-made manufactured assemblage) you'll feel differently toward hand-woven and natural materials. A few weeks ago, we had a big dinner party and I noticed our Thaibok Bangkok silk plaid pillows were threadbare at the corners. The next morning I discovered they were split wide open and the muslin casing was exposed. These pillows didn't just sit on the love seat, they were held, played with and "used" for the comfort and pleasure of several friends during the course of the evening. I bought the material thirteen years ago in Bangkok. Hating to see an old friend go, I carefully took the casings off, washed them with Woolite, and sewed them back together. They aren't new but they are friendly! Thai silk is particularly interesting when it gets worn because the warp and weft are usually two different color silks woven together to create a luminescent blending of the two. Don't be afraid of old; old can be beautiful.

Jack Lenor Larsen has clients who use only his materials for their offices and homes. One Larsen client, who is particularly attached to a heavy hand-woven natural wool from Colombia, said that his seven kids and the peanut butter only make it look better.

Make your selections with people in mind. Choose thick materials that are beautifully made for wear, and thin materials that are cleanable.

Ask yourself if you prefer to have your pattern in your rug, accessories and wall decorations, or in your upholstery. If chintz is what you're after, study examples carefully and pick one you think you won't tire of. Don't have one purple poppy protruding that you aren't happy with or it will plague you. You have to be slightly nutty about the material you select or it's of no use. Unless you "know it when you see it" and flip for one exciting material, try another tack.

You can create interest in your room, without having dominant patterns on your fabrics, through the interest in the weave, the textures and through the combination of many color tonalities. In this way you can create a wonderful mood and you don't risk tiring of your fabric.

COLOR

Your living room should be an uplifting space. The colors we use should force spring and provide inside living with guaranteed sunshine. I've been in some thrilling darkly colored living rooms and admire them for what they are but they are, to me, the difference between going to the mountains and going to the sea. You decide which type you are, in this room. The colors you select will set the spirit of the room.

Stay away from a "nothing" color. It will drain your lively colors of their energy. Purposefully decide on a lively white or beige or gray or yellow for each big and small area. I once had to choose between a rug that was yellowish beige and one that was pinkish beige. When you saw the two tones in the room, it was incredible how the wrong color beige was as sour as a trumpet blown by a two-year-old.

Stiff maroons, severe blues, neutral greens and dark golds aren't usually preferable. Be sure to study your exposures. The soft-green wall that looked great in your old house should be white in this one if you have north light. Your favorite colors don't have to be blanketed about but might be reserved for a pillow or a vase of flowers. Allow your one red tulip to command attention on your coffee table because it is the only red note. Let the eye study that until it picks up the same color in the corner of a nearby landscape. Color contrast sharpens everything and allows you the peace of focusing on one thing at a time.

Your living room should have your best disposition. It should be colored to suit you on your best day. I believe this lift rubs off on us and can get us to feel better.

ACCESSORIES

This is what separates the men from the boys. There is no faking it; when it comes to gathering things you love, they have to speak to you. No living room will ever be welcoming if it isn't expressive and revealing. If you feel most comfortable in a formal room, you still have to have a feel for the objects you put around or they won't be yours. Everyone is interested to know what kinds of things you care about. Why not show them?

I'm going on the assumption that you have an affinity for everything you put in your room; nothing is there just because it looks right. Remember, this is your most treasured room; it is a painting and your own creation. It is not a dirty old canvas you paint over in the best way you can. No one else can paint parts of your canvas if you want it to be attributed totally to you. Some of us are shy about putting many of our touches around our living rooms because we feel they're silly; others of us don't know when to stop.

Rooms, like people, should have a flaw. The Japanese have studied incompletion and have made a conscious affirmation of the understatement. We tend to snuff out the life, the vitality of a room in our attempt to complete our space and make it perfect. Anything that has soul will have meaning. Don't overdo. When you fill up your living room with one thing after another, you diminish the meaning of each separate piece. Discipline yourself to remove one object when you add another. The best place for your things is where you appreciate them most. All my favorite things are in one far corner of our living room, all together, but with space for them to have their own special place. Our first Roger Mühl painting hangs over an antique French provincial writing table we bought outside of Grasse, near where Mühl lives. On the adjoining wall is a small gilt mirror with an especially beautiful carved pediment which we bought in Italy. On the marble-top writing desk are things of special meaning to me. On the far right-hand side, I have huge branches of quince, pink and springlike, bursting into bloom. In front of my quince, I have a close friend, someone I spend a lot of time with, my dictionary. There is a delicate brass mobile which catches the passing light, some shells on stands, a huge chunk of rock crystal. One antique brass double inkwell and a crystal antique well are nestled beside my bouillotte lamp, and there is an antique lectern behind them which has a drawing of some Greek windows and a field of wild poppies. There is a box covered with book-binding paper, which a close friend gave me as a present when I finished writing this book; I attached her letter to the bottom because it said, "May this box always be brimming full" and I like to have that note with me when I work. It sounds like a lot going on but not really, just enough of my favorite things I feel good being with when I work. The accessories bridge hundreds of miles and years, emote strong feelings of memories past and fill me full of goodness, so I am at home in my own private surroundings. Accessories, when they are real, work to make you feel good. They are your friends.

Master Bedroom

The heart has eyes that the brain knows
nothing of.

CHARLES HENRY PARKHURST

The plainer your bedroom walls, the better. A bedroom should be simple. You might want to hang a textured paper in a solid color or a vinyl with a suggestion of pattern, but no more. Here, you want your background to be left free of decoration so you have the flexibility to hang pictures and mirrors.

The two key walls in your bedroom are the one behind your bed and the one you stare at while in bed. If you like mirrors the latter wall is the perfect place. If you install a mirror in front of your bed and hang a picture over your bed you get to look at your picture while you're in bed. The mirror takes the solid wall and pushes it back visually. It is most relaxing. Because our bedrooms are our most personal area of space, mirrors are nice to have so we can see ourselves, too.

In your bedroom hang something refreshing on your wall. I think a perspective picture like a landscape is good because you are fooled into being there; also, it is a good feeling to wake up to a picture that represents your ideal outlook. Let it be your window to being where you'd like to be.

Carpeting in bedrooms is practical. It warms up the room, is cozy on your bare feet and is an excellent sound absorber. A small room appears larger when carpeted.

When selecting your carpeting, walk on it with bare feet to be sure it is soft. Select a low pile; shaggy rugs get dirty quickly. The height of the pile doesn't determine a good, comfortable feel, the quality does.

A dark, plain carpet isn't terribly practical for a bedroom because the lint and dust created from your bedmaking will make your carpet look like it's constantly in need of sweeping. Twenty-seven-inch-wide, tightly woven wool carpets are wonderful for this room, and the pattern at your feet is pretty and serves a practical purpose with plain walls. But don't do anything that will upstage and interfere with your bed. Take your rug samples to your linen closet and see how they co-ordinate. If you have old sheets but plan to indulge in new ones, take your rug sample with you when you select new sheets.

A marvelous touch in the bedroom is to have individual rugs on either side of the bed so you have a cozy last step before you climb into the bed. This could be a "fun" fur or even cotton; cotton is good because it washes and fluffs dry beautifully.

WINDOWS

Again, simplicity is best. The less you do, the prettier your room will be because it won't be fussy and busy. Think of having fresh white at your windows.

If you need a totally blacked-out room for sleeping, install a light-proof vinyl roller shade as close to the window glass as possible. Then, decide whether your windows are pretty enough to be bare or almost bare. If they are, but you need something for privacy and light control, you can have white shutters or white Riviera blinds or white cotton draw curtains, which aren't lined and thus allow light to come in and yet provide some privacy.

Plants at the windows are a good idea, too. A mirror between the windows adds softness.

LIGHTING

Your bedroom lighting should be relaxing, but there should be lots of it coming from several different sources. The most flexible and practical for reading in bed are the swing-arm wall lights. They also free your end tables for books, plants and projects.

Small tensor lamps are convenient and take up no space. In addition to your wall lights, a tensor lamp is handy on your end table. Because the light is so concentrated, you can turn one on and jot down a note or read without waking your mate.

Lights inside your storage areas are essential, especially in clothes closets. A lighted cupboard can become a make-up area. Because this is your special area, you should have flattering lighting; all bedroom lighting should be incandescent or warm, daylight fluorescent.

FURNITURE

The bed is the main thing in the room. Buy the best mattress you can. Back problems are rampant; the firmer your mattress, the better. Naturally you have to feel comfortable, but soft mattresses aren't as healthy for your back as firm ones.

What you put the mattress on is up to you. If you own an old family bed, or a beautiful new bed, it may be an odd size, in which case you'll have to have it custom fitted. If you prefer a modern bed, there is no reason why you need to have a harvard frame. Possibly you'd prefer a platform made of wood or formica; your mattress fits on your platform. This is a solution when you have a small room and want it to appear larger by making the bed lower. Once your bed height is determined, everything else can be scaled to relate to this measurement.

Headboards serve the practical purpose of giving us something on which to rest our heads, so we won't soil the wall. You may have a beautiful old wood headboard, or perhaps you would prefer an upholstered headboard; it is comfortable and simple. The problem with an upholstered headboard is in deciding what to cover it with—you want your bed to be so changeable, to go with everything. If your room is modern, vinyl might be a good choice. A white vinyl platform and headboard would blend in with your white walls and disappear. The bed becomes light in feeling and the covering appears to be floating. Your headboard will get dirty, so it's a good idea for it to be washable. Select something simple you can keep fresh. Slipcover your headboard with material on both sides so you can reverse it before you have it washed. You might want to co-ordinate your headboard to your bed cover. Select a simple shape for the headboard so you can get your slipcovers to fit really tightly.

End tables next to the bed are useful, and tiered tables are handy for keeping stacks of magazines and books at arm's reach. Then, your end-table tops can be left uncluttered to contain only the essentials. A telephone, radio, clock, a plant, one flower in a bud vase. Select end tables that are large enough. If you have the space, your end tables can be large because they should be in scale with your bed. If you want them particularly large, glass table tops are a good idea. However, they get dusty next to a bed. Have a drawer if you can.

A bedroom desk can be a dressing table as well. Somewhere in your bedroom you should have a comfortable chair. It doesn't have to be big to be comfortable, but a bedroom is so personal and such a good place to relax, a chair here will probably be used a great deal. Consider having your chair swivel so you can look out the window or turn your back to the television. Swivel chairs are relaxing.

About the television. Many people have one in the bedroom, and if you do but don't use yours every day, you may want to hide it under a draped table; or on a shelf in your closet or in a cupboard. Figure this out when you position your bed.

We need places for our clothes, cosmetics and jewelry, and areas near them for dressing. Try to have your needs located close together.

Next to your closet should be a place for all the rest of your clothes. A high storage cupboard works beautifully for sweaters, blouses, make-up and jewelry, and keeps them behind doors with no surface clutter.

If you still have room left and want a table, consider a light table. By this I mean a light box, with the light inside dispersed evenly through glass or plastic. Colored objects look beautiful through light tables and African violets thrive.

Clear plexiglass and lucite are invisible and make plants appear to float. As much as I love clear plastic, however, it does scratch easily. If you use plastic, protect your surface by putting felt on the bottom of your table-top items.

A handy piece of bedroom equipment is a tray or a basket with a handle for collecting projects you want to work on in bed. It is convenient to have everything you'll need in one portable container—a sewing project, some scrapbook work, bills to pay. This can be stored under your bed. If you decide to have your bed on a platform, be sure to have drawers installed in the platform, for storage.

FABRICS

Determine what kind of activity your bed gets. Do you get out of bed and make it and never get in it again until you unmake it in the evening? Do you flop on your bed whenever you have a minute? Do you telephone in bed? Read on top of it? This will affect what fabrics you use on it.

Let's talk about sheets first. Bedrooms are for pleasure. Sleep in a garden, sleep in beauty. Enjoy all your favorite colors and changes. Instead of spending money on outer fabrics, fabrics that show, spend your money on new sheets. You could buy a complete change of sheets every third month for the next ten years, and it will cost you less than a draped and decorated fancy bed.

Another good idea for bed covers is the reversible woven upholstery material. It is rugged and won't show dirt or wrinkles. When you turn down your bed you have a pretty spread as well.

Any material that isn't quilted will wrinkle easily.

A cute idea is to line your spread with a sheet or with calico; you see the reverse side so it should look nice. Use an extra sheet as a blanket cover.

Begin your collection and enjoy interchanging and trying new combinations. As I said before, when you have basically well-defined color schemes so many of your things can happily be combined.

Focus on washable bedroom materials. The freshness of this room is essential.

Vinyl and terry cloth make good covers for a chair or a stool, so you can step out of the tub wet and not spoil the chair.

COLOR

Blues are always welcome in bedrooms because they are peaceful and fresh. For me to know what colors you'll be happiest with in your bedroom, I'd have to know you intimately. I feel we should surround ourselves with fresh, clear colors, and a good test of this would be to buy some mixed flowers and walk around your room to see if your colors are flower fresh. In a bedroom, it is especially important to have clarity in your colors. The depth of color, its value, is entirely dependent on your personality. One of my nicest clients said, "We like soft colors that are clean and happy."

ACCESSORIES

You may want to have in your bedroom the objects and photographs you love most. If you have lots of plants try having matching containers on hand so new plants can be transplanted. If your light is inadequate conceal some spots around to use during the day.

Instead of burying your pillows under a pillow sham, use them freely and stack them two and three high, two and three deep. Use baby pillows. Have fun mixing patterns. All pillows should have washable slipcovers.

Have pretty desk accessories. Book papers or lovely fabrics make appealing desk-top accessories. Some new Cecil Beaton writing paper can actually inspire you to think lovely thoughts and express them to a friend. Make your desk as inviting as your bed.

Child's Bedroom

Education is a painful, continual and difficult
work to be done by kindness, by watching, by
precept, and by praise, but above all—by example.
JOHN RUSKIN
Stones of Venice

We all try so hard to do the right thing and make the right decisions regarding our children. The easiest way to approach your child's room is to make up your mind right away that your child's room belongs to your child. It should reflect his personality, not yours. When children are twenty-four months old, they are old enough to express their own needs and become involved with the creation of their private worlds.

One of the thrilling aspects of having a child is to prepare his room before his arrival. The room you put your baby in should be a positive reinforcement, a constant support.

Then, when he is older, a child should be allowed to know himself through having responsibility for his immediate surroundings. Values are absorbed; a parent's attitude and willingness to allow his child to express his feelings fully and completely will be taught through example and love. From birth to maturity, the child moves out and establishes contact with others, learns and grows into a civilized soul. At first he is a parasite and interested in only one thing, himself, his survival, his feelings and his ability to get his own way.

I feel the healthiest way to approach a child's room is to include as many elements as you can that will contribute to his learning and growth and that will feed his special interests. Have your child set up so he is encouraged to do the things he's good at and there are facilities available for him to explore new dimensions. A child is consumed with growth. Everything is going to teach a child, but it is up to you to keep him open so he becomes perceptive to all sorts of connections and discoveries.

All this is an attitude and has nothing to do with money. Children need building blocks to create their own niches, their own cozy corners. Kids find the underneath side of tables and chairs as fascinating as the top side. Dr. Spock suggests we lie on our backs and look up at the world our infants see. What does the underneath of his table look like? Lie in his crib and study those solid bolsters blocking his vision. Try hard to get inside his skin.

The open space you might like may be frightening to a child who has a smaller world and needs it scaled down to his sights. A kindergarten table is low and sturdy. A chair is red or blue or green or yellow, offering the child a choice. It is so important that a child have his special place, his corner cupboard with his name on it and his own things inside. When your child returns home from school with a finger painting he made, isn't it important to give it a special place in his home, his world? Children learn so much in one day, it is hard to keep up with their enthusiasm. Their rooms should provide a space for them to continue what they began at school and discover new delights on their own.

One essential thing is not to get anything too set because children change and grow rapidly. Since you want a child to be as secure and happy in his room as you are in yours, try to design a room that will work for his special personality. Think of yourself, what would have been the ideal room for you when you were your child's age? How is your child different from what you were like at his age?

WALLS AND CEILING

Children's artwork can make an exciting wall covering. You could have simple, plain walls for your child so his room can be hung with his own art. When I asked Brooke, our three-year-old, what she liked most about her room, she said, "My beautiful pictures."

Use the best paint you can afford. The Swedish Emolj is superb and Scotch tape won't rip it off. If all your walls are scrubbable and as practical as a bulletin board, you'll have a larger gallery area. If Scotch tape applied directly on your wall seems unruly, have huge bulletin boards on two walls. Paint them a bright color.

Another suggestion. If you prefer a more orderly wall decoration and have some artistic talent, design a jungle scene or balloons or farm animals and have your child help you paint this scene right on the wall. In this case, use their doors for their own school pictures.

Your children's rooms have so much action they never seem big enough, so I recommend white walls or another light color. Once you have a bright sparkling background then you can add accent colors. If you have good wide wood trims, it might be fun to paint them a bold color; and a high ceiling could be painted the same bright color. Children stare at their ceilings so it's a good idea for them to be lively. Each door could be a different primary color.

Visualize all the treasures that could liven up your child's white walls. A big vinyl graphic in yellow and green on one wall could come off when your child was ready for a new design.

FLOORS

The most important thing in floors is that they can be mopped, whether they're wood, paint or vinyl. Painted floors in children's rooms are nice because they are inexpensive and easy to change. If you change your mind about the color, you can redo the room with a fresh paint job. Don't consider this unless you are willing to do the job right—lots of coats of paint and then polyethylene; this floor will get hard wear, and you don't want the paint to come up in flakes.

A wood floor doesn't have to be brown. Stain the raw wood any color and then use a wax finish. Sealers are okay, unless someone gouges them in a truck; once the sealer gets unsealed, it is messy.

Vinyl floors are rather expensive for a child's room. A decorative floor seems unnecessary because the decorations will be their toys. If you have vinyl already installed, that's fine. If you need a new floor and don't have wood, install a vinyl but pick a neutral that won't dictate the color choice for the rest of the room.

I prefer a flat surface to carpeting for kids; it's better for building castles and racing trucks. However, small throw rugs would be added for warmth, when they are sitting on the floor.

I wouldn't even contemplate wall-to-wall carpeting for children. If you insist on carpeting, choose one with texture and a blend of a few harmonious colors so you can disguise accidents. Solid strong colors are disaster for children's rooms: they show lint, dirt and crumbs.

There is an attractive multicolored rug called "candy stripe" which is inexpensive wool, and is made out of scraps of wool that were short pieces left over from expensive custom carpeting. It's perfect for children from birth to teens, and any rug dealer can get it for you.

WINDOWS

Consider leaving them bare. Have a simple pull shade or Riviera blind, but nothing elaborate. A child should be able to look out.

To frame the view, paint the window frames a bright color. Even a lousy outlook gets dressed up this way. If your color is dark such as red, blue or deep green, paint your mullions white and only frame your window in color.

LIGHTING

You need lots of light. For an infant, you should have a soft globe ceiling light so they don't stare at an open end "can" with a 200-watt reflector bulb. When they are up and about, you need strong ceiling lights so they have plenty of light on the floor. Remember, children, hippies and the Japanese do enjoy the floor! Your light has to go down lower so you need more of it.

A simple track with down cans is flexible, provides good illumination and you can get them with grillwork on the bottom so they're shatter proof. An easy and amusing thing to do is paint the funky old ceiling fixture (already there) a fun color and use frosted-ball light bulbs. You can get 600 watts from the same old fixture that Auntie Agnes used with candelabra bulbs of 15 watts each!

Depending on the child, I think children should understand about the dangers of fooling with electricity and should be given their own desk lights at age five. A tiny tensor light is fine. A clip on bed or wall light is good with a simple push on-off button.

When they are older, a strip of fluorescent lights under a bookshelf is excellent for a concentrated work surface. All this is inexpensive and hardware stores have what you need.

FURNITURE

Children should have a growing system of furniture that builds up as their needs change. Think in terms of modular building blocks. All their furniture should be scaled for small people, designed for easy operation of drawers and cupboards, should be sturdy and plain. Why saddle a two-year-old with Americana?

Children at two years can open their own drawers, open their closet door and should be encouraged to be self-sufficient. If you have their clothes hanging too high, they may try to get at them and fall. Have low closet racks.

Begin on the premise that everything in your child's room is his, and his to explore and maintain. What does a child need? A bed and space. You need a changing table. You need a chest of drawers or shelf space for his clothes. You need storage areas. Add a low table and stools for his house playing and friends and projects. Add a bookcase. Add a wall of storage with open spaces below so it becomes a work area and desk. Add files for his growing interests. Big pillows. That's all.

Sturdy, honest pieces of furniture for children are available today with exciting designs and bright primary colors. The best designs come from Scandinavia but Poland and Italy are exporting interesting things. When you go looking for furniture you want to project this into the future and question how it will grow with the child. If the designs are good and the pieces are well constructed, you have no worry. White is a color you should consider because it is more flexible than a primary color. Brown is somber for children and takes up too much visual space in their busy rooms.

Bunk beds are very helpful when you have confined space. They free the floor for play. The oldest child sleeps on top: that seems to be the special spot. Children love to go up there to sulk or to be alone. There are designs now that don't require a ladder; you climb up the end. Don't have a whole extra bed taking up floor space for friends spending the night. Instead, make a sleeping bag. You'd be amazed what a privilege it is to sleep in the sleeping bag vs. the bed on special nights. Have a platform made for a firm mattress and skip the conventional bed altogether. Stick with standard lengths when selecting sizes, so contour sheets fit. Youth beds and special sizes cause problems. Narrow widths are fine. A child doesn't need a 36-inch bed.

FABRICS

Children are feeling beings, and they should like the touch of their materials. A practical idea is to laminate the bed covers: They look marvelous, can be sponged and are rarely sat on! If you don't want your children flouncing around on their beds, vinylize the bedcovers.

Since it's hard to tell which materials your child will respond to, let him tell you what he likes and then develop his idea in other ways.

All selections ultimately should be made by the child. Preselect what you like, what you can afford, what you envision as appropriate and leave the final decision to the child. The important thing to keep in mind is to keep your material washable and inexpensive.

Sheets are a perfect material solution for a child's room. Let him pick the design. While he is in his Snoopy stage, let him sleep with Snoopy sheets. Use a sheet for a blanket cover, and if you want to be fancy you can quilt a sheet to use as a spread. When you are flexible with bed fabrics, they cost very little and require little space in the linen closet. Snoopy sheets require the same space as white ones.

Most standard beds for children are narrower than a standard twin size. You can purchase any 50-inch-wide material and if you buy 2½ yards, you can make tuck-under spreads for the children's beds. They don't need to be sewn at all. When you change the sheets, change the cover as well. Remember this when you find a remnant you like. (Later, when your material no longer seems bedroomy, you can make it into a tablecloth.)

COLORS

"I shall like to recapture that freshness of vision which is characteristic of extreme youth, when all the world is new to it." (Henri Matisse)

Your child will have every color in the rainbow in his room one way or another so don't worry about his room being bland. Someone once said, "Paul Klee seemed to handle colors and dreams as if they both came out of a box of children's toys." To get an indication of what colors your child instinctively prefers get him a supply of magic markers, water colors, crayons and colored pencils. If he clings to the same color family in all four different materials then that is a pretty accurate reading of his preferences.

Color is one of the most stimulating learning tools there is, and three-year-olds are learning to read through color recognition. Colors are symbols and tools. Children recognize colors and identify: "Green like my rug. Blue like my table." Their world is full of color and they should be allowed the freedom of expressing themselves through their selections.

Let the child talk to you about his room and let him show you where he feels certain colors should go. Once the basic colors are established, support his selection in the toys and accessories you buy for his room. This way you are developing his understanding of color as well as pleasing him. A blue typewriter for his blue room is a sure sign of love. Keep colors like violent purple for inexpensive items, because this is likely to be a phase preference. With each child there will be personally distinct room colors. When children share a room you can merge their favorites to make a cute room as well.

ACCESSORIES

You want to have lots of storage space in your children's room because children are collectors. Russell H. Conwell, the American educator, said, "The power of little things to give instruction and happiness should be the first lesson of life, and it should be inculcated deeply." Little things mean everything to little people. Samuel Johnson was quoted as having said, "There is nothing too little for so little a creature as man—it is by studying little things that we attain the great art of having as little misery and as much happiness as possible."

Children like to have lots of small containers, boxes and jars for their things. When a child likes something, he may put it in a sacred hiding place. His entire room can be a mess, but his favorite treasure is hidden away in a special spot.

Ask your child's teacher if you can observe a class. When a teacher has seventeen or so children to work with order becomes essential. You'll pick up some information about children's ability to work and play hard and pick up after each activity and also you'll discover imaginative and inexpensive storage bins for all the fun things they love to do. Think of the raw materials your child needs and then plan easy, practical and colorful storage ideas for them. There are colorful plastic drawers that you can purchase individually, and that lock into each other. There are colorful plastic cubes which can be used for everything from clothes to dolls' beds to toy storage to art-supply storage! These look so bright when stacked together against a wall. Have labeled jars and boxes for things. If they can't read "crayons" when they're two, they'll recognize the word when they're three. Make an old cigar box pretty or cover a hatbox with a favorite fabric, to make a doll's bed.

Instead of framing famous children's pictures, frame your child's best effort and hang them next to posters and prints by artists who paint in bold, strong colors. Let some of Henri Matisse and Karel Appel rub off on your daughter. I'm of the opinion that if you put the right colors around you have a good chance of having the colors sink in.

Don't clear "junk" from his room without permission. That one-armed doll might be a dear friend. Be gentle about house cleaning. After all, this is his own little world.

Bathroom

His bathroom, in contrast to the rather
portentous character of his bedroom, was gay,
bright, extremely habitable and even faintly
facetious. Framed around the walls were
photographs . . .

The bath-tub, equipped with an ingenious
bookholder, was low and large. Beside it a wall
wardrobe bulged with sufficient linen for three
men and with a generation of neckties. There
was no skimpy glorified towel of a carpet—
instead, a rich rug, like the one in his bedroom
a miracle of softness, that seemed almost to
massage the wet foot emerging from the tub.

F. SCOTT FITZGERALD
The Beautiful and Damned

. . . the primeval rhythms of the sea-shore . . .
drown out the hectic rhythms of city and
suburb, time tables and schedules. One falls
under their spell, relaxes, stretches out prone
. . . flattened by the sea; bare, open empty as
the beach, erased by today's tides of all
yesterday's scribblings.

ANNE MORROW LINDBERGH
Gift From the Sea

You have to design and build a really wonderful bathroom. The ones most of us have are old and clunky or new and antiseptic. I've yet to see a decent-sized new bathroom that wasn't a custom design.

Few of us get to design our own bathroom, unless you are building a house. Even then, you will have to be cautious with your ideas because custom bathrooms, and plumbing in general, are so expensive.

If you are fortunate enough to design your own bathroom, you should gather all your pictures and ideas and have a professional designer assist you in the planning and execution. If you can afford to create your ideal bathroom you can afford to consult with a top designer. To replace your old cracked sink for a simple new white porcelain one with a cabinet below can be expensive. An entire bathroom renovation and decoration (without swans and flowered bowls) can easily cost you as much as $12,000, so you can see the expenses are a bit out of line.

The ideas I've outlined for you here will turn an ordinary bathroom into a nice place to spend private times, without having it cost you a fortune.

WALLS AND CEILING

No bathroom could ever be big enough. With all the porcelain equipment and practical wall tiles at arm's length, it's a good idea to try and extend your walls and your ceiling. You can do this by creating open, clean spaces, uncluttered and light in color and feeling. Water is a part of all functions in this space. To assure relaxed comfort and enjoyment in your bath area, have waterproof walls and ceilings. Any wall covering you choose should be able to be splashed and not get spoiled by moisture and steam. Because steam rises, the ceiling gets badly abused. A high-quality paint like the Emolj might be more practical for your ceiling than a wall vinyl if you take lots of long steamy showers. You should analyze how each bathroom you have is going to be used. In a powder room or a room with no shower, you can hang a wall vinyl on the ceiling and not worry about the glue opening up.

Ideally, the ceiling in a bathroom looks best when it is tied to the walls because the room is small and it helps to reproportion your space. Secondly, just like kitchen walls, bathroom walls are broken up with wall tiles, usually, and having the ceiling and walls match helps to simplify the space.

Wall tiles can be so sterile looking and aren't necessary all around your room. If your tiles offend you, get an estimate on what it would cost to remove them and have a plasterer make the wall flush. This way you can envision your wall vinyl going down to the baseboard. If your tiles are old and are in poor condition, or if the color is offensive, don't worry—Emolj paint works on tiles. It won't peal off in any area except where water sits on it continually. Soap dishes should have plastic liners. We had black tiles we've painted white and they have lasted beautifully. Don't clean them with paint remover or anything too strong. Old tiles can be freshened up and should be because any white background wall covering will make your tiles look even dingier.

If you have to do bathroom construction, the wall around the tub could be installed with beautiful Mexican-Portuguese- or French-glazed tiles. I've seen mirrors used and love what it does to open the space; but they require frequent wiping with a towel because of the steam. Clear plastic installed in front of your wallpaper can work as long as you have it sealed so water can't get in between.

If mirrors weren't so expensive, I'd suggest mirrored walls in your bath. The mirrors themselves are expensive and the labor to cut and install them is sky high. We had a mirror we wanted installed and after five excessively high estimates, I gave up and hung silver paper.

In a powder room where people are in and out in a minute, you might want to dazzle them with a wild wall vinyl. I prefer the simple approach with more flexible personal touches, which are movable, but this is up to you. In the bathroom where you spend your time, don't lock yourself into colors and patterns you'll tire of quickly. A silver and white geometric or anything fairly simple which is a good background for wall hangings would be an excellent choice. If your bathroom is ugly and needs all the help it can get for very little, you have no choice but to give it a splash of color.

FLOORS

Bare feet, overflowing tubs and showers provide big and small bodies of water on our bathroom floors. A real tile floor or a simple vinyl floor is the best way to approach this area. Carpeting in a bathroom is hard to keep looking clean and fresh, unless the carpeting is selected so the dirt and carpet color blend together. A floor in a light color that can be mopped seems preferable. Pure white shows every speck of dirt, too, but is so fresh looking when clean, it may be worth the effort. Also, marbleized vinyl is very practical. Stay away from dark floors because when you powder after a bath or spill your bath salts, you'll have a real mess; and the lint from towels shows up on the dark background.

On your light, simple bathroom floor, you can use small rugs and bath mats. These should be in fresh, clear, clean colors and nothing too big so they can go into your washing machine. There is nothing more beautiful than the quilted Porthault flowered mats. As expensive and indulgent as they may seem, think of the money you'll save on decorative wallpapers or fancy vinyl floors. Use your whole floor budget on a few mats and you may be way ahead financially. If Porthault is too rich for your blood, buy simple cotton rugs. The snythetic slinky ones look great in the bath shops but they get dingy fast. If your space is tiny you can get away with bath mats on the floor, which are cheaper and so flexible; they take up very little room in your storage closet and wash easily.

WINDOWS

The ultimate in luxury is to have your toilet face a window with a nice view. On a private island, we had just this outlook when we were on a holiday. But, usually, the toilet faces the door (hung with a gown or robe) or the tub (cluttered with shampoo and Vita-bath) or the sink. So it's a good idea to come up with some deceptive measures suggesting a view beyond. Shutters, as I've already pointed out, would be ideal; another wonderful solution is white glass or plastic shelves for plants and pretty objects.

We need air in a bathroom and a window is quieter than a fan. Light, air and privacy can be accomplished by hanging a Riviera blind over operative windows. I think white for your window trims is often a good choice in a bathroom. If your glass is frosted and ugly, a blind will soften this. So much more daylight comes inside with clear glass, though, so study this choice carefully before you decide to simply cover up the window.

LIGHTING

You need enough light in a bathroom in order to shave and to make up. This can be accomplished in several ways. You can have lights on the sides of your mirrored medicine cabinet or over the top; or strong overhead lighting. I suggest you have both. There are times when you're in the tub and don't require all your light so maybe you'll want to have two separate switches. An entire ceiling of lights in a grid or skylight fixture is nice. A real skylight is heaven; you can relax in your tub and look at the clouds. Whenever you can, force natural daylight in your bathroom, it is always preferable. Corny though it may seem, try candlelight in your bathroom for a relaxed, leisurely tub bath in the evening. A bathroom should be a relaxing place to be.

FURNITURE

We also require a sink, a tub and a toilet. If you prefer a shower to a tub, this would imply having a glass shower enclosure. Showers create much more moisture than the most vigorous tub bath. A tub, however, caged inside glass doors is gloomy unless you can get the doors opened enough so you don't feel trapped. You may prefer doors for your tub so you can be modest without locking the bathroom door. The ideal tub is sparkling white, long enough so you can lie back and relax, has efficient, quick drainage, and has lots of flat surface area surrounding the tub. If you aren't in a position to have a big new tub installed, see if there is a way of creating a flat shelf at one end for plants and paraphernalia. Even if you don't intend to leave bottles around, you need to have places to put them when you are using them. If you have no room, see if there is a simple clear lucite shelf (movable) you can rest across the tub for added bathing convenience.

There are wonderful modern bath accessories that are being installed, but if you're just sprucing up your old bathroom, little things mean so much. Look into the purchase of a super shower nozzle and for a few dollars get a rubber hose for washing children's hair and misting your plants.

Think of your tub as your own private pool. You are totally private, you can regulate the temperature, add scents and bubbles and completely unwind. When your jaunt to a warm island falls through, go draw a hot tub, throw in an overdose of bath oils, turn on the radio, turn the lights down low, and have a good soak.

Your sink area can become a storage space with a cabinet below. Not only is there space to store supplies and towels, but also it makes your floor cleaning a lot simpler. White porcelain sinks with wide-enough space around the bowl to put things down on are excellent. Pretty flowered basins are beautiful too but expensive and I'd prefer a bunch of fresh flowers resting against white porcelain.

To distinguish your simple basin from those in public places you might wish to have handsome faucet handles installed. If so, get an estimate first from the plumber of his cost to install them because it might discourage you before you even price decorative bathroom fixtures. When making your selection, be sure you pick a set that is nice to feel in the hand and won't slip when you grab for it with a wet soapy hand.

FABRICS

The most important consideration when selecting bathroom materials is to make them easily cleanable. A gorgeous fabric made into a Roman shade can look sad six months later if it gets exposed to the usual dirt. I think the greatest thing that has happened to bathroom fabrics is printed terry cloth. No longer does terry cloth only come in solid colors; now, with countless designs, we can get all the patterns we'd ever want in washable towels.

Shower curtains can be simple because there are so many pretty towels and colorful mats and rugs available. A reversible shower curtain is the nicest because you look at something other than the "wrong" side when you are in the shower. A two-sided shower curtain is more flexible, is attractive from all angles.

Sometimes we have a lot to hide behind our shower curtains (diaper pails, laundry, panty hose, a tennis sweater hanging up to dry). And your tub and tiles may be old and depressing, so you may want to close your shower curtain all the time. If this is the case, possibly you want to give your shower curtain special attention. You can make a real curtain with an attractive heading, one that goes to the floor. Use the heaviest clear plastic liner you can buy. If you need the storage space you can build a cabinet above your shower rod (provided you have a high-enough ceiling to make it worthwhile).

COLORS

The fresher our bathrooms are, the prettier they'll be. Condition is important here. Silver makes a bathroom sparkle, and foil vinyls are available. A green and white garden idea is always fresh and looks well with all the white fixtures we face in a bathroom. Yellow and white geometric designs and trellis patterns make cheerful backgrounds.

The thing that is important about bathroom colors is to be able to mix and match and add new pretty towels as you find them. Don't commit yourself to colors that are limiting but enjoy the feelings you get from a movable feast of color and pattern.

ACCESSORIES

Here, little things can mean a lot. A lucite hanging shelf, a mirror and lucite door hook, a simple door knob, a lock that works, an attractive soap dish—all add to your pleasure. Think about replacing ugly towel bars and bad-looking medicine cabinets. Consider adding additional mirrored cabinets or another storage wall or a mirrored wall. Get some good hooks for hanging plants and be sure you like the pots they are in.

This intimate room should be full of small luxuries. Bubble bath, oils, soaps and lotions are important additions. They make the time we spend worthwhile, turning our daily routine into a celebration of pleasure. A cake of Caswell-Massey's almond soap is special indeed. For a bar of soap, $2.50 is high, but if you delight in its smell and it makes your bathing a joy, it may be worthwhile. Our bathrooms are functional, and we can make them personally pleasurable by the private tonics we surround ourselves with.

Hang your plants and pictures and bring in your magazines and books so you feel relaxed. Plants like the moisture and thrive in all the reflected white light. Some people hang erotic art in their bathrooms. It's a good place for masses of family and friends' pictures. The natural sponge you bought in Mikonos, Greece, and use in your baths brings the island to you; the water glass purchased from the Metropolitan Museum reproduction collection reminds you of that wonderful Saturday with the children at the museum.

Go all out in your bathroom. Put your finest touches in this little room where you spend time each day. Give your eyes a feast. Remember, too, you need only one beautiful drinking glass. It is not as though you have to buy a dozen. Any beautiful object that water won't spoil can join you here. You need very few things, but they should be special.

Bring in your bronze sculpture bird and enjoy a close view for a week or two. Bring your stone statue in from the garden so you can enjoy it during the winter months. Hang a stained-glass mobile and watch the colored lights dance around your room. Have a fresh flower in a bud vase on your sink.

A FINAL WORD

Now you are on your own. You've got all the tools you need to get started on your personal environment. Your designs for living require daily interest because keeping your surroundings in harmony with you is an ongoing project. As you grow and change, and as your family does too, you may want to change your surroundings, and I hope this book will help you, over the years, in making where you live *you*—your style for living.

Index